Massacres in the Jungle

MASSACRES in the JUNGLE

. . . .

Ixcán, Guatemala, 1975-1982

Ricardo Falla

translated by
Julia Howland

with a foreword and epilogue by
Beatriz Manz

WESTVIEW PRESS
Boulder • San Francisco • Oxford

English edition copyright © 1994 by Ricardo Falla

English edition published in 1994 in the United States of America by Westview Press, Inc., 5500 Central Avenue, Boulder, Colorado 80301-2877, and in the United Kingdom by Westview Press, 36 Lonsdale Road, Summertown, Oxford OX2 7EW

Spanish edition copyright © 1992 by Universidad de San Carlos de Guatemala

Spanish edition published in 1992 as *Masacres de la Selva* by Editorial Universitaria, Guatemala

Library of Congress Cataloging-in-Publication Data
Falla, Ricardo.
    [Masacres de la selva. English]
    Massacres in the jungle : Ixcán, Guatemala, 1975–1982 / Ricardo
Falla ; translated by Julia Howland ; with a foreword and epilogue
by Beatriz Manz.
        p.   cm.
    Includes bibliographical references.
    ISBN 0-8133-8668-3 — ISBN 0-8133-8669-1 (pbk.)
    1. Guatemala—Politics and government—1945–1985.   2. Massacres—
Ixcán River Region (Guatemala and Mexico)—History—20th century.
3. Victims of state-sponsored terrorism—Ixcán River Region
(Guatemala and Mexico)—History—20th century.   4. Political
persecution—Ixcán River Region (Guatemala and Mexico)—
History—20th century.   I. Title.
F1466.5.F3513   1994
320.97281—dc20   93-29912
                                                                                CIP

Printed and bound in the United States of America

The paper used in this publication meets the requirements
of the American National Standard for Permanence of Paper
for Printed Library Materials Z39.48-1984.

10   9   8   7   6   5   4   3   2

Contents

PART ONE: Selective Repression

PART TWO: Scorched Earth

Illustrations

Maps

Photographs *(following p. 49)*

A Kekchí woman massacred in 1982

The Xalbal River. The army crossed this river at this point before carrying out the massacre in Cuarto Pueblo in 1982

Leaving Guatemala with the bare essentials

The first refugee shacks

Food rations in the first weeks

Refugee camp in Campeche, 1985

The authority of the Communities in Resistance (CPR), the Ixcán committee's 1989 annual assembly

Games

School in the mountains

The Refugee Women's Organization. Mamá Maquín's first assembly, 1990

Solidarity between women's organizations

Twin girls in the CPR, 1990

Collective sugarcane milling

Foreword

Few places have been more studied by anthropologists than Guatemala. In the distant Indian highlands, careers have been made, theories developed, and classic ethnographies written. In many ways the field has been defined and re-defined in that troubled country. There are, however, few Guatemalan anthropologists; the two most distinguished are Myrna Mack and Ricardo Falla. I have had the privilege of knowing both these extraordinary colleagues and friends for many years. I worked closely with Myrna Mack until she was brutally assassinated by the military on September 11, 1990. I now feel honored to have been asked by Ricardo Falla to write the foreword and the epilogue to this exceptional book, surely to become one of the classic Guatemalan anthropological writings.

Until recently few ordinary Guatemalans had ever heard of the profession of anthropology. In the innumerable press reports since Myrna Mack's assassination three years ago, however, she is always referred to as "la antropóloga Myrna Mack." As a result, anthropology has become an honored, widely known, and admired profession. It has become synonymous with courage, social consciousness, and first-rate scholarship.

Like Myrna, her close friend Ricardo Falla is a remarkable scholar and human being. He is a Jesuit priest and a committed anthropologist whose work presents a challenge to a new generation of concerned social scientists throughout the world. In *Massacres in the Jungle*, Falla documents a decade of political turmoil in the Ixcán rain forest, culminating with the horrifying massacres of 1982. His copious note taking and rigorous approach—checking and double-checking every detail—result in one of the more careful historical documentations of the tumultuous decades of the 1970s and 1980s in Central America. Few anthropologists could have gained the confidence of the people or the personal commitment to participate and be a witness in the way that Falla did. His documentation is so careful because he wants to accurately convey his country's painful history and, above all, because he cares deeply about the people he is writing about. Falla declares his commitment to the poor and to the Indians along with his contempt for the criminal actions of the military, emphatically condemning when something "is not right." His high ethical standards and exceptional scholarship shine throughout the research.

Falla gathered data for this book through fieldwork in late 1983 and early 1984, mainly in the Mexican Lacandón forest refugee camps. After carefully recording the events documented in this book, Falla obtained permission from his Jesuit superiors and the Diocese of El Quiché to live with the population in resistance (CPRs) in the Ixcán. This population—displaced civilians organized into several communities—has been hiding from the military under the cover of the dense rain forest for the past ten years. In this remote and dangerous area, Ricardo Falla assumes the name of "Marcos." He reflects on the choice and explains that as Mark, the apostle, he narrates what others have told him: "I did not live through the experiences of the massacred; I am only the spokesman, the intermediary voice of these realities; I only want to leave evidence of the suffering of a people." His humility and his feelings are always evident, as are his personal reflections forged in solitude. He is a man of deep feelings, who can joyfully marvel at the beauty of nature and cry alone at the pain of others. The communities in hiding knew only that Marcos was a Guatemalan priest and a researcher; they did not know his real name nor his upper-class upbringing. In a country defined by sharp social schisms, where the oligarchy and Indian peasants would never share a roof—let alone palm branches, nylon tarps, or a hammock—Falla's immersion in the arduous living conditions in the jungle is even more remarkable.

At the time, Ricardo Falla's anonymous life in the Ixcán rain forest was known only to a handful of confidants. He occasionally requested of us small items, such as tape recorders, cameras, manual typewriters, clothing, or solar panels, to enhance his pastoral work or his research. While living among the population in resistance, under the most difficult of conditions, he completed *Massacres in the Jungle*. He presented his findings for the first time in public at a special panel of the XVII International Congress of the Latin American Studies Association (LASA) meetings held in Los Angeles, September 24–26, 1992. The book was published soon after in Spanish by the Universidad de San Carlos.

Publishing the book in Guatemala was courageous and difficult. Nonetheless, the book became widely known and an instant sensation. The book sold out immediately (even a pirated edition appeared in Guatemala). I ran across the book in the oddest of places. In March 1993, for example, a Guatemalan highly placed professional in the Ixcán showed me a book he kept under lock in his file cabinet, without knowing my association with the author of *Masacres de la Selva*. He handed me a book with a colorful cover and a religious title in Italian, *Il Vangelo di Giovanni*. I didn't understand. The discussion up to that point had been about the general conditions in the Ixcán and the return of refugees. He asked me to open the book. All of the sudden I had in my hands, hidden under an appropriate cover, Ricardo Falla's *Masacres de la Selva*. I smiled but tried to hide my joy, thinking soon he would be surprised to see the new version of that book with my foreword and epilogue. He said grimly, "Don't turn the pages because blood will spill from them." The following day he posed mischievously for a photo, as if a convict against a wall, with the bogus cover in one hand and the uncovered book in the other. (I say appropriate cover because when I told Ricardo the story he said, "How did he know? Now I am 'Giovanni' because unlike Mark, apostle John saw for himself, he was an eyewitness.")

In another instance, a rural teacher in the Ixcán, without prompting, confided to me, "There is a book you ought to read, *Masacres de la Selva*. It is an excellent book, *pero le falta mucho* (but a lot is missing). I can tell you a few things I have seen." He proceeded to talk about clandestine cemeteries, how as a volunteer fireman in his home *municipio* in the highlands he had to remove and bury hundreds of corpses, witnessing the horrible manner in which they were tortured and killed. These two incidents—among dozens on that visit—in as remote and militarily dominated a place as Ixcán, made me realize that people are confronting their past.

After LASA, Falla returned to his life in the Ixcán. An army offensive at the end of November 1992, however, forced once again a major displacement. He fled with the communities. In the assault and destruction that followed the army found a hidden deposit of material belonging to the *Equipo del Trabajo Pastoral*—the Catholic Church's pastoral team. Among the many religious items left hidden, such as hundreds of baptism records of children, were also Falla's diary, current field notes, and a list of names of victims that appear in *Masacres de la Selva*. The author of the famous book, Ricardo Falla, could now be placed among the population in resistance. The military, already stung by the authenticity of the material and the credibility of the author, jumped at the opportunity to "prove" that Falla was a guerrilla commander and thereby discredit the writings. The book became "*un libro subversivo.*"

Falla left the Ixcán to clarify the situation and took the opportunity to address the people of Guatemala. A full-page ad in the Guatemalan press entitled "Carta del Padre Ricardo Falla al Pueblo de Guatemala" was a *tour de force*. He answered the accusations, not by honoring them with a denial but by declaring instead who he is, what he has been doing for the past six years, and why. He simply stated he was a priest and an anthropologist, left no doubt of his commitment to the poor, and denounced the army persecution of a civilian Indian population. Always careful with detail, he listed the religious objects found in the cave, illustrating his own and the communities' deep religious devotion and faith. He referred to Archbishop Romero, the assassinated Salvadorean martyr, as inspiring him in his "pastoral work of accompaniment."

This response gave Falla an opportunity to further discredit and deflate the military, create an awareness in Guatemala and the world of the populations in resistance and his own work among them, and bring to the consciousness of every Guatemalan a painful hidden reality. Falla's eloquent moral arguments contrasted sharply with the military's tired rhetoric and absurd charges. In reaction to the military's provocation, the Guatemalan Catholic Church, the Jesuit Provincial order, and the academic community—both in Guatemala and internationally—all passionately jumped to Falla's defense.

Falla also made clear that in addition to his priestly functions he was conducting anthropological research, especially a detailed study on peasant economy, field notes that were found and stolen by the military. In his mind, his duties included the service he could provide to the "poor and persecuted with the scientific instrument of anthropology." To Falla, using his academic skills to aid the poor seems completely natural. He ponders, "Why did I study that discipline if I do not put it at the service of those most in need?" Those research skills formed the factual basis for his denunciations of the terrible massacres of 1982. Moreover, those skills have aided him over the past six years as he participated in community life and gathered data on the adaptability of peasants among the populations in resistance. He was particularly interested in peasant production and their high degree of organization, determination, and stability in an otherwise unstable and dangerous context.

With this edition, the English-speaking public can read and reflect on the military repression against the population of Ixcán—a repression that continues to this day—and learn of the suffering endured and the strength demonstrated by the survivors of these massacres.

Beatriz Manz
Director, Center for Latin American Studies
University of California–Berkeley

Introduction

Witness to Terrible Things

"What's this about slaughter?" I asked the witness. "What's this about people killers?" So he told me what he had seen at the military base in Playa Grande:

There are two butchers. They have a star on their foreheads and a cross on their arm and in the center of the cross a sword. They are never on duty, nor do they patrol. They are the soldiers who only wait.

Three times they took me to the pit where they burn people. I'll never forget it! … It's a large pit, about two-by-two-meters.

Other soldiers kick the poor people off the truck. Then who knows how the butchers do it. They grab them, one by one. They make them kneel and wham, they stab them. Then they take out the bloody knife and lick it!

As he told of the horror he had seen, the witness imitated the gesture of licking the knife.

"Delicious chicken," the soldiers, killers of people, say. And they grab another, and another, and another … and they go on killing them and throwing them into the pit.

The soldiers grab firewood, because there is chopped firewood right there. They dump the people into the pit, and throw more and more firewood over them. They pour gasoline over the firewood. They drench the firewood with gasoline. Then they stand back and light a match and throw it in. When it reaches the firewood, it explodes like a bomb. Bang, … a huge fire. The whole mouth of the pit is full of flames. It burns for about twenty minutes. The firewood still moves, because the dead are still kicking. Their spirits are alive. When the soldiers see that the fire is dying down, they pour on more gasoline! In half an hour the fire dies. And the corpses have become pure ash. Their hands crumble. What a lot of lard there is on their bodies! The fire sizzles with the lard, and soon consumes the poor people.

They took me to see the pit so I would give them information, but, thank God, I didn't change my story.

1

It was in 1982 that the witness saw the crematorium in a field half a kilo-meter from the Chixoy River, in Playa Grande, in the Ixcán region, El Quiché department, Guatemala, Central America.[1]

Why Write About Massacres?

Why write a book about massacres? Some may find it degrading and coun-terproductive. Why recall such unspeakable brutality and cruelty? The wit-ness gives us the key. His testimony "I shall never forget it," uttered from the depths of his harrowing memory, states an existentially positive reality for him: that he is alive. His testimony is good news. The more terrible the account of what he witnessed, the more awesome the reality that he an-nounces: I am alive. Our book undertakes to relay his message and that of hundreds of other witnesses, who are eager to tell the people of Guatemala and the whole world that, incredibly, they are alive.

I am only the conveyor of this proclamation, not a firsthand witness. But I have been entrusted by chance or by history, whatever you wish to call it, to transmit what those firsthand witnesses have seen, smelled, touched, heard, felt, surmised, thought, struggled with. They have told their as-tounding story, and I cannot keep silent.[2]

In this chain of annunciation from the witnesses through me to the reader, faith is indispensable in forging each link, because the good news can be accepted only voluntarily. In the first place, the witness believes that his testimony is worth telling. He does not merely believe in what he sees and hears, in the fire and the butchers, because he experiences them directly. But there is another important aspect of his faith, for as he de-scribes his experience he realizes that it will be difficult for many to believe that man is capable of the macabre levels of dehumanization that he has witnessed. He knows it because he and many of the victims also had trou-ble believing that the army would commit such crimes, and, as we shall see in many testimonies, this lack of faith cost many their lives.

In the chain of annunciation, I was urged to believe in those who testify and to make their stories known. I, too, crossed the barrier of incredulity. In my case, this crossing took place in 1982, when I heard the firsthand ac-count of the closest witness of the massacre in San Francisco, Nentón, Huehuetenango. There I put my fingers into the wound of the people's hands and put my hand into their sides to confirm that, as a people, they were mortally wounded but still alive. Before this experience, it was im-possible for me to believe that human beings with hearts and flesh could be capable of reaching such mindless and merciless extremes of bestiality.[3]

Yet faith in the witnesses requires a critical approach because there are false witnesses who deny reality, minimizing and hiding the facts or in-creasing and exaggerating them. Their intention is not to affirm life but rather to satisfy particular interests. Thus it is necessary to compare accounts of the same event, finding their internal coherency and establishing their value according to the witnesses' proximity to the events, their capacity to retain and interpret what they see, and their truthfulness and integrity.

In order to be understood, the annunciation also requires faith on the part of the readers. Of those people who merely glance at the title of this book, many will react by dismissing it, putting it down as out-of-date ideological rubbish. Others will feel repulsion and shock after reading only the first page. Others will delve deeper into the book, but the birds of distraction will fly away with its meaning. Still others will be moved and possibly converted, asking, "What can we do?" There will be very different reactions, but all will be related to faith in the message of the witness.[4]

Because this witnessing is an annunciation of life, readers are asked to temper their critical approach with comprehension. The book emerges from a situation that has not concluded; one cannot say that it is a problem of the past. And that is precisely why it requires faith: The acceptance or rejection of the message is a matter of life and death. The social and political context continues to be threatening and dangerous for the witnesses, which is why I have not named them for people to interview them again.

The danger of the annunciation lies in the denunciation, which is the condemnation it embodies. The witness, by proclaiming that he is alive, forcefully accuses the army of having butcher-soldiers who specialize in stabbing victims before burning them. This denunciation is a cry that awakens tremendous aggressions and may even, although it seems paradoxical, trigger new atrocities. The denunciation cries out: You have murdered the just one.[5]

The annunciation is also dangerous because denunciation pushes us toward action. What can we do? Perhaps we are not doing justice to those massacred. Are we truly fighting with all our might to demolish the wall of impunity? This fight can be tremendously dangerous: It unleashes social forces that demand that the crimes be investigated and that the material and intellectual authors of the crimes and their counterinsurgency theories and practices be brought out into the open. It brings attention to those years of dirty war at the beginning of the 1980s in Guatemala.

The condemnation spans years, decades, and centuries. The testimonies are life stories. Some are of land-starved people who sought seasonal agricultural work on the coasts of Guatemala. When the jungle began to open up as an economic alternative for agriculture, they moved. There fate or history placed them in one of the areas of greatest conflict in Guatemala: Ixcán. The witnesses, if you give them the time, will tell their stories from the beginning, culminating in their experiences of the massacres and the lives they have led after fleeing from their communities, as refugees or communities in resistance. In this book I cannot go into all the root causes. For the sake of conciseness and impact, I will concentrate on the repression: disappearances, torture, selective killings, executions of several people at a time, group massacres, and massive massacres of entire villages—in a word, genocide (Falla 1984a, 1984b).

The terrible events I focus on took place and grew in intensity between 1975 and 1982—a short period but crucial in the history of Guatemala. Many may wish to hide the facts, seeing them as denigrating their national pride or harmful to their interests.

The area of research was reduced to enhance in-depth study. The area is Ixcán, in the northern part of El Quiché; within Ixcán, I will concentrate on Ixcán Grande, which is between the Ixcán and Xalbal rivers. Covering this smaller area will permit a closer examination of events, like a camera with a zoom lens, centered on specific detail. The area of research is related to the quality of the testimonies available, as access to numerous eyewitnesses has not always been feasible in all the municipality of Ixcán.

The denunciation crosses centuries. The root causes of the massacres are from many centuries ago. The accounts of the witnesses gathered together in this book bear a great resemblance to the massacres carried out by the conquistadors 500 years ago. As we commemorate the fifth-century anniversary, we should not conceal the continuing effects of the violence of the conquest. But because this book is about the annunciation of life, I should stress that from the violence of old has sprung a people who are consolidating their identities in the process of resistance—resistance in order to live and resistance to be what they are, which paradoxically does not mean to resist change. People resist both to survive ethnically, as indigenous people and communities, and to survive as a nation, as Guatemalan people who fight for their dignity and freedom in a thousand organized and unorganized ways. This book is a humble tribute to Guatemala's indigenous people in particular and to the people of Guatemala in general.

A Glance at Recent Guatemalan History

The recent history of Guatemala, seen from the perspective of popular organization, falls into four main periods. Each period is characterized by the ebbs and flows of the great forces in conflict. The flow is the wave of popular unrest and political activity in search of a more just society. The ebb is intense repression that once again drowns these expressions into passivity. It does not destroy them utterly—that is what is incredible—because after a few years the wave starts to boil and gather force, and a new period begins.

The first period (1944–1954) began with the 1944 Revolution, which, just before the end of World War II, put an end to the dreaded dictators such as

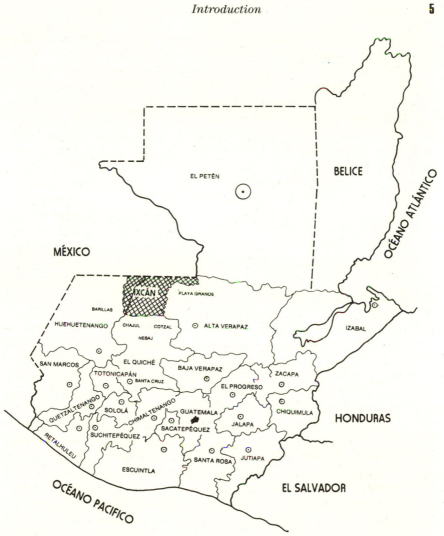

Guatemala

General Manuel Estrada Cabrera and General Jorge Ubico. There was a wave of democracy: unions were organized, indigenous people were given the vote, political parties were legalized and began to develop, new schools were created in different parts of the country, and land was distributed to the poor. This wave affected the interests of the large national and foreign landowners, in particular the United Fruit Company. The flow, which improved the life and well-being of the poor, was abruptly and violently severed when Colonel Carlos Castillo Armas, financed by the United States, invaded from Honduras. I have heard the testimonies of peasants on the southern coast of Guatemala, where the United Fruit Company had lands, telling how after the 1954 coup tractors were used to bury corpses on the Jocotén farm in Tiquisate Municipality.

The second period (1954–1966) witnessed the birth of the first guerrilla forces after the 1959 Cuban Revolution. The rebel forces were formed after the unsuccessful uprising of army officers in 1960 and unsuccessful guerrilla outbreaks as in Concuá, Baja Verapaz, in 1962. The Rebel Armed Forces (Fuerzas Armadas Rebeldes; FAR), formed in 1962, carried out activities in predominantly *ladino* (nonindigenous) areas of the country, such as the eastern coast and Guatemala City. The ebb came in 1966, when the army, this time led by Colonel Carlos Arana Osorio, attacked and dismantled the rebel forces, killing 9,000 civilians. These were the years of Vietnam, when U.S. counterinsurgency theories and techniques were being tested and perfected, both in Southeast Asia and in Guatemala (McClintock 1985).

During this period, many nonviolent movements were formed, mainly unconnected to the rebel forces. These movements prepared the ground for future guerrilla movements in the following period. The cooperative movement grew with the adoption of technical innovations such as fertilizers. The jungles, such as Ixcán in the north of the country, were opened up for colonization. Large numbers of indigenous people broke up the ground and cultivated and populated the land. As in the case of the cooperatives, migration to the jungles was an attempt to mitigate the anguish arising from the lack of land.

There was a powerful religious resurgence, stimulated by the churches, in particular the Catholic Church, that organized the indigenous peoples and motivated them to break with religious traditions that, as a whole,[6] could no longer provide solutions to the problems they faced. Grass-roots community groups emerged in villages and hamlets, and leaders were formed who first belonged to Catholic Action (the main religious organization) and then formed part of political parties that leaned toward the left at the time, such as the Christian Democrats.

The third period (1966–1982) witnessed the birth of two guerrilla organizations: the Organization of the People in Arms (Organización Revolucionaria del Pueblo en Armas; ORPA), in the highlands and the coastal lowlands, and the Guerrilla Army of the Poor (Ejército Guerrillero de los Pobres; EGP), which began to work politically precisely in Ixcán, the area where the massacres described in this book take place. The popular movement was invigorated by the resurgence of guerrilla forces, either because it maintained a degree of contact with them, converged in some aspects, or simply ran parallel.[7] The 1979 Sandinista Revolution in Nicaragua heralded revolutionary triumph in Guatemala as palpable in the near future, giving great impetus to mass demonstrations and radicalizing the actions of popular organizations. At the same time, the army began to repress social

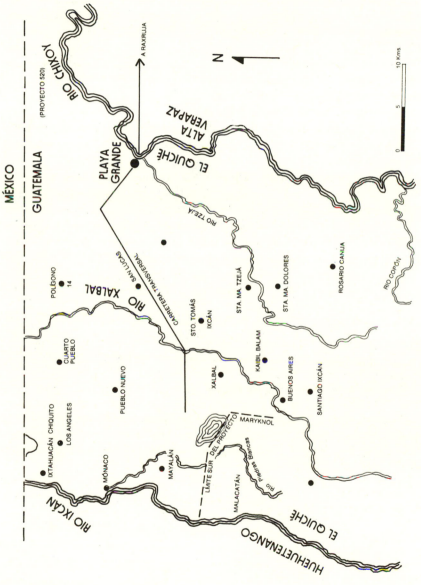

Ixcán

organization violently, and this repression escalated to its scorched-earth policy in 1982. The period ended with terrible massacres that were like open wounds in the living map of Guatemala, particularly in the indigenous areas of the country. There were 440 villages destroyed, according to the army, and the dead (primarily civilians) numbered between 10,000 and 20,000 by conservative estimate; more reliable statistics are between 50,000 and 75,000.[8]

The fourth period continues to date. In 1982 and 1983, blood flowed like water with the military regimes of General Lucas García (1978–1982) and General Efraín Ríos Montt (1982–1983). The Guatemalan National Revolutionary Unity (Unidad Revolucionaria Nacional Guatemalteca [URNG], formed in 1982) was able to rearticulate its military and political struggle and is currently in the midst of peace negotiations with the government. This fourth period in recent Guatemalan history will probably draw to a close in the near future, when firm and lasting agreements by both parties emerge from the peace talks. I hope that this book documents and reinforces the voice of the victims of the repression in Guatemala so that their human rights will be respected and a just society will be created—a society in which such crimes against humanity are not tolerated—so that what has passed will never occur again![9]

NOTES

1. The witness gave us his testimony at the end of 1983 in a refugee camp called Puerto Rico, in Chiapas, Mexico. From this camp we gathered the testimonies used for this book at the end of 1983 and beginning of 1984, in five months of "fieldwork," as anthropologists say. Most of the testimonies were recorded in writing rather than taped.

2. I am like the evangelist Mark, who spread the good news without having been a firsthand witness. Like him, I have tried to collect hundreds of testimonies, giving them an interpretative framework. The good news proclaimed by Mark is, like mine, the "unfinished account of a process which has been violently truncated," the story of a failed Jew who, nevertheless, lives on in the faith of the persecuted communities that believe in him (Bravo 1986).

3. The account of this close, and, may I say, privileged witness, who lived through the massacre from beginning to end, reflects how the people at first did not believe that the army would kill them. Once trapped, it began to dawn on them that the army did kill. In "Voices of the Survivors" (Falla 1983), I tell how I searched for this witness in the refugee camps until I found him because it seemed incredible that such a massacre could have taken place.

4. See the parable of the sower: Matt. 13: 4–23.

5. Your fathers have "killed those who foretold the coming of the Just One, and now you have become his betrayers, his murderers. You who had the Law brought to you by angels are the very ones who have not kept it" (Acts 7: 52–53). Thus Stephen denounced the Council of Jews, five years after the death of Christ, for being respon-

sible for his murder. Ten years after the events, I, too, am denouncing what I have heard.

6. We say that these traditions "as a whole" could no longer provide solutions to the problems faced by the indigenous peoples not because the traditional religion (La Costumbre) is lacking in profound values, or should not be freely practiced by its followers, but rather because it became unviable as the all-embracing, uniform, and sole cosmovision of each indigenous community as it was in the Guatemalan highlands before 1945 (Falla 1979).

7. The popular movement refers to urban and rural grass-roots social organizations that promote social change in favor of the poor, such as cooperatives, trade unions, student groups, community groups, shantytown groups, and religious groups.—TRANS.

8. See Aguilera 1986. Aguilera quotes Frank (1984) in reference to the more conservative estimates and cites Krueger (1985) as the source for the second estimates.

9. As I wrote these pages in September and October 1991, the subject of human rights was being discussed, albeit unsuccessfully, in the negotiations between the government and rebel forces. After the May 1993 coup d'état the subject of human rights is still of top importance.

PART ONE

Selective Repression

CHAPTER 1

The First Abductions

(10 June to 7 July 1975)

The First Roundup (10 June)

On 10 June, about 9:00 in the morning, planes could be heard flying over one of the small towns in Ixcán, called Xalbal. This sound was surprising to the peasants, who were far removed from the cities and large towns of Guatemala's colder regions. The planes were not war planes, but they carried parachutists. They flew over Xalbal several times and began to drop soldiers. One *parcelista* remembers, "We were pleased to see such a sight. It looked like the planes were dropping bits of rags or rubbish. But it was the army, which had come to carry out search operations."[1] The peasants in general were not predisposed against the army. They watched the parachutists come down with curiosity and delight.

But two hours later, the soldiers began to surround several houses. The same *parcelista*, who was a Chuj Indian, suddenly found his house surrounded by about forty soldiers. He was thinking about his carpentry jobs, not about war or weapons. The soldiers had a list and they asked him his name. Because his name was very similar to one on the list, they immediately threw him into a ditch, beating and kicking him: "They hit me on the head, kicked me in the stomach and back as if angrily beating a dog, that's what they did to me. They insulted me, saying: 'Guerrilla motherfucker.' I couldn't understand why they were doing this to me. So I said: 'If you want to kill me, go ahead, but I haven't done anything.' And again they said: 'You're a guerrilla.' I replied: 'I don't know what a guerrilla is. Is it a man or an animal? I don't know what "guerrillas" are.'" And he really did not have anything to do with the guerrillas who had created a support group in Xalbal.

Afterward the soldiers made him guide them to a tributary of the Xalbal River, where the townspeople were building a hanging "hammock" bridge.

The soldiers already knew that they would find the peasants gathered there and surrounded the group. Several peasants managed to escape into the jungle; the rest showed no signs of fear. Once again, the soldiers read out the list, singling out three men: Sebastián Felipe, a Mam Indian from San Ildefonso Ixtahuacán, and Juan Tomás and his son, Chuj Indians from San Mateo Ixtatán. All were originally from Huehuetenango and had emigrated, as had most of the colonizers of the Ixcán jungle, in search of land. The witness who recounted the event was allowed to leave at this point, as three men with names similar to his own had been found.

The soldiers took the three captives and went off to look for more people in their homes on their plots of land. Some were found, others were not. Those captured were tortured and made to inform on others. The soldiers went on like this day and night. Sometimes they threatened the wives, as one woman recounts: "They aimed their guns at me, sticking a gun in my chest when I was milking the cows, and asked me where my husband was. I answered them: 'If I had him here inside my slip, I'd hand him over to you.' They searched the house and my children started to tremble and cry. I was six months pregnant at the time, and due to the fright I suffered, the baby is prone to attacks."

We know that those captured were tortured because one was later released in El Quiché's main town, and he told how he was taken by helicopter and drawn into the jungle: "Every time the helicopter landed, I was beaten and kicked. They'd say: 'Tell us where the rest of your companions are.' They sat on me and tied my hands behind my back."

The Second Roundup (6 July)

On Sunday, 6 July, the army gathered in people for a second time in search of persons on their list. At about 12:30 a helicopter landed and four soldiers jumped out, running to the market to round up people. At the same time, another thirty soldiers surrounded the town and blocked the roads. The four soldiers separated the men from the women and children, lining the men up. Once in line, a man in a military uniform came up to them; he was armed and carrying equipment but wore "a cloth over his face, with little holes for his eyes," one witness remembers. He looked at the faces of the men in line, motioning at those to be captured. This soldier was not a soldier at all, but a *parcelista* from Xalbal. One of the townspeople was able to approach him and look him in the face. He says, "I recognized Francisco." Francisco was the name of the unfortunate traitor.

Three men were captured on this occasion: Miguel Sales Ordóñez, Alonso Ortiz, and Felipe Sales, all Mam Indians from San Ildefonso Ixtahuacán. Miguel Sales Ordóñez was a health promoter; his case received national and international attention thanks to his wife, who came out pub-

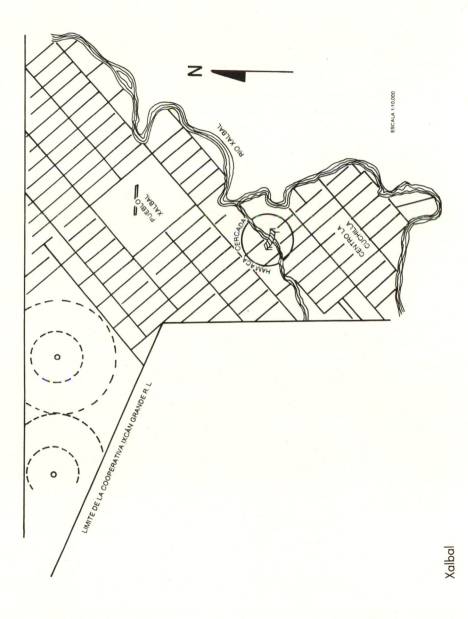

Xalbal

licly to demand the release of her husband. She even went to the Guatemalan president's office. She saw her husband for the last time the day after he had been captured; the army had hidden him in the jungle. She took him breakfast, despite the lieutenant's protests. Almost out of her mind, she went back to the lieutenant to show him her husband's identity card, hoping to prove in this way that he was innocent.

But nothing was gained. He was taken away, and she never saw him again.[2] In her broken Spanish, she expresses the anguish of not knowing what has happened to her husband. She would have preferred to simply know that he was dead.

My question is, Where have they taken him? They haven't even told me if he's dead; that's why we're sad. Are we to be killed off like chickens—killed for no reason at all?

That month, a total of about fifteen people were kidnapped from Xalbal and forced to disappear. Some of their names are as follows:[3]

Names of the Disappeared

1. Juan Tomás	from San Mateo Ixtatán
2. Baltasar Pedro	from San Mateo Ixtatán
3. Gabriel Carmelo Tomás	from San Mateo Ixtatán
4. Sebastián Felipe Jiménez	from San Ildefonso Ixtahuacán
5. Miguel Sales Ordóñez	from San Ildefonso Ixtahuacán
6. Alonso Ortiz Ordóñez	from San Ildefonso Ixtahuacán
7. José Felipe Sales	from San Ildefonso Ixtahuacán
8. Juan Ortiz Jacinto	
9. Francisco Ramírez	
10. Juan Pérez Ramírez	
11. Baltasar Tomás Torres	from San Mateo Ixtatán

Regarding abductions carried out in other parts of Ixcán, I have been able to ascertain only that one other person, Santos Vicente Sarat, was captured at his home in Santa María Tzejá on 23 July 1975. He was taken to Santiago Ixcán, where the army set up an outpost after its abrupt arrival in the area on 10 June.

National and international denunciations refer to more than thirty disappearances that took place at that time.[4]

National and International Condemnation

National condemnation began when residents of Xalbal, including Miguel Sales Ordóñez's wife, went on a delegation. The delegation received the support of various institutions and grass-roots organizations in Guatemala

City, including IDESAC (the Institute of Economic and Social Development for Central America [Instituto de Desarrollo Económico y Social de América Central]) and the CNT (the National Confederation of Workers [Central Nacional de Trabajadores]). It is probably through them that Miguel Sales Ordóñez's widow was able to be interviewed in the newspaper *La Nación*. The interview was originally going to be published in two parts, but only the first came out (on 9 January 1976) because the minister of the interior, General Leonel Vassaux, expressly forbade the publication of the rest. News of the repression in Ixcán did not reach the media until six months after it first took place. The minister of defense, General Romeo Lucas García, regarded the denunciation as slander by political opponents, arguing that if irregularities had occurred in the operations against subversives, they would have been reported to the corresponding authorities at the time they took place, not six months later (*Prensa Libre*, 17 January 1976). His response only goes to show that because the army had been able to hush things up for several months (thanks to the distance and isolation of Ixcán), it was angry that news of the events eventually did get out.

Abroad, news of the repression reached the U.S. Congress. Various interviews were carried out in Ixcán at the beginning of 1976 (including one with Miguel Sales Ordóñez's widow) by people concerned about human rights abuses. Their report was submitted to the National Council of Churches of Christ in the United States, and Rev. William L. Wipfler traveled to Guatemala on 30 January 1976 to interview government officials before submitting a formal denunciation to the Inter-American Commission on Human Rights. The Ministry of Defense did not provide him with further information except that the army had carried out counterinsurgency operations in El Quiché. Wipfler filed his denunciation and gave testimony to the U.S. House of Representatives on 9 June 1976. The testimony also included the killing of peasants in Chisec, Alta Verapaz (January 1976) and the repression unleashed in February 1976 in the Ixil area of El Quiché.

Amnesty International published information on Ixcán abductions in December 1976. President Kjell Eugenio Laugerud's response was to accuse the institution of being Communist (Amnesty International 1976).

The Political and Military Context

Why did the army so vehemently repress the civilian population of Xalbal? The answer is obvious when one recalls what the soldiers told the Chuj peasant: "You are a guerrilla." The army captured, tortured, and made disappear fifteen *parcelistas* on the grounds that they were guerrillas.

Why did the army consider them to be members of the rebel forces? From November 1969, scattered units of the FAR had been in the area, a bit to the south of Xalbal by San Luis Ixcán. But the rebels had no support base among the local population, and the army had written them off.

In January 1972, a group of rebels had reorganized, forming what would become the EGP, and entered Ixcán. The same year, the Guatemalan army, together with the Mexican army, carried out sweep operations in the jungle in search of the first fifteen rebels who had recently entered, but they were unable to find them (Payeras 1982 and 1983).

Between 1972 and 1975 the rebel forces established themselves on both sides of the Xalbal River and in December 1973 they went up into the Ixil triangle, where they clandestinely extended their political work. At the end of 1974, they ended the stage of secretly establishing their base and started to carry out open political-military actions, the phase known as armed propaganda. Their most resounding action, which was like a declaration of war, was the killing of La Perla estate owner Luis Arenas on 7 June 1975 in Chajul in the south of the jungle. Arenas was known as the "Tiger of Ixcán" because of the cruel way he treated his workers.

The army reacted immediately, not in the Ixil area but in Ixcán. On 10 June, as described earlier, parachutists landed in Xalbal and violently abducted peasants. This action was extremely important in their counterinsurgency logic, as it was an attempt to eradicate the core of the burgeoning rebel forces, putting an end to their three years of life hidden in the jungle.[5] The rebels had to be severed from their roots, which was the civilian population, so that they would not extend further into the jungle. The execution on La Perla estate made the army realize that the guerrillas had already extended as far as the highlands.

But we must not think that the army organized the operation in three days. It had been preparing for months, gathering information in Xalbal. The lists that the soldiers had when they surrounded the group of *parcelistas* next to the hanging bridge over the Xalbal tributary had been drawn up thanks to a *ladino* settler in Xalbal, who had had land disputes with the rest of the indigenous *parcelistas* in Xalbal. His name was Guillermo Monzón. He had close ties with the National Institute of Agrarian Transformation (Instituto Nacional de Transformación Agraria; INTA), which had a small office to the east of the river. Monzón was working there using a tractor to prepare a landing strip. The rebels had discovered he was an army *oreja* (spy), so they killed him in May 1975 on the river bank. The army arrived in Xalbal the following month looking for Guillermo Monzón's killers, and his relatives helped the soldiers to complete the lists. Although this was the EGP's first public action, it was never given the same publicity or political importance as the killing of the Tiger of Ixcán. On the contrary, it was the army repression that brought attention to Ixcán nationally and abroad.

The Social Context of Ixcán

What was the social context? Before 1966, Ixcán was uninhabited jungle. That year, the first settlers arrived with Maryknoll priest Father Edward Doheny to take possession of the lands in a joint Church and INTA project to buy private lands and receive allotments of certain state properties. The colonizers settled on the banks of the Ixcán River and began to clear the jungle and sow crops, battling against the heat and intense rains (six meters a year), the impenetrable vegetation, snakes, mosquitos, bogs, lack of roads, the great distances from towns and commercial centers, loneliness, and isolation. They were pioneers hungry for lands and tired of selling their labor on the large coffee, sugarcane, and cotton estates on the coast and coastal lowlands. Indigenous peasants, particularly from the Mam, Q'anjob'al, Jakalteko and Chuj ethnic groups, together with a few *ladinos*, settled on plots of 17.5 hectares each, and the fertility of the land felt like a wonderful gift.

They began organizing the first centers, one for every twenty-four lots of land, and cooperatives were later formed out of many centers. Mayalán, next to the Ixcán River, was the first cooperative to be formed. Xalbal, farthest to the east next to the Xalbal River, was the second. The jungle gradually filled with people, who organized more centers and more cooperatives until there were five cooperatives altogether.[6]

In 1975, there were 256 *parcelistas* in Xalbal, but they lived on their plots of land, not in the town. They were therefore considerably isolated from each other and were not able to be aware of the army coming down on one house, as in the case of the Chuj witness. The isolation also impeded counterinsurgency activity, as it was not possible to control the population. The army had surrounded the town on a Sunday, when the people go to market, because of this situation: Sunday is the only day when the population usually gathers together.

In 1969 Father Edward Doheny was replaced by Father William Woods, who was also a North American Maryknoll priest. He introduced changes in the project, reducing the mediating role of the INTA, indiscriminately inviting more people from the highlands, and insisting on collective ownership of the land. Thus the Ixcán Grande Cooperative was formed in 1970. It continues to be the owner of the entire project's land, bringing together the representatives of the five credit and savings cooperatives in its management council. The cooperative system provided a forum for organizational learning for this multiethnic, multilingual, and industrious pioneer group. The members of this group had had no revolutionary leanings when they came to the jungle, but the change from the sterile highlands to the rich jungle greatly changed their lives. After the army repression began, the settlers would look back and say that it had given them great joy to have owned 17.5 hectares of the country's most fertile lands, and it was no wonder that the army wanted them out so that it could distribute the lands among the rich and more powerful. (See Manz 1988a, 127–144, and AVANCSO 1992, 29–88.)

Commentaries on the Events

Again, I am moved by the urgency of the witnesses to say "You murdered the just ones." We should now analyze whether in this case the army's action was equivalent to murder and whether the people were innocent. That is, we should establish whether the people deserved such treatment in justice to law.

I do not wish to confuse the reader with the political, military, and social explanations presented in the Introduction. These are important in understanding human behavior—particularly the behavior of those in the army. The explanations are in no way intended to justify the army's criminal actions. Nor am I saying that all members of the army are criminals or that all members of the military share the same degree of responsibility for these deeds.

I would also like to make it clear that I am only analyzing the army's actions, and I refrain from passing judgment on (censuring or approving) the guerrilla actions. I remain nonjudgmental so that the analysis has greater impartiality and force. In justification of the army's actions one often hears, "Well, the rebels are hardly little angels." In this book I am not trying to establish whether they are angels or whether they are guilty.[7] However, the blood shed by the army is disproportionate to that shed by the rebel forces. In the present chapter the relation is at least fifteen to one.

We have seen that the soldier justifies capturing, torturing, and forcing the peasant to disappear by the statement "You're a guerrilla." In so doing, he is treating civilians as combatants, merely on the grounds that the former cannot or do not wish to inform on the guerrilla forces, that they may sympathize to some extent with them, or that they are in some way linked. The soldier justifies himself by shouting "You're a guerrilla" in an attempt to make the peasant feel guilty, as if his relation with the rebels (if there is one) were a crime. The result is that the peasant becomes even more impenetrable, as he knows that his life is at stake. We do not know for sure what kind of links the peasants on the list had with the rebels or who maintained such relations. But we do know that even if the civilian population did have some contact with the rebel forces, that does not automatically make them guerrillas. And if some of them did participate directly in the death of Guillermo Monzón, they could have been brought to justice by courts of law.

The peasants were captured without sufficient evidence, and with no legal warrant whatsoever. The lists were concocted during a dispute for the best lands, which was underpinned by ethnic differences. Remember that the information came from Guillermo Monzón. His accusations were heavily motivated by personal resentment: For example, Miguel Sales Ordóñez (accused by Monzón) would not let his son marry Monzón's daughter. The lists were subsequently used by soldiers unfamiliar with indigenous culture, in which a name can be repeated in alternate generations, often in memory of one's predecessors. (For example, Sebastián Tomás's son will be Tomás Sebastián and his grandson will be Sebastián Tomás.) However, the slightest similarity of a name with one on the list provokes a reaction of kicks and insults.

The evidence is insufficient, and the people captured are allowed no defense. The more that the people try to defend themselves, the more they are beaten, as the military considers them to be hiding information. The evidence is insufficient because the accusation is made without any reference to the judicial system: There is no impartial arbitrator who carries out an investigation. The army is both judge and prosecutor.

I also found that torture—in the fields and in the military barracks—is used to extract information. In other chapters this practice is documented in greater depth. Without torture, counterinsurgency is unthinkable.

Forced disappearance is a method used to conceal evidence of army responsibility in the killings, as it makes it impossible to prove that those captured have been killed. I have heard numerous testimonies that the corpses of those abducted were thrown into the canyon of the Xalbal rapids. It is difficult to ascertain whether this is true, because the bodies have disappeared. It is also usually difficult to prove that those who disappeared did not flee from the army and go elsewhere. The counterinsurgency method of forcing people to disappear tends to take credibility away from denunciations. However, in the particular case in this chapter of those who have disappeared, it is unlikely that all the witnesses are mistaken because they were related to or well acquainted with those who have disappeared and because it was also established that the men who were abducted did not return to their native lands or go elsewhere. It is very unlikely that Miguel Sales Ordóñez's widow did not know where her husband was and that the witnesses who gave us testimony eight years later did not know of Miguel Sales's whereabouts if he were alive.

Impunity has existed in Ixcán from the beginning. Forced disappearance guarantees impunity, as does concealing all information about events and threatening the local population so that the information is not publicized nationally or abroad. All these techniques allow for impunity. President Kjell's astonishing accusation of Amnesty International as being Communist also contributed to the army's freedom from punishment. To use the passing of time as a pretext to deny responsibility, as in the case of Defense Minister General Romeo Lucas García, who claimed that any irregularities in the antisubversive operations in El Quiché "should have been duly reported to the authorities," also contributes to impunity.

NOTES

1. The word *parcelista* refers to the owner of a plot of land. As there is no concise English equivalent, the Spanish word will be used.—TRANS.

2. This account is based on an interview with Miguel Sales Ordóñez's widow carried out by another researcher in December 1975.

3. The witnesses have given various names, which by and large coincide though not completely. For example, the last two names on the list appear on Miguel Sales Ordóñez's widow's list of 8, published in an interview in the daily *La Nación* on 9 January 1976. These names do not appear on the other witnesses' lists. We have omitted the name of Juan Tomás's son because, according to one witness, he managed to escape from the army.

4. A letter sent by "leaders of the community's agriculture cooperative" to the president of Guatemala, General Kjell Eugenio Laugerud, in September 1975 speaks of 37 disappeared persons. I was unable to look at the letter to see whether it included a list of their names. The letter is mentioned in W. Wipfler's testimony to the U.S. Congress (Wipfler 1976). Miguel Sales Ordóñez's widow also said in her interview to *La Nación* (9 January 1976) that more than 30 men were abducted and taken away by helicopter, though she mentioned only 8 names. Amnesty International took the matter up in December 1976, referring to the same number of victims but not giving names. I therefore believe that the estimate of over 30 is possible, given that the sweep operation took more than three months and covered many villages, apart from Xalbal. I have been unable to provide substantial evidence, however.

5. According to counterinsurgency experience in Malaya and Vietnam, Thompson (1974) distinguishes three revolutionary stages: (1) the subversive build-up phase, (2) guerrilla warfare, and (3) the war of movements. He also outlines two counterinsurgency periods: (1) when the revolutionary movement is in its first phase and (2) when the movement has not been defeated during the first phase and has moved to the second phase, guerrilla warfare. Thompson says: "Any sensible government should attempt to defeat an insurgent movement during the subversive build-up phase before it enters the guerrilla phase, and if that is not possible ... then the movement must be defeated as early as possible during the guerrilla phase" (Thompson 1974, 50). The same author distinguishes three zones: (1) urban populated areas, (2) rural populated areas, and (3) remote scarcely populated areas (Thompson 1974, 104). There is a geographical factor in the division of the areas related to the distance from the power center, the first zone being the nearest and the third zone being the farthest away. There is also respective control, as in the phase of guerrilla warfare: the first zone is under army control; the second zone is in dispute; and the third zone is under guerrilla control, although not necessarily constituting a liberated zone (Thompson 1974, 104).

By combining phases with areas during the first period, when the guerrillas are still in their subversive phase, the army should concentrate all its efforts on the remote areas, placing the guerrillas entirely under the control of the army, not the police, to put an end to subversion. The blow in Xalbal in 1975 was so strong because it was a remote scarcely populated area and because the guerrilla movement was just beginning.

6. The five cooperatives, corresponding to the five small towns, are Mayalán, Xalbal, Resurrección or Pueblo Nuevo, Los Angeles, and Cuarto Pueblo. Later, other villages were formed around the project, such as Samaritano, Zunil, Mónaco, and Ixtahuacán Chiquito to the west and Malacatán, Piedras Blancas, and Nueva Comunidad to the south.

7. Because I take this methodological approach does not mean that I do not have a political position; nor does it mean that I believe that one cannot or should not consider that only the other party or both parties together should be judged. I have chosen this path, but it is not the only one; that is why I refer to it as an option.

CHAPTER 2

Persecution of the Church

The Army "Brings Down" Father Woods
(20 November 1976)

On 20 November 1976, everyone was gathered in the church in Pueblo Nuevo. It was a Saturday, and they were waiting for Father William Woods to arrive in his small plane to give mass. "We talked to him that morning, at 6:00 A.M.," remembers a witness who was then president of the Pueblo Nuevo cooperative. From Guatemala City, Woods had asked about the weather, and they had told him it was normal. "But the time of his scheduled arrival passed and he hadn't arrived, and time went on, so we contacted Xalbal, because sometimes he would go to Xalbal first. But he hadn't arrived. So we contacted the other cooperatives, but he hadn't arrived anywhere. Finally, at 2:00 P.M. we were contacted by the Maryknolls' main house in Guatemala City and were asked if Father Woods had entered Ixcán, because they had heard that a plane had crashed. But we learned nothing further that day. It wasn't till the following day that we heard that he had had an accident." Indeed, that Saturday the plane carrying Father William Woods and four other North Americans had crashed to the north of the Cuchumatanes heights, when it was approaching the town of Cotzal. All the witnesses I have talked to invariably accuse the army of having "brought him down."[1]

Name of the Victim	Reason for Going to Ixcán
1. William H. Woods	Maryknoll missionary
2. John Gauker	Housing project in Guatemala
3. Selwyn Puig	Photographic journalist (mother of four)
4. Ann Kerndt	In Ixcán for the Direct Relief Foundation
5. Michael D. Okado	Japanese-American doctor (accompanying Ann Kerndt)

None of the *parcelistas* were direct witnesses to the army action. At first, explains another witness (a catechist), "we didn't know how he had died"; some gave one explanation and others gave another. "Some say he was shot down, others that he crashed against a tree." Several months went by before the collective opinion was formed, based on incoming information: "Much later we found out that, yes, he had been shot down by soldiers in the area."

What was the collective opinion based on? First, there are commentaries (which are not necessarily true) about the circumstances of the accident and the authorities' attitude in impeding investigations. One well-informed witness says: "The people working in San Juan Cotzal in the malaria unit said that a group of soldiers had shot down a small plane; word has it that people were near when the event took place and that the soldiers refused to let them look at the plane." Concerning the obstacles in the investigations: "His mother arrived in Guatemala City from the United States. The coffin was sealed and no one was allowed to open it. In order for no one to see him, the government put on a seal, so that they couldn't open the coffin."[2]

Second, other versions circulate about how an army officer who was very involved in Ixcán confessed that other officers were planning to kill Woods: "In 1978 Colonel Castillo said over drinks: 'I am not guilty, but other colonels planned the priest's death.'" Colonel Fernando Castillo was named national coordinator of the cooperatives by President Kjell Laugerud, and after Woods's death he became the immediate mediator between the Ixcán cooperative and the government and army. He knew the ins and outs of the army and of Ixcán. It is also possible that under the effect of alcohol he brought out the tensions between the military, which became more intense as the conflict progressed. Another witness who visited the colonel at his home on several occasions says that he confessed that high-ranking officers recriminated him during the time that President Lucas was in office: "Look, Castillo, is it true that you're in favor of the guerrillas?" This remark gives credibility to what he had said under the effect of alcohol.

Third, the collective opinion is strengthened most by the context of what happened, which is known to all. Woods was a bother to the army, not because of his personality or because of his preaching but because of his key role in the Ixcán cooperatives in obtaining lands, marketing products (using his and other small planes), and in communicating with the outside in general, thanks to his radio system and flights. Immediately after the first abductions, his license to fly was cancelled. Although President Kjell himself authorized its renewal, it was taken away on various occasions. "He was not allowed to use small planes," a witness remembers, and Woods picked up people from Mayalán who went on a delegation to Guatemala to speak to the president. His licenses were renewed, but only to go to give church services. The army took charge of marketing the community's products.

The local population also knew that Woods's house was searched on the day of the second round of abductions in Xalbal and weeks later in Mayalán. The people also knew that the army suspected Woods of being a mediator for the rebels and transporting arms, things that were never proved.

The local population also saw how the army, via Colonel Castillo and the Guatemalan air force, occupied Woods's key position in the cooperatives after he died. They made landing strips in all the cooperatives so that the army's Aravá[3] could take out coffee and cardamom and take the sick to the hospital. But the army's real intention, according to the witnesses, was twofold: to gain the hearts and minds of the local population and to implant the army in the area. The flights served to bring supplies to the military barracks that were set up in several of the cooperatives. When the following priest, a German named Karl Stetter, took up his post in Ixcán, he was not allowed to carry out marketing functions.

Before moving on to see what happened to Stetter, we should remember that the death of Woods is now interpreted as a presage that was then not understood. The catechist witness says: "We did not know what was going to happen. We thought that only he would die." Father Woods was a precursor, and his death should have been a prophetic sign of the massacres to take place. As the years followed, events put his death into context: Woods appears to have been the victim of the same perpetrators who carried out the killings later on.

Father Karl Is Deported
(19 December 1978)

On 19 December 1978, Father Karl Stetter, a diocesan priest from Stuttgart, was arrested in Huehuetenango by the army and deported from Guatemala. The catechist in Pueblo Nuevo remembers that on that day "he took his plane to the landing strip to make sure he had enough gasoline. He told the soldiers where he was going. He went first to Xalbal and then on to Huehuetenango. From there they didn't let him come back; they took him to the military barracks in Huehuetenango. We heard that when he arrived in Guatemala City they undressed him and took him to El Salvador naked. He never came back to us."

Stetter was also a nuisance to the military in Ixcán because he was witness to what the army was doing, because he was an amateur radio enthusiast who made daily contact with the world in German, because he had a plane, and because he embodied the presence of the Church, which was regarded as competition to the army in helping the local population despite that the Church was no longer involved in the cooperative, as in the times of Woods.

Twice the army tried to trap him. Soldiers dressed as rebels visited him one night, asking him to take arms from Pueblo Nuevo to Mayalán. The first time, he told a small group of catechists. One of these catechists remembers, "We asked him what they looked like. The priest answered: 'One was fat and they weren't wearing uniforms. Do you think they were really guerrillas?' he asked us. We told him they were from the military barracks. 'Why?' he asked us again. 'Because everyone knows that the rebels don't bother anyone and they don't need planes to carry arms.' 'I'll go to the military barracks right now,' he said. It was drizzling. He put on his cape and left. 'Be careful,' we told him. 'What if they capture the priest? If he doesn't come back, we'll let the centers know.' He went to the military barracks. Fifteen minutes later he came back. 'I went there to let off steam. I told them I'm not to be messed around with or to be involved in politics.'"

They laid the same trap for him for the second time on 13 December, and once again Stetter refused to transport arms.

The presence of the priest bothered the army. On 6 December there was a stormy meeting between the cooperative and Colonel Castillo. The colonel wanted the members of the cooperative to build a boarding school for the entire area of Pueblo Nuevo. He wanted to inaugurate it on 20 February 1979, in honor of Tecún Umán, a Quiché hero who died when fighting against the Spanish invader Pedro de Alvarado, according to a legend. The people rejected the idea of starting building immediately, even though the colonel had sought the support of the Evangelicals. A witness who had taken part in the discussion recalls that the colonel got angry: "You should have seen the colonel. If looks could kill!" And he threatened to take the school project elsewhere. Then the people retorted: "If you want to, take it. We aren't toys. You're only tricking us. You're a liar." They said this because the people wanted to build the landing strip first, to ensure the arrival of the building materials, but the colonel did not want this and even told them that the regular flights would be suspended.

The competition with the Church was highlighted at that meeting. The colonel wanted his school to be finished before the construction of the parochial school was completed, even though the latter had already been started. The people remembered then that Woods's flights had been suspended and that the colonel had promised to replace them and had not kept his promise. That's why they said to him, "You're a liar." The colonel replied that it was not the government but rather Father Karl who had not fulfilled his promise of providing a tractor. And the people replied that the tractor was stuck in a swamp and that the priest had fulfilled his promise.

Two weeks later the army captured Stetter and deported him from Guatemala. The local population was left without a priest.[4]

Father José María and His Sexton Are Ambushed (4 June 1980)

On 4 June 1980, Father José María Gran, a Spanish priest of the Sacred Heart congregation, whose diocese was in El Quiché, and his sexton, Domingo Batz, were ambushed by the army as they were returning from Ixcán to Chajul. A Charismatic witness, a member of a group of guitarists from Kaibil (to the east of Xalbal), remembers that Gran visited them just before returning to the highlands: "Father José María left and a few days later we heard that he had died. He was on his way from Kaibil to Chajul, visiting Santa María Tzejá first, but he never arrived in Chajul. They killed him and his sexton too. Some members of the Catholic group were happy and said: 'Let's see how the Charismatics take this. … ' From that day on, no more priests arrived."

According to an army communiqué, two subversives died in combat.

The witness from Kaibil says that there was deep division between the traditional Catholics, who did not accept the Charismatic movement, and the Charismatics. The former built another church, but Father Gran held mass only in the main church, used by the Charismatics.

The army tried to fill the absence of priests from the dioceses of El Quiché and Huehuetenango, and Colonel Castillo looked for priest friends, who visited "the Catholics" in Kaibil. According to a Charismatic, "A priest came on behalf of the government. The Catholics requested an effigy of Saint Sebastian, and it arrived by helicopter. A priest arrived and the colonel took him to bless the effigy. He also blessed the basketball court and things related to the cooperative."

The colonel also took priests to the other cooperatives, obviously only for short visits. According to a catechist witness from Cuarto Pueblo who was not a Charismatic, Colonel Castillo "later brought a priest. We were in great doubt. He brought him as the people were in need of baptisms. But the people realized that he was not baptizing according to the rules. They said: 'Do you think he is really a priest?'"

The Word of God Comes to an End

The army continued to control and threaten the Church, now no longer through its priests but through the faithful. The celebrations of the religious animators, or "animadores de la fe" (high-ranking catechists who were allowed to distribute holy communion and conducted the weekly celebration), were controlled and the lieutenant sometimes appeared for the services. A witness from Xalbal recalls: "The lieutenant entered the church, which the soldiers had surrounded. We were in a service at 11:00 A.M." He asked them if they were really celebrating the word of God or were guerrillas. He threatened them and demanded that they tell him who the guerrillas among them were: "'If you don't want to say anything, we're going to get all of you indiscriminately, including children and women, and we're going to burn down your houses.' At that time, we didn't believe him, but we were scared. That was the last day we were able to celebrate the word of God." This must have taken place in 1981. It was a premonition of the massacres to come in 1982.

The Evangelicals were also controlled and threatened. The army did not, except on a few occasions, take advantage of religious divisions as it did in other parts of the country, as we saw in Pueblo Nuevo.[5] The army distrusted everyone, Evangelicals and Catholics, traditional Catholics and Charismatic Catholics. An Evangelical witness from Xalbal recalls: "The churches were all under surveillance day and night; when there was a service, they'd come to see us. They didn't even want us to hold services. And we had to go to the military barracks to ask permission; at the end of the service we had to report back to the barracks again. When we went to ask permission, they'd say: 'You're only to drink half a liter.' They laugh at us, as if we were going to go out drinking."

The military alienated all the Christian groups. That is why with the large-scale massacres, as we shall see later on, the army chose moments when both Catholics and Evangelicals were in their chapels, celebrating their faith, to surround and kill them. It considered religion to be merely a screen for the guerrillas.

NOTES

1. In Guatemala *bajar* refers not only to lowering or bringing down but also to causing casualties or losses.—TRANS.

2. According to the Civil Aeronautical report signed by Natzul René Méndez on 25 November 1976, the accident occurred because of poor weather. But on that very day, Guy Gervais flew over the site of the accident several times and said that there had not been a cloud in the sky. The army arrived at the scene of the accident several hours later and removed the bodies, which is against the law, and did not inform the Maryknolls until the day after the accident. The aeronautical investigators only flew over the place and did not land to inspect the remains of the plane. The government refused to help a North American expert investigate the matter. Woods had said that if the army wished to kill him, it would choose that precise canyon. One of the Maryknoll priests was informed by Guatemalan friends that they had heard military officers boasting, under the effects of alcohol, about having killed Woods (Brett and Brett 1988).

3. The Aravá is a multiple-use, medium-sized Israeli plane.

4. In February 1979 another Maryknoll priest began to provide pastoral attention to Ixcán, but on a visiting basis; from time to time he would come from Barillas to visit for several weeks. He began the Charismatic Catholic movement, which grew very rapidly, had scarcely any contact with the development projects, and put the army on the alert. According to the witnesses, the army expelled him from Ixcán in 1980. But this testimony is not well documented or widely believed, although it may be true. The last time he left Ixcán was on 16 March 1980. From June that year the persecution of the Church intensified in El Quiché.

5. Colonel Castillo seems to have been aware of the existing tensions between the religious groups, and the episodes narrated here indicate that he attempted to use them. But the army did not make these distinctions when it came to the massacres. Judging from the testimonies in which the colonel is accused of being a guerrilla by other officers, it would seem that he had begun to lose credibility.

CHAPTER 3

Abductions and Torture

(1979 to 1981)

A Spate of Abductions

From 1979 to 1981, a spate of individual abductions (nobody abducted was ever released) and individual nocturnal killings took place in Ixcán Grande. I estimate that there must have been about 50, although I have documented information about only the following 22 cases:

Name	Cooperative
1. Francisco Tánchez	Mayalán
2. Luis Martínez	Mayalán
3. Julián Gabriel	Mayalán
4. Julián Ros	Mayalán
5. Julio Méndez	Mayalán
6. Mateo Marcos	Mayalán
7. Santiago Villalobos	Mayalán (Zunil)
8. Mateo Juan	Mayalán (Mónaco)
9. Alejandro Velásquez	Los Angeles
10. Isidro Pablo	Los Angeles
11. Francisco Pérez	Los Angeles
12. Raúl Solís	Los Angeles
13. Porfirio Villatoro	Los Angeles (nearby farm)
14. Prudencio	Los Angeles
15. Raymundo	Los Angeles
16. Arnulfo	Los Angeles
17. Lorenzo Méndez Pérez	Los Angeles
18. Hilario Sales	Pueblo Nuevo
19. Alonso Domingo O.	Pueblo Nuevo
20. Baltasar Juan Nicolás	Xalbal
21. Rafael Miguel	Xalbal
22. Isidoro	Cuarto Pueblo[1]

As Ixcán Grande is only a part of the municipality of Ixcán,[2] it is safe to say that the number of abductions and individual nocturnal killings surpassed 100.

What Happened in Some Cases

On the night of 28 April 1979 Alejandro Velásquez was abducted from his house on the plot of land he owned in Los Angeles. "His wife realized they were soldiers; she saw them in military uniform with their equipment," recalls a *parcelista* from Los Angeles. The woman went to the military outpost the following day to complain. The cooperative leaders called their members together and asked the lieutenant to give an explanation. The lieutenant said: "He was killed by the guerrillas." But the woman said: "You are the ones who took him." The woman went to Colonel Castillo to complain, and he sent her metal sheeting for her house, but her husband never appeared again. This abduction was the first since 1975. Alejandro Velásquez was a *cuxa* (an illegal alcoholic beverage) seller. He had had a fight with the auxiliary mayors, who put him in jail after he threatened to kill them.[3]

Francisco Tánchez, a *ladino*, was abducted at night from his home in Mayalán on Sunday, 10 June 1979. His wife did not witness the abduction, as she was with her relatives in the highlands. His children (the oldest a girl of twelve) did see their father kidnapped. So did a neighbor who went out of her house during the night to urinate; she saw the soldiers and immediately went to inform the cooperative leaders. They contacted the people from the centers close by, and "by dawn about seventy-five people had arrived" to protest to the lieutenant. He denied everything, but "the people were sure: 'It was the army,' they said. They called the military 'people-eaters': 'Cannibals, if you want meat there's a bull in the pasture.'" But they did not release Chico Tánchez and a helicopter took him secretly to Playa Grande. Even the commander at Playa Grande came to appease the people, but he achieved nothing. The colonel was very angry when he left. "The old man left in a fury," recalls a *ladino* witness. And when he went he insulted everyone, saying, "I'm leaving smeared with people," implying that the people were shit.

Isidro Pablo, a Mam Indian, was killed at night in the Los Angeles cooperative store on the Sunday before Christmas in 1980. He was the shop assistant. They stabbed him ("there was a large knife wound on his neck," according to a man who saw the body) and tried to pass it off as a common crime by taking money and merchandise. I was unable to locate anyone who had witnessed the event firsthand. But the witnesses are sure that the killers were soldiers led by the military commissioner because the latter had told the shop assistant that he was going to go to the store that night, presumably so that he would open the door for him, even if he later told other people that he had been miles away, sleeping, which was untrue because he was seen in the village at 7:00 P.M. The officer based in Los Angeles blamed the killing on the guerrillas. The army presumably killed him on the assumption that he was selling provisions to the guerrillas. That afternoon the soldiers had caught him listening to Radio Havana in the store.

Luis Martínez, a *ladino* Charismatic catechist and treasurer of the cooperative, was abducted as he was returning home from work in Mayalán on the afternoon of 5 November 1980. His wife and children witnessed the event. His wife was tied up and "the children were trembling with fear," recalls a witness from Mayalán. A group went to protest at the military outpost, but the army replied, as in the Los Angeles abduction, that the guerrillas had taken him: "Your 'parents' took him." As Luis Martínez was also the cooperative treasurer, this abduction was an attack on both the Church and the social organization. The evidence that the army had against him was that "he prays for the brothers in the bush," according to the same witness.

Hilario Sales, a Mam guitarist in the Charismatic musical group in Pueblo Nuevo, was abducted one Sunday in mid-November in the cooperative marketplace. He tried to escape from the military outpost but was captured again and violently tortured. He was returned half-alive to his parents, who took him to the hospital. "I saw him," a young friend of his remembers. "His eyes and ears were bleeding. He was a bleeding mess when they handed him over to his family." A few months later he died.

Julián Ros, a Jakalteko Indian, was killed at night at his brother's house on 29 November 1980. The army was trying to abduct his brother, who was the president of the Mayalán cooperative. The soldiers, led by an *oreja* (informer), approached the house of his brother, who was able to escape through a secret passageway. The soldiers then began to mistreat the women. Julián, who lived on the adjacent plot of land, heard the screams and thought it was his ailing mother choking. When he came in, the soldiers shot him point blank, thinking he was his brother. This event made a deep impression on the local population, given the brother's key position as president of the cooperative, and further aggravated the people's relations with the army.

I could go on relating numerous accounts of abductions and nocturnal killings. These abductions were premeditated; the lieutenant knew of them and protected their perpetrators. They were covert army actions, blamed on the rebels whenever possible. That is why they were carried out at night, when the military commissioners would secretly lead the soldiers. In contrast to events in Xalbal in 1975, the local population protested openly and fearlessly. These organized protests in turn caused more confrontations between the local population and the army, thus propagating further abductions. The kidnappings became more frequent as a means of controlling the population but also more ineffective as a way of obtaining information. They were soon to be replaced by open killings and massacres.

Torture

We will now look in greater detail at the system of torture used by the army. The analysis is based on the testimonies of those abducted, tortured, and subsequently released. Let us hear the horrendous yet awesome testimony of a Mam *parcelista*.

The army abducted Juan (not his real name) and took him to the military base in Playa Grande at the end of 1980.[4] He was blindfolded, and upon arrival the soldiers ordered him to get out of the helicopter:

> They told me: "Get out!" But how could I get out with my eyes covered? So I said, "Perhaps you could uncover my face." But a soldier threatened me: "Get out or I'll kill you." "I wish you'd kill me," I told him. "Jump," he screamed at me. So I jumped. I don't know how I did it, but I jumped to the ground.
>
> Who knows how many streets they took me through in Playa Grande. I couldn't see a thing with my face covered. But I heard when we arrived, as they took out a key and locked me inside.
>
> They took the blanket off my face and I could see. I looked upward. It was night, and I was inside a long barrel that didn't have a top. It was about five meters high. I could sit up but not lie down. I tried to sleep, but do you think my hands were free? My feet were tied too. I can tell you, the army really made me suffer. When they left me like that there was not enough room to sleep.
>
> I prayed to God: "God, forgive me! If I were stealing, then perhaps I would deserve to be treated this way. But I'm just doing my best to get by with my work." Only God can look out for me. And I thought: "Whatever they ask me, I won't say anything." That's what I decided. I just prayed to God. I was thinking: "I am going through what Christ went through when he was killed. If they want to kill me, let them."
>
> They took me out at midnight. "Out you come. Do you want me to kill you right now?" they asked me. "If my time is up, OK," I said. So he opened the lock on the barrel and unbound me.
>
> They took me to the boss. He was dressed in civilian clothing—no uniform. "You're a guerrilla, aren't you," he said to me. "How can you think that, sir?" I answered. "You know I'm not." "Are you going to talk or not?" he said, picking up a knife.
>
> "If you want to kill me, go ahead. I'm in your hands," I said. "If you talk, we'll let you go," he said to me. "I don't know anything," I said. "Let's just kill this piece of shit," he told the soldiers. They had a large blanket. They covered my face and started choking me. They laid me on the table and tied me up with a

rope. I felt as if I'd died. Everything was like a dream. When I woke up they were fanning me with a hat. I felt them untie me. "Have you woken up, Juan?" they said. Then I began to cry. I thought over and over again: "Why is this happening to me if I haven't done anything?" "You're saved this time. Go on, take him to his cell," they said.

Then I went out into the night air. When it rained, I'd get wet. Do you think the barrel had a cover?

This happened again. I was taken to make statements three times. I was there for about a week. But I never changed my story. "Listen, the guerrillas come and you feed them in the jungle at midday and in the evening," they'd say. "Who says so?" I'd reply. "Your own people." "But who? Perhaps it's slander. No one's been coming to my house," I would say. "Well, maybe you're right," they finally said.

He was released. Two soldiers took him out along the highway and told him to go west.

The Strategy of Torture

As we have seen, torture was like a combat between army and witness, and the battle was over information. The army tried to extract information by force from the prisoner, and he in turn tried to resist giving it.

The greatest torture involved suffocation; that was why Juan's head was covered with a blanket while they throttled him. They stuffed a piece of nylon down another prisoner's mouth until he began to faint and thought he would die. A third prisoner's head was submerged in a barrel of water six times. The army quickly and easily brought the prisoner to the brink of death through suffocation or choking and then brought him back, only to repeat the torture. Torture was not aimed at killing the prisoner, but at making him supply information. Torture formed an integral part of the interrogation.

The cells were very small to increase the sense of freedom deprivation; one was a barrel five meters high, and there were deep pits in all the military barracks. The cell was exposed to the rays of tropical sun, torrential rains in the afternoons, and cold jungle nights. The pits were also life threatening, as they would fill with water up to the prisoner's waist. The techniques of taking away the prisoner's freedom and leading him to near death through suffocation were aimed at breaking the personal identity of the person being tortured and, in so doing, shaking his convictions and loyalties.

Attempts were made, through the use of blindfolds, to stop the prisoner from identifying where he was being held and tortured. However, as the days progressed, the prisoners realized that they were being held at the military base in Playa Grande. Only one of the three witnesses was held and tortured in Pueblo Nuevo. Given that the military campaign was being waged in primitive conditions, the army was unable to completely dissociate the prisoner from a sense of time, as the latter could still see sunlight and count the days as they passed. In the cases studied, detentions of this type lasted between one and three weeks. But the army did try, albeit imperfectly, to isolate the prisoner from his social context and also to sever his sense of space and time so as to violate his intimate identity. In this sense, torture resembles a forced rite of passage.

Strategies to Resist Torture

The witnesses responded to the strategy of torture with a strategy of survival and resistance. If the army tried to dissociate the prisoner from his sense of space and time, the latter maintained these by listening to the soldiers talking. Even if the prisoner had been momentarily confused by his kidnappers when they dressed as rebels, he soon would identify them as soldiers because of the surroundings, the questions they would ask, the way he was treated, and from what he already knew about the army, even if he had never seen their uniforms or other distinguishing features.

If torture was aimed at making the witness supply information, the prisoner would continually deny that he was a rebel ("I'm not one of them") or that he had had contact with them ("I don't know anything about them") or that he had fed them. If the interrogator tried to confuse him by bringing in others ("they say you're a guerrilla"), the person being tortured would reply that the statement was a lie or would ask who had said that. The interrogator would try to make him contradict himself, but the person being tortured would refuse to alter what he had said. None of the three witnesses had contact with the rebels, and they were aided by this lack of knowledge. Their temptation was rather to lie to save their lives and appease the torturers, who apparently wanted them to say that they did know the rebels. The prisoners' strategy was therefore not to vacillate, not to doubt, not to change their story, and not to contradict themselves in order to make the torturer vacillate, doubt, and lie. Remember how Juan says that the torturer began to think aloud: "Maybe he [the prisoner] is right." At this moment, the person being tortured begins to win the combat.

If torture was aimed at breaking the prisoner's identity quickly by bringing him to the brink of death but not killing him, the person being tortured opted for the reverse strategy: wanting to die. To obtain inner strength, he would say, "I hope you kill me." This is the key moment of the combat, as the person being tortured, more than fighting to survive, is seeking victory over the torturer. Survival is not in his hands, but in the hands of the torturer; however, nobody can take away his desire to die, and if this desire is authentic, it can overpower the torturer, who wishes him not to die and not to wish to die so that he will talk.

If the torturer tried to control the prisoner's freedom and willpower, the prisoner would evade his domination by invoking God, recognizing His judgment as definitive by appealing to His wisdom. "Only God knows," he would say. The prisoner would give himself up to God's will, even though he was apparently completely in the hands of the torturer, and would identify with God's pain as if it were a fountain of life: "This is what happened to Christ when he was killed." However, this evasion of the capturer's domination over his prisoners was not authentic if it was not accompanied by the readiness or even the wish to die in order to live, as we said before. By identifying with God, the prisoner felt a ray of solace and love, which was life.

Finally, the army's aim to destroy the prisoner's personal identity was countered by a spontaneous response by those being tortured to affirm the faith that had been a dynamic part of their lives. This faith could be the will to work in the jungle for their families. When the interrogator accused the prisoner of harboring a faith in the rebel struggle, the prisoner vehemently denied this by asserting another faith, his faith in his work. This faith was also loyalty to his family and to the people in his cooperative, most of whom were opposed to the army. The solace and love he felt in identifying with the pain of Christ came together with the love for his family and his people; these he would affirm before the interrogator.

Although many of those tortured fell to the army's strategy, these testimonies proclaim that the poor and the weak can overcome the strategy of violence and can resist the techniques aimed at driving asunder the most intimate in a person: one's identity and loyalties.

The Context in Which the Abductions Took Place

The abductions in Xalbal were part of the army's attempts to root out the rebels. Remember that there were two stages in this attempt: The first was violent, involving abductions, and the other, civic action, was benevolent, when the army undertook to market local produce and to ingratiate itself in a thousand ways with the local population. Father Woods's death belongs to the first stage and Father Stetter's deportation belongs to the second. Both were carried out to diminish Church strength and influence.

The first abduction in Los Angeles, on 28 April 1979, heralded a new intermediary phase that contained elements of the former stage and of the stage to come. It contained the former in that it continued to try to root out the rebel forces, and it contained the latter in that the army was preparing its scorched-earth offensive. This stage finished, as we shall see in another chapter, with the combat in Cuarto Pueblo on 30 April 1981.

At a national level, repression of the popular and democratic movements intensified in mid-1978, when General Romeo Lucas was fraudulently elected president of Guatemala. The wave of repression did not reach Ixcán until 1979.

At that time the guerrilla movement was growing, particularly as a result of the impetus from the Sandinista revolution (19 July 1979) in Nicaragua. The generalization of guerrilla warfare began in the Ixil highlands in October 1979, and in Ixcán the rebels concentrated forces, which the army must have detected. As a result, the army escalated the number of abductions during those years.

But as the population grew in solidarity and became more antagonistic toward the army, torture became increasingly ineffective as a way of providing information. Interrogations became longer and more difficult because increasing numbers of inexperienced and less-trained personnel were used. (As torture became more widespread, it was carried out in small military outposts, not only at the Playa Grande base.) The information obtained was more adulterated, more people were beaten up and tortured who had nothing to do with the rebels, and discontent and hatred of the army grew. This became a vicious circle, as the local inhabitants increasingly closed ranks against the army. It is not surprising, therefore, that the outcome of this process resulted in selective and then indiscriminate massacres. Why lose time abducting and torturing? It is far more effective to simply wipe out entire sections of the population.

Counterinsurgency thus developed into large massacres.[5]

NOTES

1. The accounts of persons 12 to 16 and 21 to 22 each come from a separate source. The testimonies about persons 12, 13, 21, and 22 include descriptions of the events. We have trusted the sources because in most other aspects they have been exact. The information about the rest of these individuals was corroborated by different sources.

2. Ixcán Grande is an area between the Xalbal and Ixcán rivers. As such, it covers part of Huehuetenango and not just El Quiché, to which the newly created municipality of Ixcán belongs. The dividing line between the two departments lies between the two rivers.

3. Military commissioners are peasants chosen by the army to be its representatives. As we shall see further on, in Ixcán many of the commissioners were massacred by the army.

4. A fictitious name has been used to protect the witness.

5. According to Thompson (1974, 87), the relationship between intelligence gathering and abductions should be quite the opposite, that is, with growing results. It

ought to be a process of positive mutual conditioning: The more intelligence obtained, the more abductions, and the more abductions, the more intelligence obtained. This process culminates when relations between the population and the guerrillas diminish; the number of contacts should drop until disappearing altogether. Thus when intelligence increases and support bases weaken, persuasion becomes more useful than threats as a method for extracting information: Having complete information scares the prisoner and brings the truth from him more effectively than torture does. This is what Thompson says. But this was not the case in Guatemala.

CHAPTER 4

Selective Massacres and Terror

(1981)

The Massacre of Leaders in Cuarto Pueblo
(30 April)

On 30 April 1981, in the cooperative town Cuarto Pueblo, 15 men were killed by the army.[1] Six were forced to disappear and 9 were killed then and there.

Name	Age	Place of Origin	Occupation
Persons Disappeared			
1. Ramón Díaz Jiménez	29	Jacaltenango[2]	Health worker
2. Manuel Francisco Jiménez	28	San Rafael La Independencia	Co-op worker
3. Jesús Marcos	24	Jacaltenango	
4. Baltasar Pedro	30	Santa Eulalia	
5. Gaspar Paiz			Co-op worker
6. Félix Cumatzil	22	San Martín Jilotepeque	Co-op worker
Persons Killed			
7. Juan Pérez	26	Tutuapa	Co-op worker
8. Diego A. Marroquín	20	San Miguel Acatán	Co-op worker
9. Antonio Gómez	32	Colotenango	Co-op worker

10. Efraín López	20	Tacaná	Teacher
11. Marcos Velásquez	13	Tacaná	
12. Antonio Bravo	24	San Miguel Ixtahuacán	Co-op worker
13. Marcos López Balán		San Martín Jilotepeque	Merchant
14. Catarino López Coj	60	San Martín Jilotepeque	Merchant
15. Francisco Recinos[3]			

Combat and Massacre

On 30 April, the rebel forces attacked the military outpost in Cuarto Pueblo in an attempt to seize the barracks and distribute the weapons to form other military units. The "19 January Company" waged the battle to drive the army out of Ixcán and El Quiché, with the view to revolutionary triumph in 1982 (Menéndez Rodríguez 1981). The combatants stationed themselves in three different places, forming a semicircle around the military outpost: They placed platoons in the half-built Catholic church, on the far side of the landing strip, and near the school. The combat began at 5:00 A.M. and lasted for more than two hours. According to rebel sources, it caused 130 army casualties. They were about to seize the outpost when the air force arrived, bringing in additional troops and bombing the area.

Two warplanes and several helicopters dropped bombs over the half-built church, behind the military base, and in other parts of the town. One witness recalls: "A bomb fell near my house. It fell on a small shingle-roofed house and set it on fire." The bomb seems to have contained sulfur, as "it made clothing disintegrate: when we picked it up the fabric just fell apart and the chickens tore it to pieces." However, no one died in the air attack. Nor did any civilians die in combat cross fire.

The army carried out the massacre after the rebels had left their positions. When the reinforcements were flown in by helicopter, the soldiers killed a merchant, Marcos López Balán, shooting him in the head in his store. Then they captured the leaders of the cooperative, who had met that night to do the monthly accounts. They were taken to the military outpost. Some were later flown from there by helicopter, presumably to Playa Grande, and subsequently forced to disappear, and others were tortured and killed in the army outpost in Cuarto Pueblo. Other people were also captured and taken to the outpost to be killed. The army dressed two of the dead in olive green uniforms to make the local population think that they were rebels who had died in combat. But the local inhabitants instantly distinguished them from the three casualties suffered by the rebels (being combatants, their names do not figure on the preceding list). Nor did the townspeople take the two civilians for dead soldiers; the latter were secretly buried by the military in two large pits behind the army barracks.

Many of the women courageously went to the military outpost the following day to ask to see their husbands. One woman, unable to find her son-in-law, who was taken away by the military, remembers the slaughter in the outpost: "You should have seen the amount of blood where they'd killed the people. It was like tipping the water out of a tub." Everything was drenched in blood, as if a tub had been tipped over. "The peasants are killed inside and then taken out of doors," confirms another witness. "The place was covered in blood, as if they had slaughtered animals and dragged their corpses; there were pools of blood."

That day, the soldiers also "robbed everything from the shop and burned down Marcos López Balán's store and four market stalls," reports one witness. This act was a premonition of what the army would do to the entire town the following year—burn it to the ground.

The massacre was selective. The army killed only adult men, with the exception of one thirteen-year-old boy. Furthermore, not everyone found in the marketplace was killed. I have testimonies of men who were held at gunpoint by the soldiers immediately after the combat and were then "forgiven" by the lieutenant because he knew them. Apparently the main criterion used by the army was to kill leaders, like the cooperative's finance committee (numbers 2, 6, 8, and 12 on the list); the cooperative's shop assistant (5), who was also a catechist; the cooperative's cardamom dryer (9); the health promoter (1); and the teacher (10). Some say that the death of the two merchants, father (14) and son (13), was the result of a personal conflict with the lieutenant, as the latter had raped one of their wives. The army considered that the rest of the victims were accomplices of the rebels, as many of them had been found together at the cooperative that morning. The cooperative leaders were seemingly unaware of the imminent attack. The rebels could not have informed the villagers, as it was a surprise attack. It seems highly unlikely that the villagers would have met at the cooperative to do the monthly accounts at such a moment.

Attack on Civil Action (12 June)

The combat in Cuarto Pueblo opened a new stage of counterinsurgency in Ixcán. Civic action, introduced in 1975 to win over the minds and hearts of the cooperative members after the first abductions had taken place and to eradicate the guerrillas, had proved ineffectual. It had not managed to put an end to "subversion." Another tactic had to be used, taking the form of scorched earth.

That another tactic was needed became apparent when the army decided (albeit making out that the rebels were responsible) to destroy the hospital in Pueblo Nuevo, an army civic-action project inaugurated by Colonel Castillo during a special celebration on 3 May 1981. On 12 June 1981 the army destroyed the hospital it had sponsored. It also burned down the cooperative store and warehouse.

It was a psychological operation, mounted so that the people would blame the rebels. However, six witnesses, some of whom are firsthand eyewitnesses, have no doubt in attributing the action to the army. They also say that "the people realized it was the army." The action was therefore counterproductive because people knew that the army was destroying buildings that were designed for public benefit. It would indeed be difficult for the army to stage events so that they would not be found out when hundreds of eyes were silently observing what was going on.

What happened? A patrol of soldiers was taken by helicopter on Thursday, 11 June, from Cuarto Pueblo to a place near Pueblo Nuevo. There was no military outpost in Pueblo Nuevo at this time. Local townspeople saw and spoke to the soldiers, who entered on foot at night, trying to make themselves out to be rebels: "We're going to burn down the cooperative building, because it belongs to the rich," they said. They stole merchandise from the store, took gasoline from the warehouse, poured it over the store, and "lit a match. It was about midnight and you should have seen the flames as they burned down the cooperative store!" The store was burned to the ground, and the following day only its ashes remained.

They also destroyed the recently built hospital: "The army entered and buried a bomb in the ground; as the hospital was made of corrugated asbestos, only pulp remained," one witness recounts. The sound of the explosion reached the neighboring cooperatives. A witness from Los Angeles explains: "They threw a bomb at the poor hospital that resounded all the way over here."

The following day, the lieutenant arrived from Cuarto Pueblo, called by the military commissioners in Pueblo Nuevo. He gave the army's point of view and managed to sow the idea, for the first time in Ixcán, of setting up civilian patrols: "Look what your 'fathers' are doing," he said. "And you're giving them food. They came to destroy. Catch them and let us know. ... If the guerrillas do this again, beat them to death. If you support us, we'll give you arms, you can patrol your plots of land armed." The people said they did not want arms.

The army retired from the town in the afternoon, but shooting could be heard nearby that night. The soldiers killed a skinny little man, saying that he was one of the guerrillas who had burned down the shop. But many people had seen how they had brought the man with them by helicopter and had left him in the jungle when the patrol sabotaged the cooperative. The young man, about fourteen years old, was not from there. No one recognized him.[4]

Tensions Between the Civic and Military
Wings of the Army

The witnesses noticed a growing tension between Colonel Castillo and the troops. Some time after the rebel attack, one of the witnesses went to the yearly town celebration in Pueblo Nuevo, organized by the colonel, and was stopped by soldiers. They told the witness: "Colonel Castillo is a guerrilla," when the witness referred to the officer for protection.

The witnesses also noticed tension growing between the colonel and the rest of the military command. When the president of the cooperative in Xalbal, Rafael Miguel, was abducted in 1981 in front of the National Palace, an employee of the Coordination of Cooperatives told another witness that Castillo was furious about the abduction and had said: "Those motherfuckers [the military] kidnapped him."

It was logical that there should be tensions at a time when civic action would be declared ineffectual.

Reprisals Against Four Q'anjob'ales
(16 May)

On Saturday, 16 May, four Q'anjob'al men were seized by soldiers in Xalbal, on a stretch of the half-built transversal highway. Three of them never appeared again, whereas the corpse of the fourth was found a few days later. It was completely disfigured so as to spread terror among the population.

> The body was in the jungle. Its head had been shot off and skinned. The skull was found three meters from the trunk [body], and the corpse was placed squatting under a piece of wood.

Names of the Four Q'anjob'ales	Age	Family	Violation
1. Domingo Juan	18	2 children	disappeared
2. Ricardo Juan	16		disappeared
3. Juan de Juan Pérez	18	2 children	disappeared
4. Gregorio Juan	20	2 children	killed

How did it happen? Three days before, the rebels approached some army engineers at work on the transversal highway.[5] They took tractor parts and stopped the machine operators from working. On 16 May, the rebels tried to ambush the army in the same spot. But the army, dressed in civilian clothing, surprised the rebels, killing one of them. During the shoot-out, the army took shelter in a small store at the side of the highway and the rebels escaped into the mountains.

Four young Q'anjob'al men emerged from the same place where the rebels had earlier retreated on their way back from visiting some nearby lands. Confident of their innocence and trusting in their identification documents, they walked among the soldiers toward the little store and were captured as if they were guerrillas.

Their relatives asked about them at the military barracks in Xalbal. First they were told that the men were in Playa Grande and then that they had been released. But this was untrue, as Gregorio Juan was found dead and mutilated. Only then did they understand that the other three would never come back alive.

The four were young, all married, and three had children. Because they were already married, they were looking for plots of land for themselves.[6] This was their concern at that moment, not the rebel combat.

But the army, as in Cuarto Pueblo, opted for automatic and speedy reprisals against the civilian population, as it was unable to directly attack the rebels. It also used abductions as a way of terrorizing the population.

Abductions Carried Out to Spread Terror

A Burned Corpse in Xalbal (June)

In the months following the combat in Cuarto Pueblo, abductions were carried out not only to extract information but more and more to terrorize the population. The kidnappers no longer tried to hide the corpses but rather exhibited the mutilated bodies for the people to see. Torture was also no longer a secret practice but was carried out partly to let the rest of the community know what could happen, as in the case of Baltasar Juan Nicolás in Xalbal in June 1981[7] (his name appears on the list in Chapter 3).

> This poor man was taken out and burned that very night, his neighbors realized. Some time after they took him out, the soldiers started shouting loudly. The neighbors realized that they were torturing him. His screams could clearly be heard among the shouting of the soldiers: "Ow, please kill me instead." That night, the entire population left town.

According to another witness: "There are houses near the military outpost. The residents saw how two persons placed him on a bonfire."

This is the first time that this kind of torture and death (burned at the stake) appear in the testimonies. It was a premonition of what indiscriminately took place during the large massacres in 1982.

The terrified local population's reaction was to distance itself from the army. On the days following the event, about fifty families who lived in Xalbal began to move to the houses on their plots of land: "On one night alone, everyone left the town, no one remained except for one family." As the town emptied, the counterinsurgency policy of terror had the opposite effect of that sought by the army. What was the point of the army being in an empty town? Who was it going to control? That is why the army decided a few days later to abandon this and other villages and prepare to return with a different and more terrible kind of offensive.

Hung from Trees (30 August)

Mateo Juan and Mateo Marcos (whose names appear on the list in Chapter 3) were captured in Mayalán on Sunday, 30 August. The soldiers captured them in front of everyone. Days later, they were found, hung from trees, on the way from Mayalán to Pueblo Nuevo. The auxiliary mayor, who went with ten soldiers to bury them, remembers that buzzards had begun to eat them: "One's head was on a pitchfork, and his hands were bound. The other was tied by rope to a *cuxín* [a tropical tree]." Another witness recalls:

> Juan Mateo's testicles had been cut off and the other Mateo had had a foot amputated from the ankle down. The two corpses had been hung and were covered in worms.

Another witness remembers:

> They were falling like rotten bananas. I didn't see them, but that's what the people who went to bury them said. They gathered the flesh together and buried them there.

In reaction to the spreading terror of the army, the local population organized a network to keep guard and send messages between the plots of land to detect when and where the soldiers were arriving. The network was the beginning of a self-defense system that operated in the jungle after the large 1982 massacres.

The two men were captured after the rebels had attacked the military outpost in Mayalán. The army again attacked the civilian population because it could not get at the rebels.

The Context in Which Repression Took Place

Let us remember that the rebels had begun the stage of generalizing guerrilla warfare in October 1979 in the Ixil region. They had formed the 19 January Company and chosen Ixcán for carrying out a single attack on the army, thinking that this way they would gain large amounts of weapons and grow in force. Their sole attack (described earlier) was on the military outpost in Cuarto Pueblo on 30 April. However, the action did not turn out the way the rebels had wanted, and the company dispersed. The main guerrilla activities in the months to come were small attacks on military outposts in cooperative villages and ambushes.

As for the army, remember that the counterinsurgency operations had by now gone through two stages: the first, violently rooting out the burgeoning guerrilla force, and the second, carrying out civic action. With the killings and abductions carried out in Cuarto Pueblo on 30 April 1981, a third stage of counterinsurgency began, which consisted of preparing (in this case in Ixcán) for the massive national scorched-earth offensive. At this point, civic action proved completely inoperative in Ixcán. The army still inaugurated the hospital in Pueblo Nuevo three days later, as we have seen. The hospital would be inaugurated beneath a seal of destruction, because only a month later the army would blow it up. As it began to despair of civic action, the army started increasingly to use brute force over the civilian population, instilling terror by hanging corpses and burning and torturing civilians. The army also began to retreat because it was increasingly losing control over the population. The terrified local inhabitants moved to their plots of land and began a system of keeping guard and sending messages.

Two moments can be detected during this period. During the first, the army was still in Ixcán, repressing the inhabitants without civic action and instilling terror. In the second, the army was no longer present in Ixcán. The soldiers abandoned all their bases in Ixcán (with the exception of Playa Grande) on 17 November 1981. This had been the wish of the local population. But the army returned. The third stage came to an end when the army returned in mid-February 1982 to carry out massive massacres, as we shall see in the next chapter.

I have said that this was a preparatory stage for the scorched-earth offensive because the army withdrew so as to accumulate forces for the offensive, which would begin in Chimaltenango at the end of 1981 and would arrive three months later in Ixcán. With the offensive, the army would change its war logic at the national level and would regain the initiative.

But the retiring of the army was not perceived as such by the local population, who regarded it as a triumph in the revolutionary war heralding liberation in the near future. Ixcán seemed like liberated territory, but this would only last for a few months. As for the army, its withdrawal was precisely the condition that would allow it to regain the initiative in the conflict.

During the months that the army was absent, there was a kind of popular insurrection in Ixcán. The inhabitants sabotaged the landing strips to obstruct the return of the soldiers; they raised flags, burned down the military barracks, and prepared their self-defense strategies. This insurrection, however, left the army with little doubt that the only way of controlling the insurgency was by massively killing the population.

Here we can clearly appreciate the nature of counterinsurgency, at least in the way it has been applied in Guatemala: through the escalation of terror, killings, and massacres. It is as if the massive violation of the right to life were justified on the grounds of stopping insurgency.

And one can ask, Has the insurgency movement been detained in Guatemala?[8]

NOTES

1. The cooperative refers not merely to the store but to the organization of all the centers of Cuarto Pueblo.

2. Jacaltenango, San Rafael La Independencia, Santa Eulalia, San Miguel Acatán, and Colotenango are municipalities of Huehuetenango. San Miguel Ixtahuacán is a village in the municipality of Ixtahuacán in Huehuetenango. San Martín Jilotepeque is a municipality of Chimaltenango. Tacaná is a municipality of San Marcos, and Tutuapa is a village in the municipality of Concepción Tutuapa in the San Marcos department.—ED.

3. The total number of deaths and disappearances ranged between 17 and 22 according to the information gathered, but those interviewed were unable to supply the remaining names. I and a widow of one of the victims reconstructed the present list of 15 names. The Peasant Front (Frente Campesino) of the National Confederation of Workers (Central Nacional de Trabajadores; CNT) also denounced the massacre, listing 15 names. It is therefore almost certain to say that at least 15 men were massacred.

4. This psychological operation was copied exactly from the counterinsurgency manuals (McClintock 1985, 45).

5. The transversal highway is a large road that will cross the north of Guatemala from east to west. It still has not been finished.

6. Domingo Juan and Juan de Juan Pérez were married to two sisters. Gregorio Juan was married to Domingo Juan's sister. Only Ricardo Juan was not immediately related. They had all been born in Barillas, Huehuetenango, but only Juan de Juan Pérez still lived there. The other three lived on a plot of land in the center of Santa Cruz Xalbal at the time of the incident.

7. I do not know the exact date, only that it took place shortly after the rebel attack on the Xalbal military outpost. The attack took place "in summer [the dry season], perhaps at the end of May," according to a witness.

8. Mention must be made of the massacre that took place in San José La Veinte on 20 December 1980, although I was unable to thoroughly document this event. The information I received from a witness in 1983 seems highly reliable and includes a list of the names and ages of the victims: "Some of the victims were tortured, others had their throats slit, and others were buried alive. The soldiers came from Playa Grande. They entered the village on 20 December 1980 at 9.00 P.M. and took over the village. … There were about sixty soldiers. They forced the people from their houses one by one and took them to the outpost. After torturing them, they slit their throats and shot them. That night 17 people were killed."

Name	Age
1. Isabel Ralio	3
2. Juan Ramón Pérez	42
3. Tomasa Castro	3
4. Dominga Quixán	36
5. Martín Reynoso	25
6. Francisco Mejía	30
7. Juan Leno	56
8. Felipe Inecio	37
9. Rodolfo Monterroso	28
10. Vitalino Tun	23
11. Juan Mejía	35
12. José Tzutuj	19
13. Tomás Ralios	34
14. Domingo Pérez	29
15. Carlos Ramón Ortiz	2
16. Luciano Reynoso	26
17. Salvador Ortiz	18

A Kekchí woman massacred in 1982

The Xalbal River. The army crossed this river at this point before carrying out the massacre in Cuarto Pueblo in 1982

Leaving Guatemala with the bare essentials (Chiapas, 1982)

The first refugee shacks (Chiapas, 1982)

Food rations in the first weeks (Chiapas, 1982)

Refugee camp in Campeche, 1985

The authority of the Communities in Resistance (CPR), the Ixcán committee's 1989 annual assembly

Games (CPR, 1989)

School in the mountains. Pencils and paper were donated from solidarity (CPR, 1989)

The Refugee Women's Organization. Mamá Maquín's first assembly, 1990

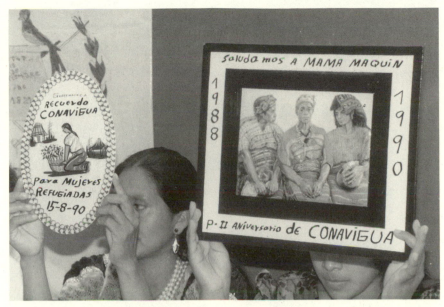

Solidarity between women's organizations (Chiapas, 1990)

More children are born. Twin girls in the CPR, 1990

Collective sugarcane milling (CPR, 1990)

Bombing of the Communities in Resistance: clearing caused by the bomb (above) and effects of shrapnel (below). Centro Santiaguito, Cuarto Pueblo, 14 June 1991

Women's collective vegetable patch (CPR, 1991)

Holy Week in the mountains. Remembering the massacres and how fraternal life was born from them (CPR, 1991)

Women watching a group enact the excesses of *aguardiente* (distilled liquor) as it was before life in resistance (CPR, 1991)

Remains of the destroyed office of the Small Landholders Committee of Ixcán in Cuarto Pueblo, 1992

Additional destruction of food supplies and agricultural implements in Cuarto Pueblo, 1992

Scattered personal and household items, along with food supplies, destroyed by government troops in Cuarto Pueblo, 1992

Family in a bomb shelter (CPR, 1992)

Woman cooking tortillas in her shelter (CPR, 1992)

Two boys with an unexploded bomb (CPR, 1992)

PART TWO

. . . .

Scorched Earth

CHAPTER 5

Massacres to the East of Ixcán

[13 to 28 February 1982]

Overall Panorama

From 13 to 28 February, according to my information, the army carried out seven massacres, killing 117 people in the east of Ixcán, between the Chixoy and Xalbal rivers.[1]

In this chapter we will see how the army began its scorched-earth offensive in the jungle. The stage of selective repression had come to a close and a new stage of counterinsurgency had begun. This new offensive commenced not in Ixcán Grande but in the eastern part of the jungle. As we will see, it was carried out in waves, from the Chixoy River moving from east to west. The massacres took place on weekends, when the army lashed out at the cooperatives' urban centers. The first wave of scorched earth and massacre took place on 13 February, the second on 20 February, and the third on 27 February.

On the weekend of 13 February, the army carried out massacres that resulted in the killings of between 12 and 17 people in Santa María Tzejá, between 27 and 41 in Santo Tomás, about 15 in San Lucas, and 7 on the road to San Lucas. On 18 February (not on a weekend, so presumably not part of the plan), the army massacred 10 people. On the weekend of 20 February, it massacred 13 persons in Polígono 14, and on the weekend of 27 February, the army went to Kaibil Balam, killing 12 to 14 people.

The army advanced toward Ixcán Grande, where most of my witnesses are from, and began to massacre on 13 March.

The Santa María Tzejá Massacre
(15 February)

The army arrived in Santa María Tzejá, east of the Chixoy River, on a Saturday, but the inhabitants had fled to the jungle. The army went out to patrol the jungle on Monday, 15 February, passing close by a group of people who had hidden. A dog barked and the soldiers surrounded the group. A frightened woman shouted out when she realized they were there. The soldiers shot her: "A woman shouted when she saw them and how they started shooting! Some were unable to escape, falling to the army. Thirteen people were killed. There was a pregnant woman. They sliced open her stomach, removing the fetus. They cut off a man's head and placed it in the woman's stomach. Her little son managed to escape. He hid under a log and later recounted what they did to his mother," according to a witness.

Following are two lists of names, the first drawn up by a witness and the second compiled by the Justice and Peace Committee (Comité Pro Justicia y Paz de Guatemala 1982).[2] By and large the lists coincide. According to both sources, 17 people were killed.

Names of Those Massacred in Santa María Tzejá

My Source			Justice and Peace Committee		
Name	*Age*	*Sex*	*Name*	*Age*	*Place of Origin*
1. Sebastián Con	93	m	Sebastiana Kanil	90	Chichicastenango[3]
2. Fidelia Vicente	31	f	Fidelia Mendoza	30	Chinique
3. Eduardo Canil	14	m	E. Kanil	13	
4. Guadalupe Canil	8	f	G. Kanil	9	
5. Estela Canil M.	6	f	E. Kanil	5	
6. Graciela Canil M.	6 mo.	f	G. Kanil	8 mo.	
7. Era Canil Juan	14	m	Eufrasia Kanil	14	
8. Cristino Canil Juan	7	m	Cristina Kanil	8	
9. Amalia Isabel Canil	13	f			
10. Martina Morales	38	f	Marta Morales (5 mo. pregnant)		
11. Vicente Mendoza	32	m	Vicenta Mendoza	35	Chinique
12. Francisco Javier Lux	8	m	Francisco Javier Lux	4	
13.			Juan Lux	2	
14.			small daughter of Cristina Morales		
15.			other small daughter of Cristina Morales		
16.			son of Felipe Perez		
17.			other son of Felipe Perez		

The Santo Tomás Massacre
(apparently on 14 February)

The army arrived in Santo Tomás Ixcán. Some were unable to flee because they were very old and "the women who had just given birth couldn't walk. … Many hid in the *chuj* [steam bath]; the army found and killed them," according to a witness.

Those who escaped crossed the Xalbal River to seek shelter with the people of Xalbal. "The people who fled came to our farm plots to seek refuge. We heard their story, they stayed with us for fifteen days. They didn't bring any clothes or food with them, so we fed them. About 400 or 500 escaped. There weren't enough tortillas to go around so we gave them fruit. The army entered Santo Tomás at 3:00 P.M.; being nearby, we could see the houses alight and hear the shooting," according to another witness.

According to combined sources, 41 people were killed.

Names of Those Massacred in Santo Tomás

My Source			Justice and Peace Committee[4]		
Name	*Age*	*Sex*	*Name*	*Age*	*Death*
1.			Margarita Marroquín Hernández	13	B&T
2. Abraham Marroquín	5	m	Abraham Marroquín Hernández	7	B&T
3. Benjamín Marroquín	3	m	Porfirio Marroquín Hernández	3	B&T
4.			Hector Argueta Marroquín	6	B&T
5.			Neftalí Argueta M.	6	B&T
6. Evan Argueta	24	m			B&T
7. Antonio Miró	65	m	Antonio Miró Sanán	73	B&T
8. Manuela Miró	60	f	Manuela Miró Sanán	69	B&T
9. Argelia Miró	35	f	Argelia Miró Galindo	41	B&T
10. Carlota Miró	40	f	Carlota Calderón de Morales	42	B&T and TS
11. Miriam Miró	7	f	Alicia Miró Galindo	6	B&T
12. Sandra de Miró	30	f	Noemí Revolorio Luna de Miró	21	B&T
13. Glenda Miró	1	f	Glendi Miró Revolorio	2	B&T
14. José Maria Lemus	65	m			S
15. Candelaria de Lemus	45	f			S

16. Tomás Lemus	18	m			S
17. Leticia Lemus	14	f			S
18. Santos Lemus	12	f			S
19. Adán Lemus	7	m			S
20. Rosalío Pinto	50	m	Rosalío Pinto	58	S
21. Lola de Pinto	35	f	Dolores Valdés	60	S
22. Luisa Pinto Valdés	13	f	Luisa Valdés	12	S
23. Fermín Pinto Valdés	30	m	Fermín Pinto Valdés	42	S
24.			Francisco Celedonio Hernández Vásquez	16	S
25. Blanca Estela de Blanco	20	f	Blanca Lidia Hernández Vásquez	32	S
26. Rosa de Marroquín	35	f	Rosa Hernández	36	S
27. Cristina Marroquín	17	f	Cristina Marroquín Hernández	17	S
28. Rosalío Marroquín	13	m	Rosalío Marroquín Hernández	9	S
29. Eulalia Marroquín	9	f	Emiliana Marroquín Hernández	11	S
30. Concepción Marroquín	7	f	Concepción Marroquín Hernández	5	S
31. Cristóbal Ramírez	40	m			B&T*
32. Cristóbal Garún	20	m			B&T*
33. Rodolfo Mazariegos	40	m	Rodolfo Mazariegos	55	B&T*
34. Lidia Gutini	35	f			B&T*
35. Dalia Gutini	16	f			B&T*
36. Engli Alvarez C.	5	m			B&T*
37. Pablo Blanco H.	55	m	Pablo Librado Hernández	55	B&T*
38. Pablo Blanco	17	m	Pablo Hernández Vásquez	19	B&T*
39. Moisés Blanco	15	m	Moisés Hilton Hernández Blanco	18	B&T*
40. Juan Blanco	15	m			B&T*
41. Nicolás Alvarez	37	m			B&T*

Note: B = burned; T = tortured; TS = throat slit; S = shot.
*Burned and tortured in the Catholic church according to my source.

The Massacre of Cardamom Sellers
(apparently on 13 February)

Seven people were massacred, probably on 13 February, on their way from Ixcán Grande to San Lucas to sell cardamom; they bumped into the army while crossing the Xalbal River on the Polígono 14 hanging bridge. The army had still not burned down San Lucas and was apparently blocking the way to the Xalbal River before attacking the village.[5] One witness recalls:

> There were two from the Champerico center in Cuarto Pueblo, a young man and woman. The other five were from the Nuevo Progreso center in La Resurrección. There were eight but one had lagged behind, having a shit. He saw how the army seized his companions, and brought the news. They hadn't reached San Lucas.

Another witness recalls:

> We went by the bank of the Xalbal River. We saw dead people's heads. A house had been burned down; I went to have a look, and there were two heads in the ashes. The heads were charred, you could only see their mouths. They were people who had been burned!

The San Lucas Massacre
(apparently on 15 February)

Two witnesses refer to this massacre, but I do not have a list of names or detailed description. I only know that, according to one witness, "On 15 February the army also gathered together the people in San Lucas, killed about four families, and burned down the deserted houses. We heard that 15 people had been killed."

The Massacre of Charismatic Catholics in Pueblo Nuevo
(18 February)

This massacre was the first to take place in Ixcán Grande. The army followed the tracks of two survivors from Santo Tomás, who had crossed the river in search of refuge and food. The soldiers came upon a group of three families of Charismatic Catholics who were praying and singing in a house. The soldiers seized them, forcing them to cross the Xalbal River, and killed them on the river bank: "They were made to lie down on the river bank. The soldiers made cudgels and beat them as if they were beating corn cobs. They killed them off, one by one," recalls a witness.

Another witness highlights how five survived. An eight-year-old girl survived because "they tied a rope around her neck and pulled. Her tongue came out so they thought she was dead." The soldiers slit a seventy-five-year-old man's throat, but he survived because "the knife touched his shirt button, but the soldiers thought it was bone, as blood spurted out, so they kicked him and left him for dead." A couple and their son also survived. They threw themselves off the bridge. The man swam ashore and the woman also survived. "She was carrying her eighteen-month-old infant; they shot at her" from the bridge but she did not die, and neither did the baby. "God is benevolent," says the witness, as five of them were saved.

Names of Those Massacred	Age	Relatives
1. Micaela Gaspar	45	2's wife
2. Diego Juan	60	
3. Lorenza Juan	35	1's daughter
4. Juan Diego	18	3's son
5. Merchora Diego	6	3's daughter
6. Gaspar Juan	40	2's son
7. María Francisco	30	6's wife
8. Isabela Gaspar	5	6's daughter
9. Isabela Segunda	2	6's daughter
10. Angelina Gaspar	3	6's daughter[6]

El Polígono 14 Massacre
(20 and 21 February)

This massacre took place a week later. After entering Santa María Tzejá, Santo Tomás, and San Lucas, the army went north to El Polígono 14, a group of farm plots on the Mexican border next to the Xalbal River. The army crossed the river from El Polígono 14 to attack Cuarto Pueblo in March, as is explained in the next chapter.

The army came from San Lucas, found two scouts sent out by the local inhabitants, and captured them on 20 February 1982. The scouts were hanged. At the same time, other families fell to the army when they left home. Others were also captured on Sunday, 21 February, on their way to market.

Names of Those Massacred[7]	Age	Sex	Death
1. Serapio Martín Pérez	55	m	shot dead
2. Rufino Pérez Matías	23	m	hanged and then burned
3. Juana Matías Carrillo	1	f	hanged and then burned
4. José Méndez	37	m	hanged and then burned
5. María Morales Felipe	35	f	hanged and then burned
6. Domingo Antonio	42	m	hanged and then burned

7. María Baltazar	35	f	ambushed
8. René Antonio Simón	14	m	ambushed
9. Domingo Morales	17	m	captured on returning from keeping watch
10. Andrés Pérez	34	m	shot dead
11. Rubén Morales	17	m	ambushed
12. Cruz Mendoza Jiménez	53	m	captured while exploring; was taken to San Lucas
13. Juan Morales	26	m	went to Guatemala City to do some errands; never returned

Kaibil Balam Massacre (27 February)

A week after the massacre at El Polígono 14, the army attacked the population of Kaibil Balam. El Polígono 14 was the place furthest north in the army offensive, and now the army was heading south, evidently to control the entire eastern flank of Ixcán Grande, including the Xalbal River, to enter Ixcán Grande. A young man from Kaibil Balam remembers:

> I wasn't there but my father told me. Soldiers wanted to surround the center of the town, but the people went south. Fourteen people hadn't left, they were about 400 meters from the village. The soldiers found them and killed two men, Andrés Gómez, thirty-three, and Tino, nineteen, as they were helping people take away their belongings. That's when they died.
>
> They killed a woman called Rosanda of about thirty-five and her three children, one three years old, another six, and the other eight. Rosanda was thrown into a cardamom oven and set alight. Another woman and her two children were shot dead. They caught a third woman alive, put her inside a *chuj*, and killed her with a grenade. A family of four was killed in the jungle, a mother and her three children.
>
> There were about 125 soldiers; at 8:00 A.M. on Sunday they set fire to all the houses.

According to combined sources, 14 people died.

Names of the Massacred[8]

My Source			Justice and Peace Committee		
Name	*Age*	*Sex*	*Name*	*Age*	*Death*
1. Andrés Gómez Sales	38	m	Andrés Gómez	37	tortured
2. Catarina Gómez	15	f	Catarina Gómez	15	tortured; naked
3. Juana Sales	92	f	Juana Sales	78	machete
4. María Claudia Aguilar	28	f	María Lucila Claudia Aguilar	27	tortured

5. Margarita Gómez	10	f	Margarito Gómez Claudio	10	tortured
6. Augusto Gómez	7	m	Augusto Gómez Claudio	6	tortured
7. Romalda Gómez	4	f	Romualda Gómez Claudio	3	tortured
8. Patricia Claudia	27	f	María Luisa Claudio Aguilar	27	tortured
9. Juana Fabiana Hernández		f	Juana Fabiana Hernández	30	
10. Cristina Fabiana Hernández	6	f	Cristina Claudio Fabián	5	
11.			Efraín Claudio Fabián	3	
12. Rosanda Ramos	47	f	Rosenda Ramos	45	tortured
13. Felipe Lucas Ramos	3	m	Felipe Lucas Ramos	3	tortured
14.			Faustino López Tomás	19	

The Way the Scorched-Earth Offensive Began

The scorched-earth offensive, launched in Chimaltenango in November 1981, reached Ixcán in February 1982. The offensive advanced geographically, according to counterinsurgency manuals, like a huge broom sweeping from the more populated to the more remote areas.[9] The army was trying to remove the water from the fish, the water being the civilian population and the fish the rebels: It was trying to eradicate the rebels' support base and force them to leave Guatemala from the same place they had entered, Ixcán.

In Ixcán, the offensive also followed the geographical movement of a great broom sweeping people from their villages. Beginning in the east, it moved rhythmically toward the west and north, reaching the point of strongest resistance in the jungle of Ixcán Grande, between the Xalbal and Ixcán rivers.

This chapter, lacking in sources though informative in lists, opens the doors to still greater massacres. Thanks to the countless number of witnesses, the following chapters copiously document counterinsurgency as it reaches maximum levels of repression.

NOTES

1. The information I have is not exhaustive for this part of Ixcán. For example, according to AID (Agency for International Development) technicians in Project 520 in northeast Quiché, "The army completely exterminated the inhabitants of La

Trinitaria, Santa Clara and El Quetzal. About 1,000 to 1,500 settlers were killed during the military action" (Dennis et al. 1984). The Justice and Peace Committee also refers to the massacre of 45 people in La Trinitaria from 10 to 12 February 1982 (Comité Pro Justicia y Paz de Guatemala 1982).

2. In this case, the informant, though not an eyewitness, was close by in Santa María Dolores, on the other side of the Tzejá River, and immediately found out what happened. We have three other sources; one is a written list of the dead people's names. The Justice and Peace Committee also has lists that by and large coincide with ours.

3. Chichicastenango and Chinique are municipalities of El Quiché.

4. I have seven witnesses, though none are from Santo Tomás. A witness handed me the following written list. He probably compiled the list after talking to various firsthand witnesses. It coincides by and large with the Justice and Peace Committee list.

5. I have six testimonies of the massacre but do not have a list of names. Only one witness remembers that from the Champerico center two victims were Juan Pérez's children.

6. There are four witnesses. At my request, one of them sought out the relatives of the dead to draw up the list. This witness tells how the five survived. Another witness, who took in the survivors after the massacre, tells how the others were killed. The witnesses are from Pueblo Nuevo. The Charismatic Catholics' house was in the Esmeralda center in Pueblo Nuevo, next to the highway. The victims were from San Miguel Acatán.

7. I have four sources, two that refer to this massacre among others and two that describe only this one. One of the sources is a written testimony, which is reproduced here. It seems undeniable that the massacre took place, although not everyone died on the same date.

8. I have three testimonies. The young man from Kaibil Balam narrates what his father told him; he was not in the village because he was out scouting for the army.

9. The technical name employed is "sweep operations" (Thompson 1974, 111–113). The author also distinguishes three major counterinsurgency operation zones: (1) densely populated urban zones, (2) populated rural zones, and (3) scarcely populated rural zones (Thompson 1974, 104). According to the manual, when the rebels are still in their subversive stage (until 1979 in the case of Guatemala), the army should concentrate on the remote zone (Ixcán). But when the rebels reach the guerrilla warfare stage, the army should do the opposite, that is, concentrate on the densely populated zones and only later on the remote zones, using sweep and then control operations.

This is exactly what the Guatemalan army did. It first started repressing the popular movement in Guatemala City, next it detected and repressed the rebel safe houses in urban areas in July 1981, then moved on to Chimaltenango and the south of El Quiché, and finally went north and northwest. The army always "swept" from the center toward the country's borders.

CHAPTER 6

The First Part of the Massacre of Cuarto Pueblo: Nueva Concepción Center

[14 March 1982]

Preparations Days Before

The last chapter closed with the army about to arrive in Cuarto Pueblo. Only the Xalbal River, which was low at that time of the year and easy to walk across, separated the army from the cooperative. The inhabitants of Cuarto Pueblo had heard that villages had been burned on the other side of the river; people had even gone to sell cardamom, coming back with stories of what they had observed on the river bank and of the skulls they had seen on the hearth of a cottage. But they still refused to believe that the army would go to their cooperative to massacre and burn down the town. It seemed out of the question. A witness recalls: "We heard a helicopter flying over El Polígono 14; we knew they killed a lot of people there, but we didn't think it would happen here."

This was in February. Around that time a message arrived (I am not sure how) summoning the military commissioners from Cuarto Pueblo to Playa Grande to talk to the army. Presumably the army wanted to find out what was going on in the area. The commissioners debated for a long time whether to present themselves at the military base. If they were to go, they could be massacred by the army; they knew this had happened in other places, as even the army no longer trusted its commissioners. But if they did not go, they would be regarded by the army as enemies or guerrillas. Among our witnesses was one of the fourteen military commissioners:

> The head of the military commissioners was very worried. "What are we going to do?" he asked. "If we don't go they'll say we agree with the guerrillas. And if we do go ... who knows what will happen to us." I told him: "I don't want to go; I'll only go if everyone does." Rumor has it that the soldiers take the military commissioners to Playa Grande and kill them there.

In the end they decided to go, but some only walked to town from their plots of land and stayed there; others went as far as the river, where they waited for the rest. Finally, no one dared continue. They returned home. The army was therefore deprived of its eyes and its hands (the military commissioners). The effect could either hinder their entrance or encourage them to enter blindly, lashing out indiscriminately.

At the beginning of March, the rebels carried out an armed occupation of Cuarto Pueblo. They brought the townspeople together and told them not to confide in the army. They also sabotaged the airstrip to impede the army's return. As noted in previous chapters, when the army withdrew its soldiers from the military outpost, a kind of joyful popular insurrection took place. Freedom was celebrated in this power vacuum. At long last, the army had left the area, leaving the population in peace. The people were tired of controls, harassment, and abductions. During the uprising, the local inhabitants burned down the much-hated military outposts, including the one in Cuarto Pueblo, and sabotaged the landing strips. In the days that followed, though, the more fearful *parcelistas* began to repair the damages, filling in the ditches that had been dug. In so doing they were also leaving the possibility open of taking their cardamom out in private planes.

During the occupation the rebels exhorted the people to reopen the ditches on the landing strip, warning them to be extremely careful, as the army would come back, and it would come back to massacre.

> They said: "This is the last time we're going to sabotage the landing strip. Lucas withdrew his army, but they have another plan for you. The army didn't leave for you to be free. They will come back to kill you! Stop holding meetings! Stop celebrating in the plazas!"

The army knew about the sabotage because red flags were hung out and graffiti appeared on the walls. A helicopter flew over the village on Sunday, 7 March, the day the national presidential elections were being held. A witness recalls how he went to the plaza that Sunday: "When I arrived, I saw that the helicopter had descended over an area sabotaged with sticks. The landing strip had also been sabotaged. Four red flags had been hung out: one in the military outpost, another in the community center, another in

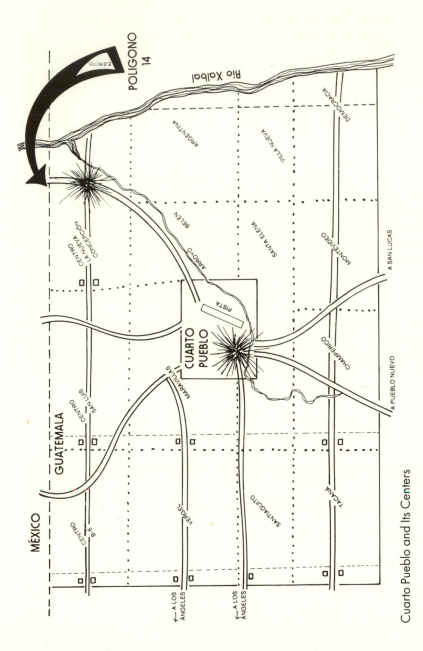

Cuarto Pueblo and Its Centers

the middle of the plaza. I don't remember where the last one was. And a skull with the inscription 'Lucas' had been painted on a smooth piece of metal sheeting on a store." Lucas, the outgoing president, had been depicted as a symbol of death. The helicopter must have seen the sabotage, although perhaps not in full detail, and confirmed that the entire Cuarto Pueblo had joined the rebels.

Very few people went to the plaza that election day Sunday, fearing that something would happen. "We thought there would be bombs," remembers a witness, "and we saw the helicopter flying overhead. That's why we didn't go." Because most people did not go to market that Sunday, they turned out in force the following Sunday, 14 March. Everyone needed to buy and sell, and the dangerous Sunday had proved uneventful. "There wasn't anything on 7 March and so the following Sunday, when the massacre took place, flocks of people went to town," recalls the same person.

Whether intentionally or not, the army took advantage of the massive turnout to fall upon the people. Remember that the cooperative members had houses on their plots of land several hours away from the town, and those who also had houses in town had abandoned them after the spate of army abductions. That is why the army had to carry out its clean-up operation at a moment when the local population was gathered together in town. The Sunday after the elections was a perfect time: The town was full of people.

One could ask why the army had not followed its advancing pace of every weekend, town by town, as it had done during the previous month. According to this rhythm, the army would have come to Cuarto Pueblo on 7 March, after the massacre in Kaibil Balam on 27 February. But it did not; that weekend was like a parenthesis in its offensive. I do not know the reasons for certain. I do not believe that the operation's surprise element had been planned. It seems more likely that national orders were given to respect voting day and for the troops to rest, thus giving importance to the elections. As far as I know, no massacres were carried out in Ixcán that day. Elections were not held in Ixcán because either the villages had been burned to the ground or the government could not enter.[1]

One thing does seem clear: The sabotage of the landing strip was not the reason for the army not entering Cuarto Pueblo on 7 March, as the raid would be carried out by the infantry. The sabotage thus served only to increase the aggression of the armed forces and not to impede their entrance.

Warning to Escape to the Jungle

Did the army take everyone by surprise in Cuarto Pueblo? It did come upon those who went to the town that Sunday, 14 March. But it did not find the people who had plots of land an hour and a half away from the town, next to the Mexican border. Although the *parcelistas* on the border had been given sufficient warning to escape into the jungle, many did not pay heed and were massacred. This was the case for many inhabitants of La Nueva Concepción center. (La Nueva Concepción center was an area of two rows of twelve plots of land each, situated on the corner formed by the Xalbal River and the Mexican border. About 200 people lived there.) That Sunday, 35 people were massacred in La Nueva Concepción and at least 3 were forced to disappear in what I have termed the first stage of the Cuarto Pueblo massacre.[2]

To understand how most of this center's inhabitants were saved while the rest died, it is important to establish how the community was warned. Remember that the witnesses' accounts always implicitly contain the good news: that they are alive.

Just as the rebel forces had held a public meeting in town with the local inhabitants the week previous to the elections, they also sent two cadres to warn the centers of the army's imminent arrival, telling them to hide in the jungle to save their lives. But judging from the testimonies of the *parcelistas* who attended the public meeting for the centers in the north, the two guerrillas were not able to cover more than two centers, as they had started out on Saturday, 13 March. They were unable to go to La Nueva Concepción center personally. They just talked to some of its inhabitants somewhere else. Our main witness is one of those who had been contacted by the two cadres.

The inhabitants of La Nueva Concepción received warning of the proximity of the army from some fishermen who detected movements over the border at 5:00 P.M. "They saw something was going on at the border," remembers the main witness.

> "Maybe they're tapirs," they thought, "as they're moving snakelike along the border." The border had recently been cleared. They were watching from the river banks. "We're going to see what it is," they said to one another. "We're going to see if it's the Mexican army or Guatemalan soldiers, but let's get out fast." So they left the beach and went up a hillock. Then they saw the soldiers coming down to the beach at a distance of 200 meters from their observation point. That was when they realized that they were Guatemalan soldiers by their camouflage uniforms.

The three fishermen ran to warn the witness. The witness was the father of one of the fishermen. His son went to tell him there was no doubt that it was the army. From above, the three fishermen had seen the army advancing along the recently cleared border between Mexico and Guatemala. It had still not crossed the river but was on its way. There were about 300 soldiers in the battalion, though at that point the fishermen had not managed to calculate its size.

When the witness received the warning, he was in the midst of hurriedly selling sugar to neighbors who wanted to stock up in case they had to flee to the jungle. He remembers: "My son came to tell me. He came running and said: 'What are you doing? Forget that rubbish! If you want to stay alive, get out quick.'" The rubbish was the sugar and its sale. The young man was very agitated and transmitted his nervousness to everyone, so the neighbors went home and the witness's family ran to the jungle, taking only "a dish and some blankets; the *nixtamal* [cooked corn] was left behind." His family set off ahead, and the witness and his son stayed behind a few more minutes, gathering together some belongings. This resulted in his wife and children getting lost and spending the night apart. Although inexperienced in "emergency plans," they abandoned their home and took to the jungle, thus saving their lives. Their house was burned down by the army the following day, with some neighbors inside.

The warning reached the neighboring center, San Luis, but it had lost the nervous charge of the messenger, who had actually seen the army advancing. A witness from this center remembers: "I received the news at 6:00 P.M. that the army was on its way, that it was crossing the Xalbal River. I was told to warn others to leave their homes. I went to warn another household and came back at 10:00 P.M. I told only one family; they were to warn another."

The witness from the San Luis center, which was a bit farther away, took the news more calmly, and judging by the time he got back home, he probably discussed the flight to the jungle at length with the family he had gone to warn. The warning, by now thirdhand, reached other families who went to the San Luis witness's home that night to seek confirmation of the news. He remembers: "Two people arrived at 11:00 P.M. and asked, 'What's going on? Have they already arrived? Is it the army or are they Mexican? Or are they *compañeros* [rebels]?' they asked me. 'I don't know,' I told them. 'They said it was the army.' That night we hardly slept."

The San Luis witness, a bright young man from Todos Santos,[3] was still not entirely convinced of the danger, and in contrast to the Jakaltekos from La Nueva Concepción, he did not leave his house. He did not even change his plans to go to market in Cuarto Pueblo the following day. How powerful was the attraction of the plaza! The plaza was a gathering place not only for economic reasons, to sell and buy, but also for social get-togethers. He had planned to go to the plaza with some relatives and did not want to alter his plans because he could not inform them of the change. The purpose of his going to the plaza was to meet some fellow countrymen from Todos Santos who lived in other centers and whom he did not see very often.

It was not until the following morning, when his brother came to warn him that soldiers were burning down houses in La Nueva Concepción, that he changed his plans and decided not to go to the plaza. With the force of having seen the houses burning with his own eyes, his brother told him to leave his home. "Let's go, and let's take blankets and dishes." Only then did he obey, seeking refuge in the jungle with his brother and uncle. This was the first time that the people left for the jungle to seek protection in groups of two or three families. These groups were the seeds of what would later become communities in resistance.

We also talked to another witness from the San Luis center, who was warned but paid no heed. He did not go to the jungle but went to the market that Sunday. In the following chapter I tell his tale. He was trapped for three days in an army siege. His testimony is invaluable.[4]

They Didn't Want to Leave

The previous testimonies have described stalling and disregard of the emergency warnings but not obstinacy. Some groups, however, were indeed stubborn. The people of Cuarto Pueblo were not united ideologically, which the army did not know. There were groups that suspected that the warnings may have come from the rebels and immediately opposed them. This was the Charismatic Catholics' attitude in this particular cooperative. For this reason they disregarded the warning, even though it had been relayed by a neighbor. Their attitude is shrouded in religious arguments. In La Nueva Concepción center the people who died were victim to this way of thinking and reacting.

The main witness, the Jakalteko from La Nueva Concepción, recalls one man who was killed in the massacre: "Martín Ramírez arrived at Chico's house to tell him not to leave. Both belonged to the MLN and fell to the army." Because the MLN (Movement of National Liberation [Movimiento de Liberación Nacional]) is an extreme right-wing political party, the two felt confident that the army would not harm them. Martín Ramírez had his party membership card and felt sure that it would protect him. He did feel the need for company, though, and went to visit his neighbor, Francisco Vargas (Chico), to convince him not to leave and not to be persuaded by the main witness. They were also both Charismatic Catholics. Martín Ramírez's children were singing and praising the Lord when the army arrived, to gather courage and to show the army that they were very religious and therefore had nothing to do with subversion. Francisco Vargas was an *animador de la fe* (animator of the faith). This meant that as Martín Ramírez exerted political influence, Francisco Vargas exerted religious influence, because animators were super-catechists who could give communion and use a stole. Both died from their misplaced belief in the goodness of the army.

Julio Alvarado, another of those killed, was also very religious; he is remembered by the witness with a sense of rage because the Charismatic Catholics did not believe him. He explains how Julio saw the soldiers coming but instead of fleeing went home to tell his family to start praying: "We're going to pray to the Lord now," he had said. His wife, however, who had a clearer sense of the situation, did not respect her husband's decision and ran to the jungle with her children and the others who were with her at that moment. But "Julio Alvarado just stood at the door, while she left," the witness recalls.

The same witness remembers yet another Charismatic Catholic, Ramón Camposeco. Ramón was a clothes merchant who on Saturday afternoon was making preparations for market day. When he was advised not to go, he answered that he was in the hands of the Lord: "'If the army kills us, Glory be to God! We shouldn't be afraid of death. If we're all to go [to the next life], that's how it must be. We shouldn't be scared.' 'Well then, so be it,' they answered." He and his entire family died in the village.

Here I am making only preliminary mention of the effect of religious ideology in not wanting to believe the word of others. As said in the Introduction, the problem of faith is present throughout the "gospel" I am writing because those who died in this center did so because they did not believe in the word of others. Perhaps I am being too simplistic in calling this attitude obstinacy or disobedience. Further on, in other chapters, I analyze the matter in greater depth, not to condemn this attitude but to try to fully comprehend it.

The Massacre

We return to the battalion wading across the river at about 5:00 P.M. on the Mexican border. After crossing the river, the military entered Mexico, camping there that night and stealing sweet corn from a Mexican cornfield. The army needed to enter Mexico to carry out a surprise attack on La Nueva Concepción the following day and to impede the inhabitants from fleeing from Guatemala and seeking refuge in Chajul, the closest village on the Mexican side. The idea was to place a kind of stopper to catch the refugees trying to flee from Guatemala. At this point it seems that the army was not yet interested in frightening people over to Mexico but rather in capturing and killing them off. Remember that the army had suffered 130 casualties in Cuarto Pueblo on 30 April 1981 and that the town had to pay back this debt to the military.

At 6:30 A.M. the army was seen by several witnesses at the crossroads in La Nueva Concepción. The south-north road leading to Mexico meets the west-east road, which passes between the two rows of farm plots and reaches the Xalbal River. The massacre took place in the houses near the crossing.

Part of the battalion stopped at the crossroads and the rest made its way toward Cuarto Pueblo, as the massacre in La Nueva Concepción was coordinated with the cooperative center massacre. The army did not enter the main town until it had finished with the people of La Nueva Concepción. The massacre in the periphery had to precede the massacre in the main town.

The first thing the soldiers who stayed at the crossroads did was to scatter in small groups to surround the nearby houses and, apparently, to take the people to a meeting in a house near the road. The house was that of Francisco Vargas, the Charismatic animator of the faith. The soldiers went to summon the people, but many houses were already empty, which in the eyes of the military confirmed that they were guerrillas. They found the Charismatic Catholics in other houses, but they obviously considered them to be guerrillas too because they killed them off.

I do not know the order in which the soldiers surrounded the houses. One house that was still inhabited was surrounded as if it had armed men inside. This house was that of MLN militant Martín Ramírez, who was there with his family. That this happened was confirmed by a couple of young men keeping watch over events and who passed by later asking for bananas without realizing that the soldiers were already inside. The young men fell into the trap at Ramírez's house and talked to the soldiers. There they found out that the army wanted to hold a meeting. Looking for ways to escape from the military, the young men said that they would call the local townspeople to the meeting. They were taken under soldiers' guard from house to house but managed to escape.

The young men told the main witness what had just happened at Martín Ramírez's house. They had left Ramírez "wearing glasses and praying," probably Bible in hand, while the soldiers kept guard over him and his sons were looking for documents to show to the military. The young men said that the soldiers rejected any kind of document, thus crushing the confidence the MLN members had placed in their credentials: "The lieutenant told them: 'Papers aren't necessary.'"

The young men "left running," the main witness recalls. They walked quickly in front of the soldiers as they led the way to the neighboring houses, and a second later they escaped. This action appears to have precipitated the massacre, as the meeting was not held. Instead of massacring everyone together in one house, the army decided to kill people off in several houses: those of the main witness, Martín, and Francisco, the Charismatic animator.

In Francisco's house the people were burned alive. I know of this terrible deed from another survivor, Francisco's nine-year-old son, who managed to escape from the soldiers when they were torturing his father. The soldiers went after the boy but were unable to catch him. Not knowing where he was going, the boy ran toward the Mexican border. There he found people from the neighboring center, San Luis, who were keeping guard. They took the orphan to some other families hiding in the jungle, and there the boy told them what he had just witnessed. One of the witnesses, who told me the boy's story, was in the group of families that took the boy in as their own. The witness remembers that the boy said: "'The soldiers are burning my father and my brother.' He explained how the soldiers burned his father in front of him, while his mother was lying down, after having recently given birth. The boy ran away, and the soldiers tried to run after him" but were unable to catch him.[5]

I believe that the army preferred other forms of death to shooting, not out of pure sadism but to avoid bullet shots, which would alert the people in the town of the army's proximity. Also, torture by fire meant that people might give information, though at that point the soldiers were not interested in finding out where the rest had gone, as the army did not stay to carry out patrols. The battalion went straight to the town. The massacre in La Nueva Concepción was a massacre en route.

The main witness remembers how the army locked several people into his empty house (he lived near Francisco) and burned them alive. He was concerned with trying to find people who had got lost and scattered in the jungle. He was also trying to see from afar what the army was doing and if it would go near his own empty house. At that point he realized that some refugees were making their way along a path to Mexico, without imagining that the army was there. They were the first trickle of the river of refugees that would soon inundate the Mexican border areas. The refugees did not take precautions during their flight and fell prey to the soldiers. The main witness seems not to have known some of them coming from the south, from Pueblo Nuevo, and mentions only a *parcelista* from another center in Cuarto Pueblo who was with them or behind them, called Ermelindo Aguilar. The witness says: "Some refugees were coming from the south, fleeing to Mexico. The army captured them. Others were with them, Ermelindo and his children. Ermelindo gave himself up. I saw the soldiers take him to my house. ... He turned himself in to them and they killed him in my house, together with Martín. They took his children away alive; who knows if they killed them later in the town."

Martín was the MLN militant whom we left "wearing glasses and praying" while the young men escaped on the pretext of calling more people to the meeting. The witness did not at that point see that Martín was in the hands of the army, but he knows that they killed him in his house because several days later he found his corpse, almost completely burned. I presume that the army took Martín to the witness's house to obtain information from him about the witness's whereabouts and that they burned him alive either because he gave false information or none whatsoever, as he did not know where in the jungle they had gone into hiding.

Perhaps among the dead refugees in the witness's empty house were the four members of a family from another center in Cuarto Pueblo, Santiaguito. A person from this center tells me how this family had been killed there on its way to Mexico. "The soldiers took him with his wife and children. They captured and then killed them. The tiny shoes of one little boy were left in the jungle." The *parcelista*'s name was Domingo Muy Ajú.

When the soldiers finished their task, at about 10:00 A.M., a helicopter was seen flying over the burning houses at the crossroads in La Nueva, where this part of the battalion had been carrying out its sweep operation. The helicopter was also seen flying over the town itself, where the other part of the battalion was about to attack. The helicopter was probably coordinating both operations from the air. As they had finished uneventfully in La Nueva Concepción, they could begin with the town. But this we shall see in the following chapter.

Convergence at the Scene of the Disaster

On Monday, 15 March, the main witness, after having found his family and seen his wife, who was about to give birth, went alone on a round of the houses at the crossroads and nearby to see who was alive and who had been killed and which houses were still standing and which had been burned down. This inspection was an instinctual way for him to define the social limits of the community and to redefine himself in this new, semi-destroyed context.[6]

But the witness also had an inner sense of urgency to know who was right: those who had remained in their houses or those who had fled to the jungle in great discomfort. The witness felt angry, thinking that perhaps the MLN militant Martín and other Charismatic Catholics were peacefully sitting at home and eating hot meals while the witness was in the jungle, hungry and suffering: "I was angry that maybe Martín was eating well, and I was suffering." Remember that he had not realized that Martín had been captured by the army or burned in the witness's own empty house, although he did know that his house had been burned down by the army.

He made his round. It turned out to be a macabre round because when he arrived at the house of Francisco, the *animador de la fe*, he "saw the corpses of Francisco Vargas and his family. They had been burned and had no flesh. Their teeth looked so ugly, like this! Oh my God! I almost wept. A

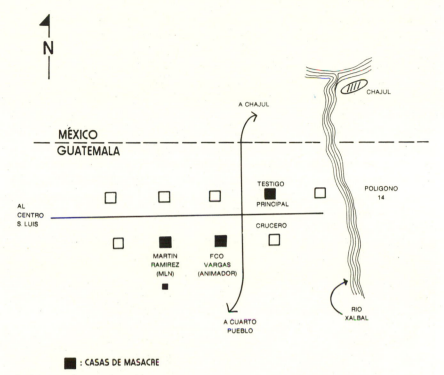

: CASAS DE MASACRE

La Nueva Concepción Massacre

great anger came over me; I felt something undescribable. There were four dead people in Chico Vargas's house: he, his wife, and children."

Indeed, as Francisco's son who had escaped the military had said, his father, mother (who had just given birth), and siblings had been burned alive by the army. The witness, upon seeing their remains, felt awe, horror, compassion, and anger all in one. Only after viewing the results of the massacre could he fathom its magnitude.

He then went to houses that had not been burned down, such as that of Mauricio Recinos (see list), who had gone to the jungle but, unable to bear the mosquitos, had gone back home, not heeding the witness's advice. When the witness realized that this house had not been burned down, his anger, which had already subsided because it was buried in horror, again began to rise: "Here's your house. It hasn't been burned down, and I am furious because my house has." But his anger was short lived, as we shall see in a minute.

He went over to inspect another house when suddenly he saw that smoke was emerging from the MLN militant's house and heard the dogs barking: "Martín's house is burning," he thought. The fire that the soldiers had made the day before was still alight, and now the witness realized that his previous suppositions were wrong. Poor Martín was not calmly eating while he was suffering in the jungle, because his house was on fire. He recalls how he went closer to have a look: "I searched Martín's house and there was a burned corpse. His children and father were on top. Then I started talking to Martín. 'This is what you get, Martín, for not wanting to leave.' I thought it was Martín's body, but it wasn't. It was a woman's corpse." The witness later realized that he had made the mistake of thinking the corpse was Martín's. At that moment he believed that Martín had been burned to death and reproached him for his lack of faith. The witness said of the children under twelve: "There was no sign of them, no bones. As they were so small, nothing was left of their bones." They had melted in the fire like small bits of lard.

The witness remembers that he found Mauricio Recinos's family in this house (it is not clear from the testimony whether this refers to the house previously described or another house of Martín's). He had previously felt angry on discovering that Mauricio Recinos's house had not been burned down, but now he saw that the family had all been burned to death: "There were eleven corpses strewn on the ground." (We do not know whether the eleven included Martín's family.)

After witnessing such sights, the informant felt numb, almost unconscious, and directionless. He puts it very eloquently when he says: "It was as if I were drunk, as if I were drunk."[7] But he still had to reach his own house.

He could scarcely search his house that day because it was still burning and wood and metal sheeting had fallen on top of the bodies. But "ten days later when we were clearing everything up we found Martín's body. He had a green sweater that was soaked in blood. He had it on and part of it hadn't burned." From the sweater he was able to recognize Martín and realize that he had not talked to his corpse ten days before. He had talked to the corpse of a woman, he learned from others.

They also found the remains of the refugees there, together with their blankets, documents, a mirror, and other personal items. The things that hadn't burned were strewn over the floor. Although the army had tried to remove all signs of identification to make the dead unrecognizable and thus create a feeling of disorientation among the survivors as to their community and frame of reference, the thousand eyes of the people almost always found clues to reconstruct the deeds and to work out who was alive and who was dead.

Lists of Those Killed

Of the following two lists, the first is based on information given by the main witness and the second is from a Jakalteko refugee who drew up his list after questioning other survivors of the massacre in this center though not consulting the main witness. They are therefore two independent lists.

Names of Those Killed

	First Source			Second Source
Name	*Kinship*	*Age*	*Place of Origin*	*Name*
From La Nueva Concepción Center				
1. Francisco Vargas		36	Concepción Huista	Francisco Vargas
2. Mercedes Gaspar	1's wife	32	Concepción Huista	Merseda Ramírez
3. Anita Vargas	1 and 2's daughter	7	Concepción Huista	Anita Vargas
4. Fabiana Vargas	1 and 2's daughter	4	Concepción Huista	Pablina Vargas
5. Juana Vargas	1 and 2's daughter	1	Concepción Huista	Manuela Vargas
6. Martín Ramírez[8]		60	Concepción Huista	Martín Ramírez
7. Baltasar Ramírez	6's son	25	Concepción Huista	Baltasar Ramírez
8. Josefa Recinos (?)	7's wife	25	Concepción Huista	Chepa Ramírez
9. Magdalena Ramírez	7's daughter	3	Concepción Huista	Malgalena Ramírez
10. Viviano Ramírez	son	6 mo.	Concepción Huista	Martín Ramírez
11. Alonso Ramírez	6's son	20	Concepción Huista	Alonso Ramirez
12. Tina Jacinto	11's wife	18	Concepción Huista	Abustina Jacinto
13. González Ramírez	11's son	4	Concepción Huista	
14. Magdalena Ramírez	11's daughter	2	Concepción Huista	Malgalena Jacinto
15. Juan Ramírez	6's son (bachelor)	17	Concepción Huista	Juana Ramírez
16. Francisco Ramírez	6's son	14	Concepción Huista	Francisco Ramírez
17. Paulo Ramírez[9]	6's grandson	9	Concepción Huista	Alonso Ramírez ("another family")
18. Mauricio Recinos		42	Concepción Huista	Maubrisio Recino
19. Jesusa Ramírez	18's wife	40	Concepción Ramírez	Jesusa Ramírez
20.	18 and 19's son	13	Concepción Huista	José Roberto Recino
21.	18 and 19's daughter	<13	Concepción Huista	Catalina Recino
22.	18 and 19's son	<13	Concepción Huista	Humberto Recino
23.	18 and 19's daughter	<13	Concepción Huista	Maruca Recino
24.	18 and 19's daughter	<13	Concepción Huista	Valentina Recino
25.	18 and 19's son	<13		
26. Pascual Recinos	18's son	20	Concepción Huista	Pascual Recino
27. Felisa Manuel	26's wife	16	Concepción Huista	Feliscia Gómez

28. Mauricio Recinos	26's son	1	Concepción Huista	Maubrisio Gómez
29. Clemente Gaspar Vicente	30's husband	19	Concepción Huista	Gaspar Clemente
30. Juana Recinos	18's daughter	18	Concepción Huista	Juana Recinos
31. Julio Alvarado		28	Concepción Huista	Julio Albarado

From Belén Center

32. Ermelindo Aguilar[10]		60	Tacaná	Ermelindo Ramírez
33. Juan Aguilar	32's son	23	Tacaná	
34. Francisco Aguilar	32's son	18	Tacaná	

From Santiaguito Center

35. Domingo Muy Ajú		23	Mazatenango	
36.	35's wife		La Libertad, Huehuetenango	
37.	35's son	3		
38.	35's son	1[11]		

NOTES

1. The presidential elections of 7 March 1982 were fraudulent, despite an agreement reached between all the political parties to respect the results. The fraud and subsequent protests headed by the three losing parties put the "pacification" of the country at risk. Two weeks later, on 23 March 1982, the army carried out a coup d'état against Lucas García and General Efraín Ríos Montt came to power.

2. Most of the Nueva Concepción inhabitants were Jakaltekos from Concepción Huista, Huehuetenango. Thus they call their center in the Ixcán "La Nueva Concepción" (the New Conception).

3. From the Mam-speaking Todos Santos Cuchumatán municipality of Huehuetenango.

4. To systematically study warning processes it is useful to refer to disaster sociology. The arrival of the massacring army can be compared to the arrival of a cyclone, when the people's reaction to the alert is of utmost importance. Factors to be taken into consideration include previous experience of similar kinds of disaster, in this case massacres; long- and short-term preparations (attitudes toward the army and emergency plans); identification of the perpetrators of the disaster, in this case the army; communication of the alert; confirmation of and belief in the imminent danger (as can be seen by the *parcelistas* seeking confirmation from the witness who sent out the warning); conflicting sources of information; and the situation in the community (Barton 1969). A review of studies on this subject may be found in Kreps (1984).

5. Another witness also told us of the boy's account of his family being burned alive by the army.

6. Massacres can be analyzed in the same way as natural disasters, in which sociologists place great importance on the emotional impact, on the coming together of

the population in the place of the disaster, and on the emergence of new forms of social organization. For this reason I have followed the feelings of the main witness upon arrival at the crossroads and have mentioned that the first groups of families in the mountains will sow the seeds of the new form of organization, the Communities of Population in Resistance (Comunidades de Población en Resistencia; CPR). The sociology of disaster involves many enlightening hypotheses. Massacres are "unnatural" disasters.

7. I found that the sole surviver of the San Francisco massacre in Nentón, on 17 July 1982, used the exact same expression. The day after the massacre, as he was fleeing to Mexico, he walked as if drunk, without realizing that he was covered in blood and looking as though he had slaughtered a cow (Falla 1983).

8. According to the first source, the mother of no. 6 did not die in the massacre, as she was in Concepción Huista at the time.

9. The boy's father lived in Xalbal. The boy was visiting his grandparents when he was killed.

10. For nos. 32–34 I have preferred to use the testimony of another witness from the Belén center. He lists only two sons, including their names and ages. According to him, Ermelindo was, as in the first source, Ermelindo Aguilar (no. 32). According to the main witness (first source), there may have been another son of no. 32 who was killed. The main witness does not remember no. 34's name. According to the second source, no. 32 had three sons, but he does not include names.

11. I have tried to be meticulous in providing the information because I am constantly thinking of the deceased's friends and relatives, perhaps grandchildren and great-grandchildren, who in the future will also read this book. I express my greatest respect for them. Each name is a person and a constellation of people.

CHAPTER 7

The Second Part of the Massacre of Cuarto Pueblo: Cuarto Pueblo

[14-16 March 1982]

Heavy wines spill
And mix
In ruby splendor

—Alaíde Foppa,
"Bougainvillea"

I have chosen a verse of the Guatemalan poet Alaíde Foppa to start the terrible account of this massacre, one of the largest and bloodiest in Guatemala's recent history. Because I believe that I am also proclaiming good news, I hope not only to convey the horror of the event but also to transmit the radiance of the blood that was shed, which was like heavy wines. Blood gives life and in the long run produces profound hope, like the most precious rubies, which paradoxically adorn the people of Guatemala.[1]

The Various Witnesses

We now return to the army burning houses in La Nueva Concepción and another large part of the battalion making its way from Mexico to the town, to catch unawares the people gathered together for Sunday's economic and religious activities.

My account is based on four groups of witnesses, described in chronological order. The first group is composed of those who fled when the army
entered the town shooting indiscriminately, trying to crush the population
in a pincer movement. The second group consists of those who witnessed
the army actions during the entire three-day massacre, unable to escape
from the army siege but not massacred because they were able to hide on
the ground. From their hiding places, the witnesses heard and saw some of
the things that occurred. Their witnessing of the massacre was more auric-
ular than visual. The third group comprises witnesses who, after fleeing
that Sunday, observed the army actions from the jungle nearby. They are
scouts. Finally, the witnesses of the fourth group are those who went back
to the town after the soldiers had left nine days later. As in La Nueva Concepción, they would bear witness to the main sites of massacre and burning. These, then, are the types of witnesses who will tell us about the massacre in the town of Cuarto Pueblo, where, according to my lists, 324
people died or disappeared.

The Layout of the Town

To facilitate the account, it is necessary to describe the layout of the town
and go over the scene of events. In the center of the town was the marketplace, a small square with a tree in the middle. There were 75 to 100 small
stalls for peasants to sell their produce under the shade of the tree, and
around the square were about 15 small stores and places to eat. The
marketplace reflected the dynamism of the local economy and the emergence of social classes. The marketplace was later razed to the ground.

The marketplace was in the middle of a small hollow surrounded by a
crescent-shaped hill. The hill opened out to the airstrip, running northeast
to southwest. Some of the town's main buildings (almost all made out of
wood) were set out on the hilltop in the following clockwise order: the cooperative warehouse, the community center (which the Catholics used as a
church), the cooperative offices, the half-built Catholic church, the military
outpost (burned down in November 1981), the new school, the old military
outpost, and the Central American Evangelical Chapel, where many people
were later burned alive.

The cooperative store was halfway down the hill; further down still and
near the airstrip was the old school, which would become a bonfire for the
corpses. Next was the auxiliary mayor's office and jail, where some children would be burned to death, and then there was a large shed with a machine to dry cardamom and the clinic. Finally, the witnesses also mention
an open loading shed next to the airstrip.

Behind the crescent hilltop were a hundred or more houses. Every
parcelista had a lot in town, and although their main houses were on their

farm plots, many had built houses in town. All these houses were burned
down.

The lower part of the village was bounded by a stream or small river with
clean water. On the other side of the stream was another hill; from there
one could see the airstrip and, further in the distance, the market and military outpost. The scout witnesses observed what was going on from this
hilltop.

There were five paths or roads leading from the town on all sides to the
cooperative centers. Two are important: the one from La Nueva Concepción in the north, on which the army advanced at 10:00 A.M. to surround
the village, and the road to the extreme south of the airstrip, leading toward Pueblo Nuevo, on which many people traveled to escape the military
encirclement.

One can see the town on the map, drawn by a witness and added to by
many others.

Unexpected and Violent Encirclement

What kind of operation did the army carry out? What were its intentions?
How was it seen and interpreted by the witnesses? How did the people react? To answer these questions, I have woven together the testimonies of
several witnesses, including one I shall call the main witness of Cuarto
Pueblo. Thus I will try to give an overall view of the events without losing
dramatic individual perspectives. The main witness, a Q'anjob'al Indian,
knew of the army's approach, as he was from one of the centers bordering
Mexico. However, a dream he had had that morning made him decide to go
to the plaza. I shall call him Felipe (not his real name).

His dream sent him to be a witness and made him see the unthinkable
things that were to occur, though at that moment he did not know what he
was letting himself in for. "My dream told me that the soldiers were going
to come to kill people; you can go and see if you want." Although the dream
was not an order but an invitation, it compelled him to go, even though his
wife tried to dissuade him. He went to see what was going on, apparently
with the intention of then warning a friend of the danger. But this specific
situation would lead him to a wider mission: to tell the world what he had
seen.

Felipe recalls how he arrived at the market at 9:30 A.M. People were
busily buying and selling: "There's bread, there's everything, beans, lime-
stone. They're selling tomatoes, chile, eggs, hens, tamales,[2] everything. The
market's lively and full of things to buy." Therefore when "a blue and white
helicopter passed overhead," when it "came to have a look," the people did
not interpret it as a sign of danger. As a young *ladina* woman recalls: "We
thought it was just flying around." The helicopter flew over the town twice

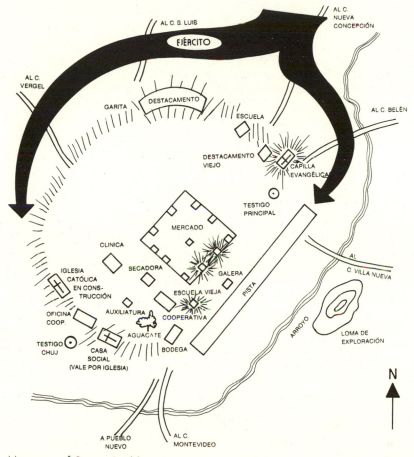

Massacre of Cuarto Pueblo

and then left. No one suspected that its presence was a precursor of the military encirclement to come.

Felipe had gone to the plaza to have a look and was confident that he would detect the army in time. He did not go to the Charismatics' religious service in the community center: "I didn't go to the service because people make a lot of noise there." The Charismatic Catholics pray out loud and clap. "I didn't go because I wouldn't be able to see the soldiers coming, because I was waiting to see where they would come from."

He was against the army and believed that everyone should flee. When the military commissioners, *parcelistas* like himself, tried to convince the people not to run away, he argued with them, even though they were his elders. "The commissioners were in the marketplace talking to my people. 'Don't run,' Commissioner Santos said. 'Don't be afraid, fellows. We're going to just stay when the soldiers come.' 'Maybe they've come to kill,' I said to them, because they had already killed people in El Polígono 14. 'No, you don't know anything about it, you're just a kid. The soldiers don't do any harm.'"

I will call the second most important witness Joselino (not his real name). He too got trapped in the encirclement, and like Felipe he was another firsthand witness. Joselino was a Chuj Indian and lived in another center. He was more naive than Felipe and did not take precautions to defend his life. He was more submissive, not to the army but to the Charismatic catechists, who took the stand of not running away from the army. Therefore when some "devout men" told him to go to the temple, he obeyed, "because if they were to kill us there, they'd kill us while listening to the word of God." He witnessed the drama of those religiously controlled people, and from the open church he saw the line of soldiers advancing along the airstrip with heavy knapsacks. He then fled, but the Charismatic Catholics did not budge, even though they had time to escape.

Felipe, on the contrary, did not see the soldiers in time because he was in the marketplace and "the marketplace is in the hollow," whereas the Chuj witness, who was on the hilltop, was able to see them. Before Felipe knew it, the soldiers were already on top of him. He did not know where to run, because another column of soldiers had stealthily advanced behind the hill and was already reaching the top and blocking off the exit. He remembers: "First the soldiers came along the airstrip, and then more came in on another path above the landing strip, because the army entered from two places." He was therefore surrounded.

It is impossible to say what came first: the people trying to flee or the barrage of bullets. What is certain is that the soldiers' approach was accompanied from the beginning by shooting. Perhaps some soldiers shot into the air whereas others aimed to kill those escaping, because Felipe remembers the guns pointing in different directions. But the bullet that grazed him was certainly intended to kill: "The army opened fire on me twice. It didn't get me, but one bullet grazed my shirt, so I fell to the ground, as though dead." Many people were killed then, though the majority escaped unharmed.

Panic mounted as everyone started running and trying to escape through the only exit. A Jakalteka woman who saw another woman fall next to her found herself trapped by the escaping crowd. Sudden and intense panic overcame her. Her disjointed account combines the word "fright" with the insistency of "we left." "We left, we left" runs through her entire testimony. "We headed toward the jungle; we left. My heart ached with fright. I was really frightened when I saw the shooting. A girl fell down next to us and we left." The woman was amazed that when the crowd ran past the Charismatic Catholics they did not budge, even though she tried to use her influence over them (she was the wife of an animator) by calling out: "Leave, leave, the enemy is killing us." She was amazed and still cannot understand how the people could reply: "We're not leaving, because our papers are in order." She did not stop running, though. "We left with my son and daughter-in-law. We left! But my husband stayed in the marketplace. … My husband didn't listen."

Then the woman began to weep, remembering her husband. She recalled how she prayed for her salvation, forming the words with her dry mouth as she ran along the road: "We only thought: My Lord Jesus Christ. Maybe we'll be saved! My mouth was dry from fright."

In the meantime we have left Joselino, the Chuj witness, in the community center, among the Charismatic Catholics. He heard the religious leaders intersperse the words of God's will with mention, which we also heard in La Nueva Concepción, of some form of identification or "papers." "When we were at the service, the catechists said: 'We don't need to run, we haven't done anything wrong, nothing. We have papers. We are all Christians. Let the soldiers kill us. We are here on earth by God's grace.'" They also argued that for them a life in the jungle, homeless and exposed to the elements and the mosquitos, was out of the question. "They said: 'If we run, there's nowhere to go. If we go to the jungle, we'll die of hunger, we won't be able to stand it. On the other hand, if the soldiers kill us here, we'll die at once.' That's what they thought. The soldiers killed them. Not one of them ran away." The catechists, sadly deceived, urged their followers to stay and thus became instrumental in their deaths.[3]

But Joselino had more common sense. In a taped interview he says: "I was thinking that perhaps I wouldn't let the soldiers kill me. I wasn't going to let the soldiers kill me; it was better to run. Everyone was on their knees and I decided to leave. I was barefoot—I didn't have my shoes on. So I put on my shoes and started running. … I left, but the people stayed on."

However, as in the case of the main witness who was trapped between the two columns of soldiers shooting, he was unable to escape. He lay as if dead. Despite his common sense, he took time in deciding to escape, and when he did try he "could no longer get past." He fell to the ground so that they would not notice him. Both men were caught in the encirclement at opposite points of the town. The main witness, Felipe, was in the north, near the Evangelical chapel, and the Chuj witness, Joselino, was in the south, near the community center.[4]

Commentary on the Military Encirclement

The striking feature of this situation is the instruction not to flee. The reactions to this command allowed the army to determine who was for and who was against it. There is no doubt that this instruction was from the army: It was spread by the military commissioners and also by the soldiers, who on entering the town shouted out: "Don't run away."

But the way that they communicated their message produced the opposite effect. Not everyone could hear what they were saying (they did not use loudspeakers from a helicopter). Nor did the soldiers seem friendly. Some insulted the people ("don't run away, you bastards"), which instead of reassuring them made them even more frightened. Furthermore, the instruction was given after the shooting began, even though the first shots might have been in the air. These first shots were followed by shots at the people as they ran, which created a generalized sense of panic that was overcome only by those grouped together and controlled by the intensity of their prayer and the reassurance of their religious leaders, both among the Charismatic Catholics and the Evangelicals.

As we shall see later on, the instruction was not intended to save those who obeyed but rather to control and massacre them.[5] Those who perceived this intent escaped as quickly as possible. Others failed to distinguish it through their frightened haze of religious feelings of self-sacrifice and total surrender to God. The Jakalteka's testimony clearly shows that the people in the community center could have escaped because she was able to escape, albeit heart in mouth.

The Evangelicals reacted in a similar manner. The man holding the service answered the person who came to warn them: "If you don't trust in God, pray so that your fear will pass." But because their chapel was farther north, the Evangelicals were trapped as soon as the army entered by way of the airstrip, and it would have been very difficult for them to escape.

Family ties reinforced the choices made, which in the final analysis were political choices that were veiled by religion. The ties joined people from different centers into a network. For example, Diego Ramírez, thirty-nine, was the Charismatic leader who persuaded the people to stay in the community center. He was from Concepción Huista, as was Martín Ramírez, the MLN militant from Nueva Concepción who also spoke of the "papers" that would save him. Both had the same last name: Ramírez. Diego Ramírez's wife, María Vargas, also from Concepción Huista, had the same last name as Francisco Vargas, the Charismatic animator from Nueva Concepción who was mentioned in the previous chapter. Francisco Vargas was married to a Ramírez who was also from Concepción Huista. One can therefore detect strong family ties, as well as political and religious connections, between the Ramírez and Vargas families.

It was not only because of ideological beliefs that people did not leave but fell into the hands of the army. There were other factors, such as sales (not wanting to leave one's merchandise), solidarity between spouses (looking for the other), curiosity, and indecision, as can be seen in the witnesses' accounts.

Sunday: The First Dead
and Burning the Marketplace

Those who fled escaped southwest by the road to Pueblo Nuevo, which had not been sealed off by the military. All those who remained in the town were massacred or disappeared except the two witnesses who managed to survive.

We will now follow the main witness, who had hidden under a log, his face bitten by ants. He witnessed the entire four-day massacre. I will interweave his testimony with the account of the other trapped witness and those of the scouts. The sequence of events is not always clear, in part because the main witness did not remember and in part because the account is disjointed. Also, because he was hidden he could only catch glimpses of what was going on, like tableaux that became imprinted on his mind. From these, I can only deduce what happened.

From his hiding place the witness caught glimpses of the army's various encirclements: The soldiers surrounded the town and also places where the people had gathered together, like the community center and the Evangelical chapel. In this way the soldiers were able to immobilize and control the people. The army placed sentries in key places, such as at the Evangelical chapel door, which the witness had seen. At the opposite end of the town, the other witness remembers how the army surrounded the Charismatic Catholics gathered together in the community center.

The Chuj witness then caught a glimpse of a group of people who had already been surrounded. He says that they were women and children: When we asked whether there were men among the group he said, "There were no men, only women, and kids hiding behind their mothers." This testimony tallies with other reports by witnesses (not eyewitnesses) that the soldiers separated the men from the women after surrounding the places of worship. At this point, the women still had their children with them, but during another stage of the operation, which we have not been able to place in the testimonies, the children were snatched away from their mothers.

The main witness continues to relate his story, jumping from one event to another as he associates images rather than following the course of events. As he visualizes the children hanging onto their mothers, he remembers something else he saw. From what I can make out, it took place after the soldiers had surrounded the town but before they rounded up the people at the places of worship.

It was a terrible scene: a child next to his dead mother. It seems that the child was a baby in his mother's arms, but the testimony is not clear. A soldier, who perhaps felt incapable of looking after the child and was conscious of the order to kill everyone, grabbed him by the leg and smashed his head against the ground, killing him instantly. In his broken Spanish, the Q'anjob'al Indian relates: "There was a child and the soldier grabbed him. He said, 'We must kill him.' He grabbed his leg and smashed his head on the ground and left him lying there." To see if he was sure of this, I asked him whether he had seen it happen, as sometimes witnesses mingle what they have seen with things others have told them about. "I saw it," he said. "It happened in the marketplace. As his mother was already dead, the child was crying. The soldier only did this with his leg [making the gesture of smashing] and his head slammed against the ground. And he left the child lying there. He was no longer crying."[6]

Then the interrogation took place. The main witness did not hear or see it, but as we shall see later on, he did hear the lieutenant referring to the interrogation, so I presume that it began on Sunday, once the men were separated from the women. The lieutenant explained to his soldiers that everyone should die because during the interrogation those captured merely answered that they did not know. The interrogations were therefore fruitless. The words that the witness heard the lieutenant utter were the following: "We ask them questions and they say they don't know. Bullshit!" The interrogations appear to have taken place in the cooperative offices.[7]

Something else made a deep impression on the witness. He went into great detail about how at midday, after securing all the positions, the soldiers ate everything in the market. While the witness was suffering from hunger and thirst, the soldiers were stuffing themselves. Remember how they had stolen sweet corn from the Mexican field. They arrived hungry and their hunger made them get on with their job quickly: "The market was deserted, so they ate there. They ate cookies and bread. They drank Pepsi. As it was Sunday, there was everything in the market."

It would seem that while some soldiers were cordoning off groups of people and starting interrogations, others were given the task of preparing a large meal for later on. Both witnesses, hidden at opposite extremes of the town, mention that the army killed fowl, pigs, and a sturdy bull. "The army ate meat—it killed pigs and cattle," recalls the Q'anjob'al witness. The Chuj Indian remembers the conversation he overheard between the lieutenant and one of the soldiers in charge of looking for the animals: "Have you found anything?" asked the lieutenant. "Yes, there are two pigs and four turkeys." "Is there anything else?" "Yes, a big bull." And they went to get it in the afternoon. It was a very fat black bull; I do not know who it had belonged to. The soldiers stole everything they could eat and forced the people to get firewood.

Another tableau engrained in the memory of one of the witnesses is a helicopter that landed and then took away ten *quintales* (1,000 pounds altogether) of cardamom. That Sunday morning the witness must have seen the local men and women bringing their pounds of cardamom to the marketplace to sell to the merchant, Benedicto Escalante. The local inhabitants used the money earned by selling cardamom to buy basic consumer goods and food supplies. The witness now saw how "the army took the cardamom away by helicopter." He does not say whether the local merchant was killed, but the merchant's name appears on the lists of those massacred that were drawn up by other witnesses.

That afternoon, at about 3:00 or 4:00 P.M. according to the Chuj witness's estimates, the shooting massacre began. The Chuj witness explains that he did not see the massacre but only heard it taking place. He determined that many people were being killed. "I heard but couldn't see it." He heard how the lieutenant separated the soldiers from the local inhabitants, making them stand on a kind of a hillock, and shouted, "'One, two, three, hallelujah!' and they began the shooting.[8] And what a shoot-up! 'That's enough,' the lieutenant said, and the shooting stopped. It seemed like maybe the army had killed everyone." And about half an hour later he heard the lieutenant say: "'Let's get the other groups.' And a little while later the shooting began again. And again what a shoot-up! The people were obviously killed."

The Chuj witness associates this recollection with that of a strange smell. I do not think that the smell immediately followed the shooting, but there seems to be a sequence of events in which the army, after killing the people, threw them onto a fire. The witness smelled the bodies burning. "Smoke appeared; I could see it where I was. What a lot of smoke! And what a smell! A horrible smell!" We asked him what kind of smell it was, but he didn't want to say. He only replied: "Firewood, the smell of. ... Perhaps they were throwing the people onto the fire."

The main witness also smelled burning flesh and confirmed that the soldiers were burning people, apparently in the marketplace. The burning started that evening, around 6:00 P.M. The fire burned all night long. He could see it as he was lying down looking upward because the sky was illuminated by the fire: "The market buildings were burning all Sunday afternoon and people were burned in the market on Sunday afternoon. A fire was burning in the marketplace all night long. The night was very clear because of the fire. ... The people were already dead when they burned them. There was a good taste [smell], like burning pork."

The soldiers also burned down the cooperative store and the community center that night, "pouring diesel fuel over the buildings to make them catch fire." And while they were burning, the soldiers said: "We have to get rid of all this and sweep it all away," an expression apt for the sweep operation they were carrying out.

That night the main witness was awake and heard the lieutenant ordering the soldiers to place sentries on all five roads leading to the town in order to capture the guerrillas or hungry people returning from the jungle for food: "'At night we're going to keep watch over the houses. The guerrillas are going to get very hungry.' His plan was that they were going to return out of hunger and they'd get them then. That's why they placed sentries on all the roads. The lieutenant gave this order at about 9:00 P.M. and then went to see another group, gathered together in the community center."

The witnesses deduce that the soldiers were gathered in perhaps three large groups. They were able to situate two of the groups, which were at opposite ends of the town: one was at the community center, near the Chuj witness, and the other was next to the Evangelical chapel, near the main witness. The commanding position seemed to be next to the main witness, as many soldiers gathered there the following day to listen to a long speech.

On that same night, while the sky was lit by the market and houses on fire, the main witness recalls that the soldiers were raping women. "They entered the schoolhouse with the women. The women were screaming that night. Perhaps they were fucking them." He did not see this firsthand but confirmed his suspicion when he heard two Kaqchikel soldiers talking to each other near where he had hidden: "Utz ixok chiré," he heard them say. Because many Kaqchikel Indians lived in his center, he had learned a bit of their language and was able to understand what they were saying. The soldiers had said: "These women are attractive." He also heard the officer reproving the Kaqchikel soldiers for speaking in their native tongue.

The Chuj witness confirms that women were raped, as he heard a similar conversation near him, although he refers to the women being locked up in the shed used for drying cardamom. A soldier "was coughing all night long. Every now and then cough, cough, cough. ... Perhaps he had a cold. He didn't move at all. Then the other soldier said: 'Let's go fuck the women. Let's go fuck them, they're attractive; I've already been once.' 'No,' said the one who was coughing, 'no,' he said." The witness highlighted the difference between the two soldiers, the one who did want to and the one who did not. It was not clear whether the one who said no did so out of respect for the women or because he was ill. This witness, like many others I have interviewed, makes a distinction between the behavior of the soldiers: for example, between the cruel and the compassionate and between the aggressive and fearful soldiers.

Monday: The Lieutenant Justifies the Massacre

By dawn on Monday, many people had already been massacred, but not all, perhaps not even the majority. So the lieutenant gave a pep talk to the soldiers to inspire them to finish the people off. The main witness, still hidden under a log, his face swollen from ant bites, remembered much of what he said. The subjects covered are of great interest, as they give an idea of the army's plan and intentions. And they became engrained in the witness's mind because they helped him to understand what happened and to explain it to others. Thus during my interview with the witness he repeated the lieutenant's speech various times.

The first thing the lieutenant said was that the soldiers had to wipe out the entire town because it supported the guerrillas: "They are friends of the guerrillas, but they aren't saying so. We have to finish them all off, to put an end to the guerrillas. The women are preparing their food. If we finish them all off, things will soon calm down. The men are helping them. But when we ask them about that, they say they don't know anything. Lies!" The witness well understood the army's intention, to kill the entire town, men and women, so that "things will calm down"—in other words, to pacify the country. He remembers how the lieutenant went on: "All the commissioners are their friends. That's why they don't say anything. We're going to do in the lot of them. That way they won't be able to help out the guerrillas. If you finish off the people, there's no one left to help them." From this statement it appears that while addressing the local inhabitants the lieutenant identified them as guerrillas, as we have seen in other chapters, but when addressing his troops he made the distinction perfectly clearly between the guerrillas and the civilian population.[9]

The second subject was how to establish the people's sympathies with the guerrillas. One technique used, interrogation, failed: "They don't say anything." But the main proof was a list the lieutenant brought with him of the villages that should be destroyed. As in the 1975 abductions, which were carried out according to lists of persons, so now the massacres were taking place according to lists. The witness well remembers that the lieutenant said to the soldiers: "We have a list of guerrilla villages. We already know which entire villages are going to be wiped out. We'll finish this town first and then we'll go to others: Centro Uno, Kaibil Balam, Piedras Blancas. ... We have to finish off the lot of them and then do the same in El Petén." It is clear, therefore, that the decision to massacre was not taken by the officer on the ground: The orders came from above. Responsibility lay with the material culprits who carried out the massacres and with the intellectual culprits who planned them.

A third subject is the argument used to encourage the troops. Some soldiers were doubtful and also feared a guerrilla attack. Even in his sorry state, the witness laughed to himself on discovering that there were also frightened soldiers. They had undoubtedly heard about the guerrilla attack against the military outpost in Cuarto Pueblo in April the year before. To raise their morale, the lieutenant told them, "We're going to win, don't be afraid. A small plane will come to help us, and a helicopter." The rebels do not have planes, but the army does. The infantry's morale depends highly on the air force. He also said to them, "Thanks to the United States helping us, our soldiers won't be wiped out." Although the United States had cut military aid to Guatemala because of human rights violations, the lieutenant felt the moral support of the North Americans in this large-scale offensive.[10]

Monday: The Children and Women Die

Let us go to other witnesses for a moment. I have already said that as of Monday men approached the town to observe from on high what the army was doing. According to a young scout, that Monday "the children were in the auxiliary mayor's offices, alive but locked up. They were separated from their mothers and the army set fire to the building filled with children. They probably poured on diesel fuel and set the building alight." The value of the witness's observation is not comparable to those of the two trapped witnesses, as he was about 200 meters away from the events. But he was very certain about what he had seen.[11]

According to the main witness, that Monday the army also dismantled the Evangelical chapel and burned it the following day: "On Monday they were breaking up the chapel; they were taking the wood apart." It was probably on that day that the army killed many of the women. The witness remembers hearing desperate cries and says that when they were burning the chapel on Tuesday, the women were already dead. Although he does not remember when they were killed, he does recall that they burned their bodies there: "Who knows what time they killed them. On Monday afternoon the people were screaming. The people were already dead when they burned them."[12]

Tuesday: Only a Few Remain

Thus little by little the people were exterminated. According to the Chuj witness, on Tuesday (it seems), there were still some women and young people alive who were taken to the drying shed at night, where the soldiers said: "We're going to go have a fuck." He believes that during the four-day massacre the old people were killed first and then men and women because the "young women" were useful as cooks, according to a comment he heard the lieutenant make. "'What are we going to do with these women?' a soldier asked the lieutenant. 'That woman will stay to make bread [because she was a baker] … and that's how we'll do it, a woman in each place, in every place. There are two soldiers here, so two women will stay here. Another there, another over there, and over there, where the soldiers are. One woman for each pair of soldiers.'" Thus apart from the two or three main army concentration points there were also small sentry posts of two or three soldiers each, which were perhaps located on the outskirts of the town. The women served them as long as the army remained in the town.

On Tuesday the scouts found the town quieter: "When he went out exploring on Tuesday," another witness says, referring to a scout, "there was no longer the noise of children and the soldiers scattered in groups around the town," as the previous witness had said. The scout also saw that they were still killing people, no longer on a large scale but one by one. "He saw the soldiers take a peasant from the drying shed; the soldiers were holding more people inside. When they took him to the old school you could hear him moaning 'ow, ow!' The peasant did not return. And a while later a soldier took out another peasant and took him to the school to finish him off. You could hear them screaming only when they arrived at the school. Then the screams stopped."

According to another scout, on Tuesday the soldiers also took out "dead people on a cart" from the cooperative offices to the old school, which they then set on fire. He also saw how there were still a few people alive who they pushed into the building. "They were screaming in the school, but their voices were no longer loud." Perhaps they killed them there.

Wednesday: Everyone Has Been Exterminated

By Wednesday almost everyone had been exterminated, with the exception perhaps of the young women who cooked. Another scout says that he saw soldiers in the marketplace but that "we no longer saw any people," that is, civilians. He says that "from afar you could see the dead and there was no longer any screaming, only the shouts of the soldiers laughing."

That day the main witness and the Chuj Indian managed to escape from the town. The former says: "I dragged myself out slowly on Wednesday at about 1:00 A.M. The soldiers still had the lights on. They heard me make a noise and said: 'It's an opossum.' Then I got to the road leading to the Argentina center and I left." Thus the main witness made his way to freedom.

The Chuj Indian was able to leave earlier on the same Wednesday. Just before he left he heard a heartrending cry and thought it was his son calling him. It was the voice of a fifteen-year-old boy, deeply anguished, crying out for his father: "'Ohhh, Daddy, Daddy,' he cried. The boy was crying: 'Daddy, Daddy.' It could have been my son they were killing." That was the last thing he heard, and it pierced his heart. With great sadness and uncertainty he decided to try to escape to freedom despite the surveillance, which by that time was probably not very strict.

Returning to how things began, the Chuj witness remembers that his son was in church (the community center) when the soldiers arrived. His son stayed there, but he managed to leave.

The army stayed in Cuarto Pueblo for another five days after the four-day massacre. Why, if there was hardly anyone left? The likely explanation is that the army was not only waiting for the rebels and the townspeople who had escaped to return hungry in search of food but that it also needed time to burn down the houses.[13] They burned down about a hundred houses. Once the town had been razed, the survivors would have no reason to return. Nor would there be any point in the army staying on any longer.

Horror: Reconnoitering the Deserted Town

The army left on 23 March and the town was deserted. The first scouts who ventured back described the state of the town. Let us listen to the testimony of a Kaqchikel *parcelista*, who walked through the razed town in a state of shock: "The army isn't here now, only dead people; only a few remains of dead people can be seen." I asked if there were any corpses left untouched.

> No, not a single corpse had been thrown in the jungle because they were in the town. … We reached the large school and beneath it there was a pit. We went to it and saw it was covered with earth. There were bones in the pit. We dug around and saw that the bones had flesh. There were a load of bones that had not been burned. Most of the dead were thrown into that pit. It was in the school.
>
> And another place was the chapel. We reckon there were about a hundred people there. The Evangelicals were gathered together with their loudspeakers when the army arrived. The Charismatic Catholics had also gathered, but there were no remains of bones in their chapel. They burned down the Central American chapel. They burned down the loudspeakers. There we saw several freshly severed heads. We also found women's *trajes* [typical costumes] with ribbons in the chapel. They hadn't burned well. There were also the *cortes*[14] of the dead women strewn around. There was a wooden fence around the chapel and in the town there were plenty of metal barrels filled with gasoline and kerosene. Maybe they used them to light the fire.

The witnesses remember most of the burned corpses being in the Central American Evangelical church. Two of the witnesses estimate that there were about a hundred corpses. Another says: "That's where they burned most of the people." There were so many bodies crammed together, one on top of another, that they did not burn well, and that was why the witnesses were able to find the remains of the women's belongings: necklaces, bits of *corte*, ribbons. These remnants made a deep impression on several of the male witnesses. Although the witnesses presume that this building was the site of the burning of the Evangelicals who were celebrating their religious service, it is probable that the chapel was used for burning other bodies as well.

The second place mentioned by the witnesses was the old school, near the landing strip, which the scouts saw burning. The soldiers dug a ditch or pit by the school to hastily bury the half-burned corpses and calcinated bones. According to another witness, they gathered the children in the school building and set it on fire. This version may not contradict the story of the scout who said that the children had been locked up in the auxiliary mayor's offices, as there may have been two groups of children. In any case, although they differ in place, the stories coincide in that the children were separated from their mothers, locked up, killed, and burned.

The third place where burned corpses were found was two houses or market stores. And the fourth was the clinic.

Perhaps other places were used to burn people. But it is important to note that the army used only a few buildings as crematoriums or ovens for burning people alive. They did not burn indiscriminately but according to some system. They probably chose large wooden enclosed places, which would burn well with the help of diesel fuel and gasoline from the drying machines. People were not burned in the community center, which also served as the Catholic church: It was open and did not have a fence around it. The half-built Catholic church was not burned down either, as it was made of cement blocks. The fact that the ovens were concentrated in a few places also indicates that many people were killed in one place (for example, those shot dead on Sunday) and burned somewhere else.

All the scout witnesses agree that people were burned alive. They saw people being thrown into the burning buildings. The soldiers played with the men as if they were footballs: They left them in the sun and then picked them up and "threw them into the old school, which was on fire," one witness explains. He adds that the women were thrown "into an oven." "You could see that the people were still walking when they were shoved into the houses," which were then set alight, another witness says. They also report having heard the screams of people inside as the buildings were set on fire, like in the Evangelical chapel, according to a third witness. One could argue that at such a distance the scouts could not definitively confirm what they saw. But some of them stress that they could see "clearly" or that, although not hearing the precise words of the soldiers speaking, they could hear them when they shouted. And the screams of the people on fire were perfectly audible.

The persons named in the list in the following chapter should be regarded as individuals who disappeared rather than as dead people whose bodies were recognized. As said earlier, the corpses were unrecognizable, half burned, buried, or piled on top of each other. And although a man would probably have been able to recognize a bit of his dead wife's clothes, for example (as in the smaller massacre in La Nueva Concepción), there were so many corpses that it made the search for and recognition of remains nigh on impossible. Hardly a single witness recognized anyone. Furthermore, very few returned to the town because of the danger of falling into an army ambush. The lists compiled are therefore limited in these ways. The witnesses who drew them up gave the names of those who never returned from the town center.

The army did not take anyone with them when they left except a few men to carry things. The women who had been doing the cooking were not taken. The soldiers probably would have liked to take them but they could not because the operation had only just begun in Ixcán Grande with Cuarto Pueblo. They still had to move on to Los Angeles, Pueblo Nuevo, and Xalbal. People in Los Angeles who saw the soldiers and even talked to them saw only three or four civilians carrying loads. The military had thus wiped out everyone in the town.

The only exception was that a few young men were taken away by helicopter during the first days of the massacre.[15] Three witnesses mention this, though none saw it happen. Two say the young men were taken away on Tuesday: "The helicopter arrived on 16 March to pick up the young men. They only took young men with them. Who knows why they took them away." The third says the helicopter made three trips, taking the young men to Playa Grande. It would seem logical that they were taken there to be interrogated and tortured, as they were young and therefore more likely to be suspected as connected to the guerrillas. What did the army do with them after that? They figure on the list of the disappeared. The witnesses have given them up for dead, but I have not found a single person who identified their corpses.

It is possible that some people on the lists survived, as the army could have spared their lives or they could have decided to collaborate with the military. I doubt that they could have escaped, though, because they would have turned up before, as in the case of witnesses who were taken to the secret detention centers (see Chapter 12). It is therefore necessary to investigate the whereabouts of the disappeared.

NOTES

1. Bougainvillea is a red or purple flower (there are also white and yellow species, which are not so common). The plant is a bush that is used to embellish fences, walls, and houses. The flower is not big—it is smaller than a rose—yet all the flowers together give the impression of a purple waterfall. In some countries the name is veranera. Note, though, that it is not a jungle flower. The Guatemalan poet Alaíde Foppa was abducted in Guatemala City in December 1980. She did not write "revolutionary" poems, but being an authentic poet she recreated life not partially but in its totality. I have found hidden meanings in her poems about flowers (Foppa 1982). The wounds of the people of Cuarto Pueblo are awesome, as the survivors show them while being alive and resurrected. The witnesses, too, by telling their stories, weep

once more as their wounds are again opened up. The wounds give meaning to the living.

2. A dish made of corn meal with chicken or meat, wrapped in corn husks or banana leaves.—TRANS.

3. The attitude may seem rather excessive, but think of the widespread image of Jesus handing himself over to his enemies and not trying to escape, as if it was God's will. What happened in Cuarto Pueblo serves in theological terms to reflect upon the meaning of voluntary surrender and the meaning of fighting for one's life in the face of adversaries and taking security measures—that is, the opposite of "tempting God."

4. In the counterinsurgency manuals, special importance is given to "surround and search" techniques. There are two moments. In the first, called the encirclement (as was done in Vietnam), the area, which was usually a village or a hamlet, was cordoned off, generally at night, to increase the element of surprise. The surrounding forces had to be prepared to face not only the villagers but also any enemies caught in the trap as well as a possible attack by the enemy. In this case, reinforcements would be brought in from the outside to free those trapped (Tho 1980, 92).

5. A comparison can be made with the instructions given during the encirclement of the Vietnam village Ben Suc, in the Cedar Falls operation. According to journalist Jonathan Schell, through loudspeakers the army advised the local inhabitants: "Don't escape or you will be shot as Viet Cong sympathizers. Stay in your houses and wait for instructions." They dropped leaflets that could be handed in as safe-conducts. But despite the more sophisticated techniques and sheer brute force (the attack was carried out by sixty helicopters and 500 U.S. soldiers), the journalist says the operation turned into "destroy and search" instead of "search and destroy" as planned, because in the first few moments alone the army caused 24 civilian casualties (Schell 1967, 21).

6. This is comparable to a scene witnessed by the sole survivor of the San Francisco massacre: "Then they took out the last child, a small boy of perhaps two or three. He was small; I saw it happen. The poor little kid was screaming. There was a trunk of a fallen tree. The man grabbed the poor little boy and smashed his head against the trunk. He cracked his head open and threw the boy inside [the house]" (Falla 1983, 651).

7. The second moment of the "surround and search" pacification technique was the search. The soldiers in charge of the search were different from those in the roundups, as the former were more powerful and the latter had more contact with the population. The task of searching was planned to the last detail: The village in question was divided up into sectors and each search group was assigned a sector (Tho 1980, 92). In Ben Suc, the North Americans laid siege to the village and the Vietnamese soldiers searched. The villagers were divided into groups according to age, sex, and how suspect they seemed. All men between the ages of fifteen and forty-five were evacuated to the provincial police headquarters that same afternoon. The North Americans interrogated about forty men on the first day. The Vietnamese also used torture during their interrogations. The North American captain makes the excuse: "They are so intermingled in the population that you can't say who is Viet Cong" (Schell 1967, 58).

8. The witness says in Spanish: "Uno, dos, tres, júbilo." "Júbilo" means joy.—TRANS.

9. According to the counterinsurgency manuals, the first pacification aim was security, that is, to destroy the main enemy force and "eliminate enemy infrastructure." Infrastructure referred to the noncombatant population. A distinction was made between the indoctrinated party members and party sympathizers; the latter were ordinary people who had been persuaded to collaborate with the Viet Cong. The elimination policy would be applied in different degrees accordingly. In practice, however, under the Diem presidency, secret orders were given to leaders in the provinces to dispose of the Viet Cong infrastructure, including carrying out extrajudicial killings: "The task force members *indiscriminately* [my italics] slaughtered every Viet Cong infrastructure member they hunted down" (Tho 1980, 72). But infrastructure members continued to be killed off after Diem's death in 1963. In 1967, according to Tho, 5,615 people were eliminated (Tho 1980, 72–73). In the Cuarto Pueblo massacre, the Guatemalan armed forces killed indiscriminately: They massacred children, old people, women, guerrilla sympathizers, and nonsympathizers alike.

10. The United States cut its military aid to Guatemala during the Carter period. At the beginning of 1982 Alexander Haig, then secretary of state, declared that the United States put it clearly to the government of Guatemala that it should take measures to stop the continuing human rights violations. In spite of this cut in aid, the lieutenant lifted the morale of the soldiers by invoking U.S. backing.

11. Counterinsurgency practices in Vietnam led soldiers and officers, such as Lieutenant William Calley, to say: "Everyone was Viet Cong there. The old people, women and children. Babies were all VC or would be VC in three years' time. And inside the VC women I imagine there were thousands of little VC" (Sack 1971). Officers from Huehuetenango also said that the infrastructure had to be exterminated from "the seed" when they threatened people before the July 1982 scorched-earth offensive in Huehuetenango (Falla 1984a).

12. Another scout, however, says that some people were burned alive in the Evangelical chapel: "On Tuesday I was able to get near the Evangelical chapel. It was the same day they set the people on fire. I came by the jungle, not by the road. I could hear them setting fire to the chapel at about 12:00 midday and could hear the people screaming inside." We asked him if everyone inside was alive. He answered: "Perhaps a few had been killed beforehand and others were thrown onto the fire alive. And the soldiers were shouting and laughing."

13. It seems that the army burned down only the houses in the town, not on the plots of land, although some nearby farmhouses may have been destroyed.

14. Wraparound skirts made from typical Guatemalan cloth, used with a sash by indigenous women.—TRANS.

15. It is interesting to contrast this army operation with the one carried out in the village of Ben Suc in Vietnam. There, many men were taken in Chinook helicopters to the provincial police headquarters on the same day the village was cordoned off. The following day, the inhabitants of Ben Suc were taken to another village that was being used as a camp for more than 5,000 people who were by now regarded as refugees. However, they were not massacred, as in the case of Cuarto Pueblo. On the fourth day, 100 men who had been taken away by helicopter were returned. The journalist does not say how many men did not return. Afterward Ben Suc was razed:

Homes were burned down with gasoline, tractors were then brought in, and even the cemetery was destroyed. Finally, the entire village was bombed intensely to ensure that even deep tunnels, if there were any, would be demolished. Physical damage was greater in Vietnam than in Guatemala, but the genocide of Cuarto Pueblo is incomparable to the number of deaths in this particular Vietnamese village (Schell 1967, 64).

CHAPTER 8

The Living and the Dead: Cuarto Pueblo

Let us return to the living in this chapter. A few survivors managed to escape from the army that tragic Sunday, but most of those who survived stayed at home and did not go to the plaza in town. The situation of the orphans is particularly dramatic: Their parents went to town and never came back.

Orphans and the First Groups to Flee to the Jungle

After the massacre, several men went from house to house on the farm plots to seek survivors and take them to the jungle. They did this on their own accord. Thinking the army might extend its scorched-earth policy to the centers near the town, they went to the farm plots, where they found relatives of the massacred who did not know what to do. The following testimony is of one of the men who gathered together groups of survivors. These groups, unlike the ones we saw in the centers on the border with Mexico, were not formed of two or three related families. They brought together a larger number of families, many of whom were neighbors and not necessarily relatives. Let us hear part of his testimony:

> We went to warn the people to leave, to take their corn with them, as the army was going to burn down their houses. We arrived at a house where there were three children around seven or eight years old. They started running away from us. We followed them. They were frightened. They thought we were the army. We asked them where their mother and father were. "They went to market, they went to church," they answered. We said they wouldn't return home, as the army had killed them. We told them that they could stay with a widower who was in his home.

The widower was lying down inside the house. Two of his children, aged fifteen and ... had gone to market. He said he had gone to fetch firewood, had cut his leg, and was unable to walk. That's why he hadn't gone to market. He wept as he thought of his children. We left him the three children and told him that his sons would not return. That's when he began to weep.

We found a woman in another house. She was pregnant. Her husband and two children had gone to market. Only two children had stayed behind with her. We told her to leave, as her husband had already been massacred. "Take your things and your corn with you, and go with this brother to the jungle to form groups." She went to the jungle.

We found an eight-year-old girl. She was alone in the jungle. She was Q'anjob'al and didn't speak Spanish. I talked to her. Her parents and brothers and sisters had all gone to market. She began to cry. We sent her to the widower and they took her to the jungle.

We went to another house. There was a woman who had given birth about fifteen days before her husband died. ... She began to cry. She was with her two small children, a girl of about five and a boy of three. She said her husband had gone to church. "He won't be coming back," we told her. She started to weep. So she left. ... There were four young men, about seventeen or eighteen years old. ... They hadn't gone to market. She went with them to the jungle.

The testimony of this generous man continues; he refers to more destroyed homes that he found during his search. He remembers that he was in such a state of shock that he lost his appetite and did not eat for several days. His testimony gives an insight into the problem of orphans.

The following testimony is not of a person who served as an intermediary trying to bring the survivors together but of one who merely sought out his relatives and neighbors. At first, he and his brother went in search of their sister. Later, his brother took in various orphans. The testimony brings us in contact with specific kinship relationships.

We looked for our neighbor, to coordinate with him, but he was no longer there. He had gone to Mayalán with his father-in-law. But we managed to coordinate with all our other neighbors.

Afterward we went to look for my sister. We thought, "She's probably been killed"; that's what we thought. She lived in another center. We went to look for her two or three days after the army had left Cuarto Pueblo. "Perhaps she's lost," we thought. My brother [who has since passed away] and I went to see her. My mother wanted to go too, but she is very old and can't run.

We reached her house and found no one. We found some chickens. The dishes were there and the corn grinder had been put up. My brother and I began to weep. There was a pot of food next to the cooked corn, but it was seventeen days old and was rotten. We thought she must have gone to the plaza that Sunday.

He then remembers that his brother, who had accompanied him on that visit, was given some orphans to look after. The orphans were alone in a house and unalarmed. They had been lighting fires and cooking together, without realizing that the smoke could attract the soldiers' attention. They were playing and shouting, unaware of what had happened. They thought their father had got drunk and that was why he and their mother had not returned from market.

> The children were aged four, six, and eight. They were calm. They thought their parents were still in town and had got drunk. They had their cooked corn. The eight-year-old was looking after the smaller ones. They had *panela* [unrefined brown sugar] and sweet corn *atol* [a hot drink]. The sweet corn in the fields was ripe. They also ate a chicken, but they didn't know how to kill it because they were small. They put it in the pot alive and it tried to jump out. That's what the kids told us. The children were alone for exactly eight days.
>
> They gave the orphans to my brother. My brother had four orphans: the boy from La Nueva Concepción who escaped while his parents were being burned to death and these three from the Maravilla center.

Threshold to a New Life

Life continued amid the debris. A few men, like the witnesses, took the initiative to bring together the people who were dispersed on their plots of lands, taking them from their homes, because this was the only way to protect themselves from the army. Their aims were to avoid being killed at home by the soldiers and to avoid being forced to become informers and guides to root out the people hidden in the jungle. They therefore formed small groups that became the seeds of resistance.

The way the first witness talked to the survivors may seem harsh, but it helped protect the people by getting them to leave their houses. On each visit, he used the same approach, which contained three essential aspects: (1) to ask about those absent in order to gather information, (2) to listen to the survivors' accounts in answer to his questions, and (3) to assume a hard line by taking away all hope of their relatives being alive.

Taking away all hope helped to sever the survivors' emotional bond to their homes. Why stay here if your loved one will never return? The witness's cold and sincere words define the situation of the survivors—disoriented and at a loss as to what to do. The witness's definitiveness made those listening to him burst into tears, not because of the harshness of his words but because it was only then that they assimilated that their loved ones were dead. Their weeping also weakened their resistance to leave, and that was when the witness advised them to seek survival in the jungle. He recommended that they take their corn with them, and although the testimony is not explicit, he probably told them to take their dishes, corn grinders, clothing, and blankets, which were all necessary for the new situation.

Thus the weeping marks a turning point, as it is the beginning not only of a psychological state but also of a new life-style. The community had been rendered apart. Immediately after the massacre the survivors were confused, unsure, and numb, as if drunk. They could no longer recognize the parameters of their social environ because they did not know how many people had been killed. But the survivors emerged from this state of disintegration on realizing that their relatives were indeed dead. At that point they would break down and weep. One witness describes this twofold reaction of numbness and weeping after the massacre: "At the time of the massacre we hardly felt a thing. It was only when the army left that we began to feel. Only then did my massacred brother's family begin to cry. Only then did we realize which families remained."

Weeping also gave way to powerful feelings, such as rage (not hatred), that led to action. Thus the same witness says: "What made me most angry was that the army killed so many children. I haven't forgotten that anger, which is why I liked the idea of setting traps, which some people later suggested." Weeping also gave way to solidarity and love: The orphans became the children of new parents and family boundaries opened up. There is a hidden force in the reaction of weeping that manifests weakness and despair but gives rise to fighting on with love.

The First Refugees

After the Cuarto Pueblo massacre, the first refugees left Ixcán Grande and went to Mexico. They, too, would restructure their lives, creating new forms of social organization based fundamentally on solidarity. The main witness relates how he escaped to Mexico in search of his wife, whom he believed to be dead but who had crossed the border with some neighbors in search of safety. Why stay in Guatemala if her husband was no longer alive? The witness went to Mexico, where local peasants took him in with great compassion. He recalls: "My wife told herself 'My husband is now dead' and began to cry. She didn't think that I could still be alive. She hid in the jungle with a neighbor of mine and then went to Mexico. 'I no longer have a partner, he stayed there,' she said. Then I arrived in Chajul, Mexico; I got as far as that. 'What happened to you?' the Mexican asked me. 'I'll give you two eggs.' 'Thank goodness you made it,' he said. 'You're going to work with me.' 'Thank you for putting up my wife,' I told him, 'I'm going to work with you.' 'No,' he said, 'now you're going to rest; I don't want you to work now. Another day you'll come with us to work, alright?'"

The hospitality of the survivors hidden in the jungle is mirrored by the Mexican peasants who used to give the *parcelistas* work before the repression. Given the witness's suffering, the Mexican establishes another kind of relationship from that of boss and takes him in without asking anything in return. The idea of reciprocity is on his mind, as he thinks that now he is taking the Guatemalan in but perhaps tomorrow the Guatemalan will take him in. Reciprocity between peasants is the basis of wider relations that were formed later between the refugees and Mexicans.

Very soon relations were established with the Mexican government, and immigration officials authorized the refugees to stay in Mexican territory. The Mexican government also offered solidarity. The witness remembers: "News arrived that all the refugees would be issued documentation. I received mine on 18 March; I went to Mollejón to get it. There were already a lot of us—over a hundred received documentation cards." Thus were created the first seeds of the refugee camps on the border with the north of El Quiché.

The Dead

Following is a list of 324 persons massacred in Cuarto Pueblo. I have left it in the middle of the book rather than including it as an appendix to give the reader an idea of the extent of the massacre by reading the names page after page. We also wish to be meticulous in providing sources because every name is a person, and both the dead and their living relatives deserve great respect.

The 38 persons who died on the same day in the Nueva Concepción center do not figure in the list.

The list contains endnotes detailing how the names were obtained. Two main information-gathering processes were used: (1) through witnesses who talked to me directly and told me of the dead in their centers and (2) through a witness (S2) who drew up the remaining centers' lists. Each center had between fourteen and thirty-three plots of land (and families), so it was easy for a member of a center to recognize the dead. However, the member was not always able to supply the names of everyone, particularly children. In some cases, the refugees I spoke to in the camps and others who drew up the lists received additional lists from other refugees to complete the information. In all, I consulted twenty-three different sources to make up the overall list. To avoid duplication, I asked for additional information concerning age, place of origin, and relatives. In this way I was able to exclude repetitions.

Finally, it is important to remember that the witnesses took for dead the ten or fifteen young men who had been taken away alive to Playa Grande by helicopter during the massacre.

The massacre had several specific characteristics: The first and most notable is that persons from different ethnic groups were killed. This was not true of the San Francisco, Nentón, massacre, where all those killed were Chuj Indians. In Cuarto Pueblo, both indigenous people and *ladinos* (from

Tacaná, La Democracia, La Libertad, and elsewhere) were massacred. People were killed who had been born in different parts of the country, particularly Huehuetenango but also San Marcos, Chimaltenango, and Jutiapa. People from different municipalities and speaking different tongues (Mam, Q'anjob'al, Jakalteka, Chuj, Kaqchikel, and Spanish) were killed. This diversity gives the massacre and others carried out to the east of Ixcán a national transcendence, making, I believe, a historical impact on the future consciousness of the Guatemalan people.

Another distinguishing feature of the Cuarto Pueblo massacre is that, compared to the San Francisco massacre, for instance, fewer children were killed in proportion to the total number of those killed. In San Francisco, 27 percent of those killed were children aged seven or under, compared to 16 percent (49 of the 314 victims whose ages we were able to document) in Cuarto Pueblo. Many children stayed at home on their plots of land when their parents went to market that Sunday. Hence the problem of orphans but also the force that they will nurture in the future.

A third feature is that, compared to the almost 90 percent of the inhabitants (352 out of 390) of the San Francisco village-estate killed, here only 14 percent of the population (362 out of 2,500) was massacred. I estimate the total population of Cuarto Pueblo at around 2,500; that is, 6.7 persons per plot of land and 376 plots.

Finally, it is evident that the centers nearest the town were hit the hardest. Their proximity to the town probably meant that more people went to the plaza that Sunday. It is also evident which centers received warnings in time, in particular B-6 and San Luis, where the inhabitants were better protected. La Nueva Concepción also received the warning, but the center was more divided ideologically and thus did not heed the alert.

The geographical location of the centers that offered better conditions for escape does not seem to bear on the number of people killed, as in the high number of dead in the Santa Elena center close to the town. Those who were able to escaped in the opposite direction of the approaching army, which was shooting profusely. They did not necessarily take the usual roads out of town.

There were victims from the two neighboring cooperatives, more from the smaller one in Los Angeles than from the larger and main Pueblo Nuevo cooperative. The economic attraction of Cuarto Pueblo on market day was greater for the former than for the latter.

Those Massacred in Cuarto Pueblo (14 to 17 March 1982)

Name	Age	Origin	Other
B-6 Center[1]			
1. Jorge Matías Jerónimo	30	Todos Santos	Evangelical

2. Marcelino Matías	40		auxiliary
3. Andrés Vásquez	60	San Ildefonso Ixtahuacán	"an old man" (S2)

San Luis Center[2]

4. Angel Roldán	27	La Libertad	"They were going to have their photos taken in the market" (S2)
5. His wife			

Nueva Concepción Center[3]

6. Ramón Camposeco	50	Jacaltenango	
7. Magdalena Vargas	50	Jacaltenango	6's wife
8. Jorge Camposeco	20	Jacaltenango	6 & 7's son
9. Rosa Marcos	18	Jacaltenango	8's wife
10. María Camposeco	1	Jacaltenango	8 & 9's daughter
11. Victoriano Tomás	62	La Libertad	
12. Juana Maldonado	50	La Libertad	11's wife
13. Rocael	18	La Libertad	11's grandson
14. Julio(?)	12	La Libertad	11's son
15. Tavo Tomás	25	La Libertad	11's son
16. His wife	18	La Libertad	15's wife
17.	9 mo.	La Libertad	15 & 16's son
18.	30	La Libertad	11's daughter; "already a widow"
19.	16	La Libertad	11's child
20.	<16	La Libertad	11's child
21.	<16	La Libertad	11's child
22.	<7	La Libertad	11's child

Vergel Center[4]

23. Julián Gómez	36	La Democracia
24. Arminia Gómez	11	La Democracia
25. Magdalena Pérez C.	35	La Democracia
26. Carmela Gómez	9	La Democracia
27. Elías Gómez	1	La Democracia
28. Gregoria García	60	
29. Diego Ramírez P.	28	Concepción Huista(?)
30. Anacleto Domingo	55	La Libertad
31. Arminia Díaz	48	Jacaltenango(?)
32. Manuel Diego M.	26	San Miguel Acatán
33. María Jiménez	40	Jacaltenango
34. Isidro Castanieda	23	Jacaltenango

35.	Matías Ramírez R.	28	Concepción Huista	
36.	Diego Ramírez	39	Concepción Huista	Charismatic catechist
37.	María Vargas	39	Concepción Huista	36's wife
38.	Francisco Ramírez R.	18	Concepción Huista	
39.	Manuela Ramírez R.	12	Concepción Huista	
40.	Carlos Pérez G.	60	Tacaná	
41.	Evertina Pérez	14	Tacaná	
42.	Angel Morales	33	Tacaná	
43.	Rafael Morales	12	Tacaná	
44.	Simona	63		
45.	Ermitanio Roldán	46	La Democracia	4's father
46.	Juana Hernández	17	La Democracia	
47.	Elisio Roldán	20	La Democracia	
48.	Anselmo Roldán	17	La Democracia	

Maravillas Center[5]

49.	Gregorio Ramírez	51	Jacaltenango	
50.	Angelina Cardona	41	Jacaltenango	
51.	Eulalia Ramírez	10	Jacaltenango	
52.	Manuel Ramírez	13	Jacaltenango	
53.	Alonso Ramírez	50	Jacaltenango	
54.	Ana Cardona	50	Jacaltenango	
55.	Gabino Ramírez	17	Jacaltenango	
56.	Pablo Ramírez	15	Jacaltenango	
57.	Juana Ramírez	10	Jacaltenango	
58.	Alonso Ramírez	20	Jacaltenango	
59.	Balvina Díaz	18	Jacaltenango	
60.	Angelina Ramírez	2	Jacaltenango	
61.	Andrés Ramírez	6 mo.	Jacaltenango	
62.	Ana Pascual	57	Santa Eulalia	
63.	Antonio Lorenzo	21	Santa Eulalia	
64.	León Lorenzo	18	Santa Eulalia	
65.	Fabiana	18	Soloma	pregnant, 63's wife
66.	Santos Luis	40	Tacaná	
67.	Genaro López	65	Tacaná	
68.	Rufina López	20	Tacaná	
69.	Laureano López	30	Tacaná	
70.		20	Tacaná	69's wife
71.		7	Tacaná	69 & 70's child
72.		<7	Tacaná	69 & 70's child
73.	Marcos Díaz	30	Santiago Chimaltenango	
74.	Petrona	27	Santiago Chimaltenango	73's wife
75.			Santiago Chimaltenango	73 & 74's child
76.			Santiago Chimaltenango	73 & 74's child
77.		7	Santiago Chimaltenango	73 & 74's child

78.	<7	Santiago Chimaltenango	73 & 74's child
79. Ofalio Aguilar	20	La Democracia	
80. Elonoria Aguilar	18	La Democracia	
81. Viviano Baltasar	33	Santa Eulalia	
82. Dominga	30	Santa Eulalia	81's wife
83. Crescencia Escalante	40	Tacaná	
84. Félix Velásquez	19	Tacaná	
85. Filomena	38	Tacaná	
86. Leonel López	19	Tacaná	
87. Felipe Fabián	56	Todos Santos	
88. Secundino Fabián	19	Todos Santos	
89. Luis Fabián	16	Todos Santos	
90. Teodora Fabián	12	Todos Santos	
91. Juan Mendoza	40	Todos Santos	
92. Isabela Mendoza	20	Todos Santos	
93. Emilia Mendoza	3	Todos Santos	
94. Eulalia	35	Santa Eulalia	pregnant; 91's wife
95. Cecilia	15	Santa Eulalia	
96. Eduardo Escalante	35	Tacaná	
97. Margrita	30	Tacaná	
98. Pascual López	80	Tacaná	
99. Silveria Escalante	75	Tacaná	
100. Eugenio Bartolón	18	Tacaná	

Belén Center[6]

101. Nicolás Felipe	48	San Miguel Acatán	
102. Diego Gaspar	18	San Miguel Acatán	101's child
103. Lucía Fabián	23	Todos Santos	"my wife" (S10)
104. Marina Mendoza	3	Todos Santos	S10's daughter
105. Rosalbina Mendoza	8 mo.	Todos Santos	S10's daughter
106. Andrés González	42	Concepción Tutuapa	
107. Flavio López	58	La Democracia	*ladino*
108. Clemente Valásquez	34	La Democracia	*ladino*
109. Alvina Roldán	27	La Democracia	108's wife
110. Héctor Velásquez	13	La Democracia	108 & 109's son
111. Jorge Velásquez	12	La Democracia	108 & 109's son
112. Pedro Lorenzo	24	San Miguel Ixtahuacán	
113. Mariano Lorenzo	12	San Miguel Ixtahuacán	112's brother
114. Marta Rafael Cinto	31	Tacaná	
115. Mariano Orozco	8	Tacaná	114's son
116. Bartolomé Velásquez	19	La Democracia	
117. Pedro Diego	26	San Juan Atitán	

118. Benedicto Escalante	39	Tacaná	
119. Isamona Escalante	38	Tacaná	118's wife
120. Josefina Escalante	13	Tacaná	118 & 119's child
121. Juana Escalante	12	Tacaná	118 & 119's child
122. Ignacia Escalante	10	Tacaná	118 & 119's child
123. Emilio Escalante	7	Tacaná	118 & 119's child
124. Elena Escalante	5	Tacaná	118 & 119's child
125. Cecilio Escalante	3	Tacaná	118 & 119's child
126. Alberto Escalante	19	Tacaná	118 & 119's child
127. Florinda Aguilar	26	Tacaná	125's sister-in-law
128. Rogelio Escalante	5	Tacaná	126's son
129. Domingo Escalante	3	Tacaná	126's son

Argentina Center[7]

130. Nicolás Francisco	51	Santa Eulalia	
131. María Marcos	49	Santa Eulalia	130's wife
132. Miguel Francisco	27	Santa Eulalia	130 & 131's son
133. Juana Francisco	24	Santa Eulalia	130 & 131's daughter
134. Andrés de Juan	20	San Juan Ixcoy	130 & 131's son-in-law
135. Isabela Francisco	17	Santa Eulalia	130's daughter; 134's wife
136. Pascual Francisco	14	Santa Eulalia	130 & 131's son
137. Genaro Francisco	11	Santa Eulalia	130 & 131's son
138. Nicolás Nicolás	23	San Miguel Acatán	
139. María Nicolás	29	San Miguel Acatán	138's sister
140. Juan Hernández	43	Tacaná	
141. Juana Velásquez	46	La Democracia	
142. Andrés Pedro	55	Soloma	
143. Juan(a) Andrés	50	San Miguel Acatán	
144. Teresa Pedro	21		142 & 143's daughter
145. Pedro Nicolás	28	Santa Eulalia	
146. Andrea Felipa	24	Santa Eulalia	145's wife
147. Felipe Nicolás	6	Santa Eulalia	145 & 146's son
148. Anita Nicolás	4	Santa Eulalia	145 & 146's son
149. Romana Nicolás	2	Santa Eulalia	145 & 146's daughter
150. Juan Díaz	34	Jacaltenango	
151. Lorenza	34	Jacaltenango	150's wife
152. Guillermo Díaz	12	Jacaltenango	150 & 151's son
153. Oscar Díaz	8	Jacaltenango	150 & 151's son
154. Marta Díaz	3	Jacaltenango	150 & 151's daughter
155. Andrés Martín	55	Jacaltenango	
156. Antonia Pérez	54	Jacaltenango	155's wife

157. Francisco Pedro Antonio	31	Santa Eulalia	
158. Anita Nicolás	29	Santa Eulalia	157's wife

Santiaguito Center[8]

159. Andrés Díaz	43	Jacaltenango	*parcelista*
160. Balbina Díaz	20	Jacaltenango	159's daughter
161. Ireneo Matías	35	Todos Santos	*parcelista*
162. Eustaquio Morales	37	Chiantla	*ladino parcelista*
163. Emilia Morales	16	Chiantla	162's daughter
164. Mariselda Morales	14	Chiantla	162's daughter
165. Rubén López	18	Cuilco	
166. Amparo		La Libertad	165's wife
167. Ovidio López	11	Cuilco	165's brother
168.	2		165 & 166's son
169. Jesús Domingo	45	Jacaltenango	*parcelista*
170. Magdalena Jiménez	42	Jacaltenango	pregnant; 169's wife
171. Angel García Godínez	38	Colotenango	*parcelista*
172. Juana	29	San Pedro Necta	171's wife
173.	9 mo.		171 & 172's son
174. Juan Alvarado	47	Jacaltenango	*parcelista*
175. Manuela Alvarado	12	Jacaltenango	174's daughter
176. Carmelino Domingo	20	Jacaltenango	
177. Agustín Domingo	18	Jacaltenango	176's brother
178. Vinicio Domingo	17	Jacaltenango	176's brother
179. Baltasar Domingo	34	Jacaltenango	*parcelista*
180. Félix Domingo		Jacaltenango	179's son
181. Sebastián de Sebastián	45	Santa Eulalia	*parcelista*
182. Ana	43		181's wife
183. Lorenzo Sebastián	17	Santa Eulalia	181 & 182's son
184. Sebastián Sebastián	14	Santa Eulalia	181 & 182's son
185. Alberto Tomás	31	San Miguel Acatán	*parcelista*
186. Nicolás Marcos	19	Jacaltenango	185's son-in-law
187. Angelina Tomás	17	San Miguel Acatán	186's wife
188.	4	San Miguel Acatán	186 & 187's daughter
189.	1	San Miguel Acatán	186 & 187's son
190. Magdalena		Santa Eulalia	"a married woman"
191.	14	Santa Eulalia	190's son
192.	1	Santa Eulalia	190's daughter

193. Felipe Manuel	30	San Miguel Acatán	*parcelista*
194.	27	San Miguel Acatán	193's wife
195.	2	San Miguel Acatán	193 & 194's son
196. Hugo González	25	Soloma	*parcelista*
197. Agustín José Juan	40	San Miguel Acatán	*parcelista*
198. Aura	45	Jutiapa	197's wife
199. Alberto	20	Jutiapa	197 & 198's son
200. Diego Andrés	32	San Miguel Acatán	*parcelista*
201.	28	San Miguel Acatán	200's wife
202. Emilio Morales	33	Tacaná	*parcelista*
203. María	40	Tacaná	*parcelista;* previously abducted
204.	10	Tacaná	203's daughter
205.	12	Tacaná	203's daughter

Santa Elena Center[9]

206. Pedro Gómez	55	Santiago Chimaltenango	
207.	45	Santiago Chimaltenango	206's wife
208. Paulo Cardona	50	Jacaltenango	
209. Ramona Cardona	35	Jacaltenango	
210.		Jacaltenango	208's child
211.		Jacaltenango	208's child
212. Gaspar Cardona	25	Jacaltenango	
213. Ana Martín	18	Jacaltenango	
214. Antonio Cardona	3	Jacaltenango	
215. María Cardona	15	Jacaltenango	208's daughter
216. Vicente Lorenzo	30	Santa Eulalia	
217.	28	Santa Eulalia	216's wife
218.		Santa Eulalia	216 & 217's child
219.			216 & 217's child
220. Cándido Matías	50	Jacaltenango	
221. Francisco Simón	25	Santa Eulalia	
222.	23	Santa Eulalia	221's wife
223.		Santa Eulalia	221 & 222's child
224.		Santa Eulalia	221 & 222's child
225.	7	Santa Eulalia	221 & 222's child
226.	<7	Santa Eulalia	221 & 222's child
227.	<7	Santa Eulalia	221 & 222's child
228.	75	Santa Eulalia	221's mother
229. Diego de Diego	32	Santa Eulalia	
230. Magdalena Gaspar	30	Santa Eulalia	
231.		Santa Eulalia	230's child
232.		Santa Eulalia	230's child
233.	±7	Santa Eulalia	230's child
234.	<7	Santa Eulalia	230's child
235.	<7	Santa Eulalia	230's child

Villa Nueva Center[10]

236. José Francisco	45	San Miguel Acatán	
237. Manuel Francisco	25	San Miguel Acatán	236's son
238. Domingo Velásquez	35	San Rafael	
239. Andrés Pérez	50	Jacaltenango	
240. Antonio Pérez	18	Jacaltenango	
241. Pedro Pérez	16	Jacaltenango	
242. Gilberto	32	San Ildefonso Ixtahuacán	
243. Ovidio Pérez	13	San Ildefonso Ixtahuacán	son of Francisco Pérez, who was killed previously by the guerrillas
244. Manuel Ramírez(?)	24	Todos Santos	
245. Juana(?)	20	Todos Santos	244's wife
246.	3	Todos Santos	244 & 245's daughter
247.	1	Todos Santos	244 & 245's son
248. Mateo Tercero	32	Santa Eulalia	
249. Diego	12	Santa Eulalia	248's son
250. Juan Velásquez	40	San Juan Ixcoy	

Tacaná Center[11]

251. Antonio Agustín	42	Soloma	
252. Victor Agustín	14	Soloma	251's son
253. Alfredo Agustín	10	Soloma	251's son
254. Domingo Miguel	21	Santa Eulalia	
255. Juana Domingo	15	Santa Eulalia	254's sister
256. Nicolás Sales	16	San Sebastián Huehuetenango	
257. Antonio Marcos	45	Jacaltenango	
258. Trinidad López Montejo	38	Jacaltenango	257's wife
259. Ana Montejo	18	Jacaltenango	257 & 258's daughter
260. José Silvestre	1	Jacaltenango	259's son
261. Nicolás Marcos			
262. Angélica Tomás			
263. Antonio Marcos Torres			
264. Jesús Domingo Marcos			
265. Juana			
266. Alicia Marcos			
267. Rosario Marcos			
268. Jorge Montejo			

269. Alicia Montejo
     Marcos
270. Felipe Vinicio
     Domingo

271. Sebastián Tercero	30		
272.	2		271's son
273. Alonso Ramírez	50	Concepción Huista	
274. Juana Gaspar	40	Concepción Huista	
275. Francisco Ramírez	25	Concepción Huista	
276. Juana Ramírez	5	Concepción Huista	
277. Sebastián Diego	30	San Juan Ixcoy	

Champerico Center[12]

278. Man. Rafael Alvarado	50	Jacaltenango	animator
279. Domingo Tun	30	San Martín Jilotepeque	
280. Teodoro Matías	25	Todos Santos	
281. Leonora Aguilar	17	San Marcos	
282. María	35	Santa Eulalia	
283.	13	Santa Eulalia	282's son
284. Gabriel Silvestre	23	Jacaltenango	
285. Lola Tomás	20	San Miguel Acatán	284's wife
286.	6	San Miguel Acatán	284 & 285's child
287.	3	San Miguel Acatán	284 & 285's child
288.	1	San Miguel Acatán	284 & 285's child
289. Félix Marcos	15	Jacaltenango	257's son
290. Belisario Ramírez	35	Cuilco	S2's neighbor
291. Amado		Cuilco	290's son
292. Flora de Escalante	28	Tacaná	

Montevideo Center[13]

293. Gumercindo Mateo	40	San Sebastián Coatán	
294. Valentín Mateo	19	San Sebastián Coatán	293's son
295. María Mateo		San Sebastián Coatán	293's daughter(?)
296. Angela Hernández	18	San Miguel Ixtahuacán	
297. Hipólito Ramírez	35	La Libertad	

La Democracia Center[14]

298. Santiago Ramos	36	Todos Santos	
299. Alejandro Ramos	14	Todos Santos	298's son
300. Rosa Ramos	8	Todos Santos	298's daughter
301. Dominga	25	Jacaltenango	
302.	5 mo.	Jacaltenango	301's son

303. María Gómez	35	Santa Bárbara (Huehuetenango)	
304. Cayo Gómez	8	Santa Bárbara (Huehuetenango)	
305.	6 mo.		303's son
306. Juan Recinos	28	Jacaltenango	
307. Juan Ramírez	24	San Sebastián Huehuetenango	
308. Manuela Ramírez	15	San Sebastián Huehuetenango	307's sister
309. Agustina Calvo	26	Todos Santos	
310. Eduardo Fabián	12	Todos Santos	309's child
311. Ambrosio Fabián	6	Todos Santos	309's child
312. Vicente Fabián	4	Todos Santos	309's child
313. Matías Fabián	8 mo.	Todos Santos	309's child

Los Angeles Cooperative[15]

314. Manuel López	28	Santa Ana Huista	commissioner S21; San Pedro center
315. Mateo Sun	14	Cobán	San Pedro center
316. Telésforo Mendoza	15	Todos Santos	S21's neighbor; San Pedro center
317. Benjamín Herrera	22	La Libertad	Palestina center
318. Gaspar Aguilón	30	Kaqchikel Southern Coast	Pentecostalist leader (S22) Santo Domingo center (S21)
319. Doroteo Jiménez	23	Todos Santos	San Francisco center
320. Raymundo Carrillo	40	La Democracia	
321. Francisco Martín	35		
322. Raúl Solís	25	southern coast	
323. Juan Martín	28	San Ildefonso Ixtahuacán(?)	

La Resurrección Cooperative[16]

| 324. José Sales Clavio | | San Sebastián Huehuetenango | La Libertad center |

GENERAL NOTE ABOUT THE SOURCES

The numbering of the sources (S1, S2. ...) does not correspond to the order of the testimonies in the chapter's text.

The order of the centers goes from west to east and from north to south. The order of the lists within each center follows the order given by the informants or as they appear on the main list; often the order is not haphazard.

With regard to the places of origin: For adults, this refers to their place of birth. In the case of children, it refers to their parents' place of birth. The place of origin indicates the language spoken and social identity of those massacred.

NOTES

1. *S1:* The informant or witness from the B-6 center, originally from Todos Santos. He went to the plaza on the Sunday but managed to escape.

S2: The Jakaltekan informant from the Santiaguito center.

N.B.: According to S2, no. 3 was from San Pedro Necta, in the municipality of Huehuetenango.

2. *S3:* Informant from the San Luis center, originally from San Martín Jilotepeque.

S4: Informant from the same center, originally from Barillas. He is the main witness referred to in this chapter.

3. *S5:* Informant from the Nueva Concepción center, originally from Concepción Huista.

S6: A member of the center (a contact of S2's) who drew up a list.

N.B.: Only S5 mentioned the name of no. 10. Regarding nos. 11–22, S6 gives the names of only nos. 11 and 12, saying that they were killed with their eleven children but not giving the latter's names. According to S6, no. 11 was Victoriano Pérez, not Tomás. S5 does not mention no. 12's last name.

4. *S7:* List drawn up by a member of the Vergel center through a contact of S2. He did not mention the places of origin.

S2: Provided information as to the places of origin.

N.B.: S7 also mentions no. 45's son, Angel Roldán, mentioned earlier (no. 4).

5. *S8:* A member of the Vergel center (a contact of S2's) who drew up a list.

6. *S9:* A contact of S2's who drew up a list. The list does not include family ties or places of origins.

S10: Informant from Belén born in Todos Santos, with whom I reviewed the list. He thinks the list of names is complete, and he added places of origin and family ties. S9 does not include family ties but does group the relatives together.

7. *S11:* A contact of S2's who drew up a list. The list does not include places of origin, family ties, or nos. 150–158.

S12: Gives the places of origin, family ties, and names of nos. 150–158.

N.B.: S9 and S11 are the same person: Their lists are in the same handwriting and the names are organized in a similar way. However, the person may have used different sources to draw up the two lists.

8. *S2:* See note 1.

9. *S12:* A contact of S2's.

10. *S13:* Informant from Cuarto Pueblo, born in San Martín Jilotepeque and apparently from the Villa Nueva center.

S2: See note 1.

N.B.: S13 drew up the entire list, except no. 250. S2 provided six names: nos. 236–237, 239–241, and 250. Nos. 238 and 250 may be the same person.

11. *S14:* A member of the Tacaná center. The list provides the names of twenty-two people without places of origin: nos. 251–272.

S15: A contact of S2's. The list gives eleven names, only six of which (nos. 251–256) are included in S14's list.

S2: Also provided the names and places of origin of nos. 257–260.

N.B.: S14 gives the last name of nos. 252 and 253 as González. S15 calls no. 256 Vicente Sales, aged nineteen. I believe him to be the same person. Nos. 271 and 277 may be the same person.

12. *S16:* Informant born in San Martín Jilotepeque, a member of the Champerico center.

S2: See note 1. He provided the names of nos. 285 and 289, who had already been identified by S16.

N.B.: According to S2, no. 290's name is Belisario Domingo.

13. *S17:* A contact of S2's.

S2: Provided the places of origin and family ties.

14. *S18:* A member of the Champerico center (a contact of S2's). The list goes up to no. 308.

S2: Nos. 309–313. No. 316's surviving husband gave S2 the names.

15. *S19:* A member of the Los Angeles cooperative who compiled a list (nos. 314–323), written up by S2. No places of origin have been given.

S20: The informant is from Los Angeles center, originally from Todos Santos. He provides the places of origin on the list.

S21: From San Pedro center, Los Angeles, and provides the information concerning nos. 314, 315, and 321.

S22: Explains who no. 318 was.

16. *S23:* From La Resurrección, San Miguel center.

CHAPTER 9

Respite in the Spate of Massacres: Los Angeles and Pueblo Nuevo

(23 to 30 March 1982)

The army remained in Cuarto Pueblo until dawn of 23 March 1982. When it was still dark, the soldiers left the town that they had razed to the ground and went west to another cooperative, called Los Angeles. As the officer had said in his pep talk, they were advancing, town by town. On the map, the advance of the scorched-earth offensive followed a back-to-front incomplete Z: in a horizontal line from Cuarto Pueblo to Los Angeles and then from Los Angeles through Pueblo Nuevo until Xalbal in a diagonal line. The back-to-front Z would have been completed had the army advanced from Xalbal west again to Mayalán, but it did not do this.

We Are a Different Army: We Don't Kill

In this chapter we will follow the army's course as it leaves Cuarto Pueblo until it reaches Xalbal. The strange thing about this part of the army's incursion is that the soldiers do not carry out massacres either in Los Angeles or in Pueblo Nuevo. There was a respite in the offensive, at least with regard to genocide. Why? We shall see as we go on.

On the way to Los Angeles, the soldiers captured some negligent peasants who had not left their houses on the plots of land. The army officers gathered them and some other people together for a meeting. The officers first confessed to the peasants that they carried out the Cuarto Pueblo massacre on the well-known pretext: "We went to screw those fuckers from Cuarto Pueblo, as they're all guerrillas." They also added that they were no longer going to kill: "We are no longer going to kill people, because that was President Lucas's army. But we got rid of Lucas. This is now Ríos Montt's army; we no longer kill people."

That same day young army officers carried out a coup d'état, deposing President Romeo Lucas García after the fraudulent elections on 7 March, and placing General Efraín Ríos Montt as the head of the military junta. The officers in charge of the troops gave this reason to inspire the local population's trust; indeed, they did not carry out massacres in Los Angeles.

What was the real reason? How can it be best understood? I believe (as I do not know for sure) that in part what they said was true but that there were also other reasons.[1] One reason was that the operation in Los Angeles was not planned to be like the one in Cuarto Pueblo: It was not carried out on a Sunday, and it did not involve cordoning off or massacring on a large scale. Then, too, when the soldiers captured the first peasants on the morning of 23 March, Lucas had still not surrendered. Lucas surrendered at 3:30 P.M. Therefore the change of government could not yet have been the motive, and if the battalion had been given instructions to exterminate the local population in Los Angeles, as it had in Cuarto Pueblo, it would have killed people from the first day, as it did when it passed through La Nueva Concepción. This means that planning previous to the coup d'état influenced the officers to treat Los Angeles differently to Cuarto Pueblo.

In any case, by 24 March the officers would have found out about the coup. At that moment, if they still had doubts about whether to kill the local inhabitants, the political change probably influenced them to be less cruel. I do not believe that they received orders directly from Playa Grande, still less so from Guatemala City, to discontinue the massacres. It seems more likely that, irrespective of Ríos Montt's harder line or greater leniency regarding the policy of massacre, at the moment of transition the army's power structure weakened, which led to an easing up of repression. There are signs of the army's weakening structure: For example, the witnesses noticed the differences that existed between soldiers and officers when some of the soldiers disobeyed the captain and did not go in search of a man to his home. Also, the hierarchy of the officers was not being respected, as the lieutenants had taken the initiative over and above the captain (I found out in an interview that there were eight army officers in the battalion). If we are to presume that the soldiers were tired of massacring, as killing was hard work, then we reach the conclusion that the officers themselves felt that it was an uphill struggle to undertake another massacre in Los Angeles like the one in Cuarto Pueblo. They did not have high-ranking officers putting pressure on them to go on with the hard job of massacring, which involved the effort and tension of killing people, burning bodies, and subsequently waiting in the cooperative town. The soldiers did not feel like carrying out another massacre.

Another aspect of the coup d'état may have influenced the battalion not to begin another massacre. On hearing of the coup, the officers probably wanted to return to their barracks to find out what was going on and how the military command would be restructured. I deduce this from the army's haste in Los Angeles to gather the people together and organize the first strategic hamlet. Indeed, the battalion stayed in Los Angeles for only one day, as on 25 March it left for Pueblo Nuevo at dawn. Los Angeles was the point farthest away from Playa Grande in the offensive and the officers would not want to dally there.

Apart from the weakening of the military structure and the haste to return (which were effects of the military coup), the response of the local population, in particular of the witness who told us of the meeting, must have appeased the officers. The latter would sometimes be enraged and other times remain calm. This time, those who were captured collaborated as much as they could with the soldiers, and when it was a question of informing on others they resorted to all sorts of evasion strategies. Another point in their favor was that the witness knew one of the lieutenants when he had been posted in the cooperative in 1980 and the lieutenant seemed to trust him.

An Attempt to Organize a Strategic Hamlet

Instead of massacring, the officers tried to organize a strategic hamlet and civil patrols. The attempt failed because the army did not return to Los Angeles until three months later and the population organized by the army was far away by then.

The local inhabitants, who were dispersed on their plots of land, were brought together to live in the town to be more easily controlled. The people could be brought together in two ways: either by persuasion or through fear. In this case it was through fear, as they were captured in their homes or on the paths dividing the plots of land. The soldiers also forced them to go to town by threatening to kill their closest relatives (women and children) who had already been captured or threatening to kill their neighbors, whose lives depended on the local inhabitants complying with the army.

After gathering the people together, the soldiers placed more emphasis on persuasion and on instilling confidence that they would not kill. But this confidence had its price: The local inhabitants had to prove their sincerity with deeds. They had to undo the sabotage on the landing strip. And the officer insisted that they should inform on the infiltrators among them, saying that there were three guerrillas in the meeting and that the rest should point them out. However, the people did not do this; nor did they give themselves up in an act of repentance. Sincere repentance could have cost them their lives because the army, instead of accepting their conversion, could have eliminated them. But this they did not do. The officer tried to get the population to change their loyalties. To this end he used ruses such as getting a man nicknamed "Cuco," who had come with the army, to tell the story of how he had been a rebel in Ixcán but had given himself up to the army in Escuintla. The officer also tried to change their attitude by saying that the people had been taken in: "You aren't bad, you've been deceived; we'll forgive you for that." He promised them the lands of those who had fled and a wonderful life in contrast to the hardships of being a rebel. By promising the lands, the army was clearly trying to deeply divide the community in order to dominate it. However, behind the persuasive arguments lay implicit threats, as at certain moments the officer lost his patience at the people's passivity and returned to threatening. He claimed that Cuco knew who was infiltrated and tied two people up, creating a scene of terror, after which he himself admitted that it was not true.

The relation that the village was to maintain with the army was also established. The landing strip should remain in good condition so that provisions could be brought in to the new detachment, which would defend the local population from the guerrillas. The soldiers would defend the population in the same way that they did during the meeting. (At a given moment, they had gone out to check out a supposed guerrilla attack. The captain had ordered the people to hide in the ditches of the sabotaged airstrip.) But not only the soldiers would be in charge of defense: The people themselves should also defend themselves from the guerrillas. An imitation civil patrol was to be organized to carry out night duty. Their weapons, the officer said, would be sticks. Each patroller would have a stick.

The army appointed five men to be in charge of informing them periodically of everything going on. If the group of forty were to disband, the five men in charge would be punished by the army. To save their skins, the five would try to carry out orders. They were to ensure in particular that the people live in the town, that they collaborate with the army, not the rebels, and that they provide information.[2]

Pueblo Nuevo Is Empty:
The Army Does Not Massacre

The army did not carry out massacres in Pueblo Nuevo either, but for a different reason: The local inhabitants had retired to their plots of land and nobody went to market on Sunday.

On Thursday, 25 March, the battalion set out for Pueblo Nuevo at dawn, arriving in the town on the same day. It tried to organize a meeting, as it had done in Los Angeles. That day, a man was captured who had gone to the town unawares. The soldiers told him to summon the local inhabitants. As he was leaving, they threatened and kicked him: "'If you don't come tomorrow ... ,' they said to him, and they kicked him." But he did not return, and news spread to "be careful."

· The soldiers remained in town on Friday, Saturday, and Sunday, waiting for people to come to the plaza on the Sunday. But nobody came. "The army was waiting for the people on those days, but because it had carried out the massacre in Cuarto Pueblo, nobody went," recalls a witness.

On Monday, 29 March, the army left Pueblo Nuevo, making its way to the Xalbal River and then heading south, more or less following the river. On its way it burned down a few houses and killed cattle and other animals and also a *parcelista* who crossed its path. "They killed a relative of mine. They grabbed him and cut him into pieces until he died. His name was Ventura Jerónimo and he lived in the Santa Rosa center. He was in the Galilea center, fleeing from the army; that's where they killed him. Later they took him to a house, which they burned down with him inside," remembers a witness from Pueblo Nuevo. It would seem that the army, after its frustration in Pueblo Nuevo and perhaps after receiving orders from Playa Grande, returned to its scorched-earth policy several days after the military coup.

Attacks on the Camps

The army changed tactics after leaving Pueblo Nuevo. It not only returned to scorched-earth operations but also adopted guerrilla techniques in seeking out people who had fled to the jungle, as it did not find them in the town.

On the night of 29 March, the battalion set up camp on the banks of the Xalbal River and on 30 March it captured three peasants. Two of them served as guides to harass the population in the jungle the following day. The third witnessed how the people were attacked. Because he was made to accompany the battalion, he could see from the inside how the army mounted the operation and the intentions it had. Let us listen to his testimony.

At 3:30 A.M. on 31 March, the lieutenant began to wake up the soldiers. At 4:00 they left, taking us with them. Romaldo and Rufino [the other captured peasants] were also taken. They began showing the army where the people were hiding. A lieutenant ordered some soldiers to stay put: "If we all go, we won't capture the people in the camp. Half an hour after we leave, start building a big fire. While you make noise here, we're going to sneak up on them over there."

The officer divided the battalion to take the camp by surprise. The witness refers to the people seeking refuge in the jungle as in the "camp." The witness knew that the groups were made up only of civilians, as he would say later on. But as the army and rebels had skirmished the day before, causing two army casualties, the officer thought that a guerrilla military unit was hiding there. He wished to catch it off guard.

The lieutenant told the soldiers who went to root out the people: "Look, we're going to go in darkness, no lights, no cigarettes, so that they won't detect us." Half the battalion left [about 150 or 175 men], and we were taken with them. Romaldo and Rufino went ahead. Romaldo found a path leading to the camp; they took it but advanced very little since they couldn't see. There was a stream with a steep bank to one side, but Romaldo didn't know the way well [he was from another center]. There was a landslide. "Don't you know the way?" the lieutenant asked him. Finally, they hit him with a rifle butt and he fell down; they did the same to Rufino. And the soldiers turned on a flashlight to light the path and we continued.

The camp was about seventy *cuerdas* [about 2,000 meters] from the road. We reached a large river with the water above our knees. The soldiers didn't want to get wet and began to look for logs to help them cross the river. But as it was sandy there weren't any. By then it had grown light; it was about 6:00 A.M. They finally crossed the river, but there were so many of them they made a huge din as they crossed. And when they got to the other side, they took off their boots and wrung the water from their pants. It was even lighter by then; it was about 6:30. And now we were only about twenty *cuerdas* [600 meters] from the camp. Then I felt pity. I felt really sad! I knew there was no military unit in the camp and that they were going to exterminate the poor people. Only God could save them! But when the army crossed the river, the persons keeping guard realized and the people got out in a hurry.

We entered the first camp and there weren't any fresh tracks. "Where are the signs of the people?" asked the lieutenant. We went to the second and there were no tracks there either. We reached the third camp and there was a fire. We reached the fourth camp and there were also bundles. But there weren't any footprints leaving the camp. The soldiers hacked the clothes with machetes and broke the corn grinders. They looked to see where the people had left but couldn't find anything. There were no footprints leaving the camp! "How did the shits leave?" asked the lieutenant. "Why can't we find anyone?" he said to the soldiers. "Look over there, you turds!" "There's nothing over here, sir," they told him. But the people from the fourth camp had returned to the third and escaped from there.

They asked Romaldo where the path leading to Xalbal passed by. He showed them and they took out their machetes, hacking an opening in the undergrowth. The blades of grass were really sharp! The undergrowth was dense and short, and there were hollow tree trunks full of ants. When they started to hack at the undergrowth they got covered in ants and when they hacked with their machetes, they cut themselves with the blades. They took turns opening up a path, they could hardly stand it. They managed to advance about five *cuerdas* [150 meters]. It was 10:00 or 11:00 A.M. by then, and there was still a long way to go to get to the road. The lieutenant was very light skinned and he got covered in ants. They reached a part of the jungle where the undergrowth was sparser and then a cardamom field where there were human tracks. The tracks were fresh. What a lot of mud there was! "The shits came by here," said the lieutenant. But perhaps God didn't want the people to die. The people were nearby but the army returned to the third camp and that's when the soldiers realized that the people had escaped through there.

They again tried to tail the people. "Silence," said the lieutenant, and they went on walking. And by now they were frightened. They were walking in the jungle. At times leaves would fall and they would get scared and sit down. They'd sit for about ten or fifteen minutes and the lieutenant would go have a look. "There isn't anything," he would say, and they would go on.

We reached a downhill slope. There was a dog tied to a trunk. He was muzzled and was trying to free himself. Now there were no tracks to be seen. But the dog knew where the people had gone. So they cut the rope and the dog rapidly followed the people's tracks, and the soldiers found where the people had gone. "Oh my companions," I thought to myself. They were about ten *cuerdas* [300 meters] away. But the people killed the dog when it caught up with them, so the soldiers only found the dead dog. "What sons of bitches. Those shits are smart! But careful, the guerrilla unit is there. Everyone cock your guns," the lieutenant said. But the soldiers didn't run; they approached slowly.

The people reached a clearing, and the army followed their tracks. They crossed another path and their tracks were lost. Then the soldiers started searching for them and about four *cuerdas* [120 meters] away a boy cried out. They went running in that direction. They had bound my hands and tied me to a soldier's knapsack harness. The soldier made me run; he started running and I had to run along with him. I climbed on a fallen tree trunk; he jumped but I didn't and I fell. I banged my face three times against the ground and my mouth began to bleed. I wanted the harness to rip so that I could escape, but it was made of canvas. My face hit the ground three times.

There was no one where the boy had shouted, but a bit farther up stood a member of the group. A soldier shot at him. They shot at him, but they didn't hit him. And when they reached the place where he had been, there was nothing there.

Finally they got tired and we reached the dividing line of La Unión center. We were now in Xalbal. They saw the time: 1:00 P.M. It was late! So they started to catch some chickens and roast them. And the lieutenant made contact with the other platoon. It was about 1:30 P.M. when the other platoon arrived.

The aim of the operation was to cordon off the camp where the officer believed there was a guerrilla military unit and to wipe out the guerrillas and the civilian population, which he considered to be guerrillas, according to what he had said in Cuarto Pueblo. Therefore the population had to be exterminated, as in Cuarto Pueblo. I believe that the change in government would not have stopped the army battalion from carrying out the massacre now that it had changed tactics and was seeking in vain the inhabitants it had not found in Pueblo Nuevo. This was proved true that very day (31 March) and the next day, when it massacred around 30 people in Xalbal, as we shall see in the following chapter. The witness was also convinced that the army was going to kill the people in the camps. That is why he felt so sad when they drew near and trusted in God to save them.

But when the army reached the four camps, it realized that it had been foiled. The surprise element did not work. So it started another stage of the operation: searching and pursuing the people, following their tracks. But the troop's morale was not high. It was uninterested, tired, and fearful of the slightest sound—even that of a falling leaf—which gave the people time to escape.

The tactic of destroying the people's personal belongings was evident in the camps. One would imagine that all the belongings were easily movable, but the people did not manage to take them with them in their haste to escape. That is why they left their corn grinders and bundles of clothes. These the army destroyed to keep the people from surviving in the jungle, compelling them to eventually give themselves up to the armed forces, starving and threadbare. In this way it prepared for a slow withdrawal of the "water surrounding the fish," causing immense suffering to the people.

I found this population to be more organized than the people of Cuarto Pueblo and Los Angeles. Let us recall that the army had killed a group of Charismatic Catholics on 18 February in a Pueblo Nuevo center. Probably as a result, the people were more on the alert and had abandoned their houses on their plots of land to form groups in which they, like road builders or lumberjacks, lived in improvised housing. Their houses were "little shelters hidden in the jungle," according to one witness. They were little tents, perhaps made from plastic or leaves, that could be put up and taken down easily. Their mobility was essential. The people's main form of self-defense was being able to be in one place today and another place tomorrow. Their movements were determined by those of the army. They tried to remain at a distance so that the voices of children would not carry and the tracks on the entry paths would fade.

The camps were composed of civilian population, that is, noncombatant population. The witness calls these people "population," distinguishing them from the guerrillas. He sometimes refers to them as "companions," which is appropriate because of the solidarity developed in the jungle. The only kind of weapon a few of the *parcelistas* had was a .22-caliber hunting rifle. Again, their main source of defense was not arms but flight and information as to the army's whereabouts.

There were four neighboring camps, which must have been connected in some way. Each camp tended to have its leaders, usually the men who had gone out to look for survivors on the plots of land to bring them together. In this case, two of the four camps were from Kaibil, on the other side of the Xalbal River; they had returned to their plots of land several days before the army had discovered their tracks. The other two were from Pueblo Nuevo centers, one from each center. The way of organizing through cooperative centers was continued in the jungle. Considering that each center was made up of about twenty-five plots of land, there must have been a maximum of twenty-five families (nuclear and extended) per camp.[3]

The Country's Political Context

As said in the previous chapter, fraudulent elections were held on 7 March 1982 and the official candidate was heralded as winner. The opposition political parties united despite being on opposite extremes of the then-electoral spectrum, taking to the streets to protest. But Congress, predominantly composed of progovernment deputees, elected the fraudulent winner during the second round of elections on 13 March. As there was no hope left among the opposition of a political solution, it planned a coup to overthrow Lucas García and his governing generals on 23 March. The coup was supported by 900 army officers. After troop movements for ten hours in Guatemala City, Lucas surrendered at 3:30 P.M.

The young officers created a military junta with General Efraín Ríos Montt at their head. Ríos Montt had been the real winner in the fraudulent 1974 elections and had also been minister of defense. The main measure taken by the military junta was to suspend the Constitution to restructure the state for facilitating counterinsurgency. The army's cohesion, achieved by the coup, would increase its counterinsurgency capacity in the country's rural areas.

The URNG, formed on 7 February 1982 and bringing together the four revolutionary organizations, declared that the coup d'état was "a new reactionary strategy." The EGP declared that "the faces change, but the regime continues to be the same."[4]

The restructuring of the state followed the lines of the National Security and Development Plan, which was presented to the main members of the government and army on 5 April at a meeting in the Center for Military Studies. The main thrust of the plan centered on the definitive eradication of subversive activity. To achieve this end, it insisted that military action was not enough, because "existing contradictions" had to be tackled "that were the result of historic processes, which communism exploits in its favor." Thus the policies of security and development were intimately related. The plan set out to cover four main areas: political, economic, psychosocial, and military.

The plan did not have an immediate effect on Ixcán in political, economic, or even psychosocial terms, where "the participation and integration of the different ethnic groups that make up our nationality" was considered. The only immediate effect was the army's renewed enthusiasm for military operations to "eradicate in the short term" guerrilla groups, as it feared a military impasse that could go on for years, and it foresaw "the possible fall" of El Salvador into "the hands of international communism." The ensuing military operations indicated no change with respect to scorched-earth policies.[5]

Indeed, condemnation of the large-scale massacres continued—for example, when the Committee for Peasant Unity (Comité de Unidad Campesino; CUC) and the Popular Front 31 January (Frente Popular 31 de Enero [FP-31]) occupied the Brazilian Embassy on 12 May. They issued a public statement protesting that "since 23 March we have seen that far from an end to the massacres, the Junta's army has continued to carry out massacres. The army has occupied our communities and has carried out an increasing number of massacres in Chimaltenango, all over El Quiché, in Sololá, Huehuetenango, Alta and Baja Verapaz and other places too. More than 3,000 people, men, women, children and old people, have been massacred in the most barbaric fashion over the past month and a half alone. They have been tortured, their throats have been slit, or they have been burned alive in their homes."[6]

NOTES

1. I am here presenting the other side of history; that is, I am trying to reconstruct events as perceived by the people, which usually does not happen. Yet I believe that it is also important to investigate the deeds from the perspective of the army—to see both sides of the coin and to discover those intellectually responsible for the large massacres.

2. According to counterinsurgency manuals, the pacification process comprises three phases: security, control, and development. The scorched-earth tactic belongs to the security stage. In the second phase, follow-up is given to the first phase with control operations. Without these, the sweep operations would be rendered useless, as the zone would return to its original state upon the government force's withdrawal from the area. Different types of local forces are organized during the control phase. The organization of civil patrols is designed to ensure counterinsurgency control.

3. The numbers varied later, when the refugees left for Mexico in large numbers.

4. See Noticias de Guatemala, 4/12/82; and Inforpress Centroamericana, 4/1/82.

5. National Security and Development Plan, 1982.

6. See Noticias de Guatemala 5/15/82. The press release mentions the names of the villages and municipalities in Chimaltenango, the south of El Quiché and the Ixil Triangle, Sololá, Alta Verapaz, and one municipality of Huehuetenango (Chiantla). No reference is made to the jungle massacres. Because of the remoteness and military control of the area, it is probable that the CUC was unaware of the massacres in Ixcán, although at the time of the Brazilian Embassy occupation the refugees in Mexico were already making public condemnations.

CHAPTER 10

Massacre in Succession: Xalbal

[31 March to 2 April 1982]

Let us now leave the army in its frustrated attempt to pursue the civilian population in the camps on the morning of 31 March, when it was about to take the road to Xalbal, the cooperative furthest to the southeast. In Xalbal the army would commit another massacre, which I have referred to as "in succession," as this massacre was not the result of a massive cordoning-off operation but rather of the successive capture of families and persons, one after another, in such a way that the capture of one led to the capture of the next and so on. But first, let us refer to events prior to the massacre.

Misleading Meeting (13 and 14 March)

The army entered Xalbal twice several days before the massacre. The first time was on election day, Sunday, 7 March. It entered from Kaibil, through La Cuchilla center to the south of Xalbal, apparently in search of people who had fled from Kaibil. The army killed Petrona Ramírez in La Cuchilla when a group of people returning from market in the afternoon accidentally encountered the army. Everyone fled, including Petrona, but the soldiers fired a barrage of bullets and wounded her in the knee, making her unable to run. The army finished her off with a couple of machete blows to her head. A witness who found her corpse on his return from the market remembers what happened: "On catching sight of the army she fled. They shot at her, and a bullet hit her foot. When we got there, some dogs were eating her leg. Some other neighbors went to have a look. Her leg was missing and her head had been slashed twice with a machete."

The following weekend, the army arrived again from Kaibil. This was the weekend that the battalion carried out the massacre in Cuarto Pueblo. However, the army did not arrive in Xalbal to massacre but to force the people to attend a meeting, at the end of which food was handed out to those present.

About thirty soldiers[1] arrived in Xalbal at 5:00 P.M. and found a group of people gathered together with their guitars, getting ready to go to a religious ceremony on one of the farm plots. "A group of Charismatic Catholics was gathered together in the church; there were about forty people. The soldiers surrounded them and the group of musicians who were also there. They seized the president and the treasurer … who were on their way to celebrate the Word in another village, in La Cuchilla center," recalls a witness. After talking to them, the army took them to the church.

The soldiers shut them in the church all night and then the patrol leader talked to them. The essence of his message, which was meant to be transmitted to other centers afterward, was that the army did not kill: It looked after the civilian population, and everyone should therefore return to town. If the people were all together, the army could protect them from the guerrillas and organize them, as the officer had told the *parcelistas* in Los Angeles. The patrol leader gave them a deadline, after which the army would return to ensure that they had followed its instructions. As in Los Angeles, he also told them that they should remove all guerrilla propaganda and fix the sabotaged landing strip.

The Charismatic catechist Pascual Paiz agreed not only to stay in the town but also to convince the people who had fled to return. Although I do not know whether the officer threatened him specifically, the tone of the meeting was threatening, as the military launched the same accusation as always ("you are guerrillas"). The capture lasted for an entire day and night, and the people were forced to sing for hours on end and were not allowed out to eat.

Early Sunday afternoon the lieutenant released the captives, giving them food. One witness recounts, "'We're going to give you food,' the lieutenant said. 'Maybe it's true, maybe it's not,' thought Pascual. They had entrusted themselves to the hands of God. Then the helicopter arrived, one of those big ones, with a basket of tamales. They made a big show out of it. The soldiers gave them bread, which they ate, and then they gave them more." And according to another witness: "They gave the president of the Charismatic Catholics [Pascual Paiz] an *arroba* [25 pounds] of salt and an *arroba* of sugar from the helicopter" so that he could not leave on the pretext of going to Barillas for provisions.

Pascual Paiz mobilized the network of catechists to advise the local population to return to the town, as the army was not going to kill. He even visited the houses farthest away, those of influential people such as an "old

Evangelical man." He also insisted that the president of the cooperative send "a note to the leader of each center, asking him to bring the people from their center to Xalbal, and not to worry, as the army was going to help them."[2]

And What Were the Rebels Up To?

The rebels have been absent in all these events. One could ask why they did not defend the population from the army massacres. The answer is straightforward: They did not have the necessary strength to contain the army. That is why one hardly hears of military actions during the army's route. In the absence of a military force, the rebels' main contribution in defending the people was to convince them of the need to hide from the army to avoid being massacred.

The Sunday after the staged meeting with the Charismatic Catholics, 21 March, the rebels carried out an armed occupation of Xalbal to persuade the local population to leave town. "The talk lasted for about two hours; it was in the auxiliary mayor's offices," according to a witness.

The result of this action was not wholly successful, as "some stubbornly refused to leave" and some Charismatic Catholics "did not obey," which would cost them their lives.

In addition to insisting that the people flee from the army, the rebels carried out an armed ambush at the entrance of Xalbal on 31 March in the afternoon. This action could have contributed to holding back the army as well as alerting the population, through the noise of shooting, to flee. But like all weak military actions, it could also be counterproductive, succeeding only in enraging the army, which in turn could react indiscriminately, putting the population that had not fled in danger.

A witness shows the positive aspect of the ambush: "I was in the town when the shoot-out began, so I ran away. My entire group left for the jungle." His group was made up of about six families who lived close by in the same center.

The next witness, to the contrary, illustrates the army's rage. We left this witness in the previous chapter when the army was pursuing the population. Now we find him at the head of the battalion bound to two soldiers, one in front of him and one behind. "The one in front was shot and wounded but not killed. 'I've had it,' he said. And soldiers from behind began to open fire indiscriminately." After the shoot-out a male nurse arrived to heal the wounded soldier; he gave his knapsack to the witness, who was already carrying two. "Then they gave me the other knapsack. Now I was carrying three! 'You're a guerrilla! They want to free you,' they told me. 'It's obvious that you're not just anyone' and they started kicking me. But I put up with it, even though I felt I was dying at times and then I'd come to again. We arrived in Xalbal like this."

A Bird's-Eye View

The troop arrived in Xalbal and started to kill. The massacre took a week, from Wednesday, 31 March, to Monday, 5 April, and 37 people were killed. This massacre is complicated to narrate, as there are a large number of testimonies with differing degrees of accuracy and because it was carried out successively.[3] To follow the thread of the massacre, we will study four days. The first three days, which were consecutive, cover the army's arrival in Xalbal, the initial captures, and the burning of the first families (31 March); the army's sojourn, the capture of a youth who was used to search and ambush others, the burning of more people, and the burning of the town (1 April); and the army's withdrawal from Xalbal, the ambushing of others, and the terrible massacre in Kaibil when the army was leaving the area (2 April). Finally, on the fourth day (5 April), after the army had left, a bomb exploded under a corpse and killed one of the grave diggers.

A bird's-eye view gives us a photographic image of the quadrilateral town. Inside are the landing strip, the market, many houses and buildings, the army outpost, the Catholic church, two Evangelical churches (Mamand Q'anjob'al), the cooperative store, the clinic, and other buildings. These can be seen on the map, drawn by a witness. A road reaches the quadrilateral from the north and divides two rows of farm plots, so there are houses on both sides of the road. The road leads up a hill before reaching the town. The rebels ambushed the soldiers on the hill, as they were approaching the town from the north.

Captures and the First Families to Be Burned
[31 March]

After the ambush the army immediately went to the house of Pascual Paiz, the president of the catechists. His house was adjacent to the town, on the right-hand side of the entry road. It was the first inhabited house that the army found and took over. But the catechist, who had been asked to gather the people together, was not at home. The soldiers found only his wife, who was ill, their seventeen-year-old unmarried daughter, and two younger children.

Near Pascual Paiz's house lived the Torres family, also Charismatic Catholics, but Sebastián Torres was not at home either. The army asked in both households where the head of the family was and the women replied that they were out, each at a religious ceremony in separate houses. So the soldiers captured the families, probably suspecting that the men were out

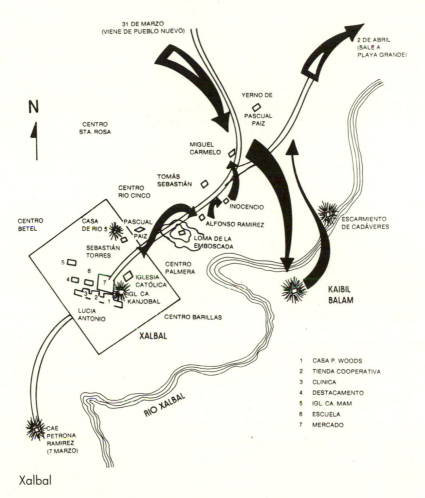

Xalbal

making clandestine contacts and that the women were covering for them. Both families were then taken to a nearby small meetinghouse made of palm and were killed and burned that night. There, two days later, Mrs. Torres's brother saw the burned remains of his sister: "I saw my sister. Only bones remained—there was a big pile of bones. They took her to a palm hut and burned her alive. About six people were killed. Their remains were clearly visible and we saw that some were children's bones." The dead woman's son also saw the remains of his mother, recognizing her by a bit of *corte* (skirt): "I found a sizable piece of my mother's *corte*. It was drenched in blood; it didn't burn, as there was so much blood. When it rained, the blood came out."[4]

Shortly after the army arrived, Pascual Paiz appeared from the other end of town. On hearing the shooting during the ambush, Pascual feared for his wife, and instead of fleeing he went into town in an attempt to save her. He told a daughter who was with him at the religious celebration: "Stay here, I'm going to see if they have killed your mother. I'll hand myself in; if I don't come back, you, like a seed, will remain." According to another witness he said: "I'm going to see if your mother has been killed, I'll give up my life for her."[5]

This was the way Pascual Paiz bade farewell to his daughter, suspecting that his death was near. He then entered the town to face the soldiers and try to save his wife and family. The soldiers were already in the market-place, where they captured him: "They kicked him while his daughter looked on from a height." The army detained the famous Charismatic cate-chist and it seems he never got home nor saw his wife again.

Sebastián Torres and his twenty-year-old son were also attending a reli-gious ceremony when the shooting began. Like Pascual Paiz, they were never to return home, as they were captured in the town center. A witness deduced their fate when he found the son's identity card and guitar: "Some people picked up the young man's identity card at the corner of the market, on the road leading to the Evangelical chapel." The witness presumes that Sebastián Torres and his son, like Pascual Paiz, were taken to the Q'anjob'al Evangelical chapel to be burned the following day: "Only men were found piled on top of each other in the Evangelical chapel latrine; they were black with soot, maybe gasoline had been poured over them." While some soldiers were burning the men, other soldiers were burning the women elsewhere. Men and women had again been separated for interro-gation purposes, as presumably the soldiers wanted to extract information about the rebels before killing them.

Apart from the three men, another Chuj *parcelista* was captured in the town. His name was Tomás Sebastián. On leaving one of the religious cere-monies, he decided to go through the town to do some errands. He wanted to go to Barillas the following day to sell several *quintales* of coffee and he needed to collect his mule, which was grazing by the landing strip. He had heard the shooting of the ambush but thought that the shots had come from afar, so he confidently entered the town. In contrast to Torres and Paiz, who lived in the quadrilateral or next to it, he lived on a farm plot and did not need to enter the town to go home. But economic worries dis-tracted him and made him go look for his mule, even though a friend tried to put him off. To assure himself, he used religious arguments: His wife was a prophetess, a kind of seer, and she had encouraged him to go for his ani-mal, saying that according to her vision it was safe to do so. The vision proved false and her husband was captured that day and burned the next in the Evangelical chapel.[6]

More People Are Burned (1 April)

In the morning of 1 April, the army first captured Tomás Sebastián's son, then burned 9 people in the Q'anjob'al Evangelical church, and finally began to burn down the entire town. It was probably afternoon when they killed another 4 people in the same church. That day, a total of 13 people were killed by the army.

At about 7:00 A.M. the army captured Tomás Sebastián's son, an eighteen-year-old scout who had gone out to look for his father. His name was Sebastián Tomás.[7] He and another young man made their way to a hillock near the entry road to the town to observe what the army was doing. They "were coming along the road, but the army was lying in wait and seized Sebastián." The other youngster was detained by a strange premonition that made his whole body uncomfortable, so he stayed behind and was saved. He hid and watched from about forty feet away how the soldiers frisked Sebastián, finding a note from a man we will call Inocencio (not his real name). The note provided the soldiers with the clue to ambush Inocencio's house that night and to use Sebastián as a guide to capture others in this chain of dispersed massacres.

Sebastián's companion fled after witnessing the plight of his friend. He went to tell Sebastián's mother, who was the prophetess, that she should give up her son for dead. "Then his mother began to cry," realizing that her visions of the goodness of "the brother soldiers" had been fatal, leading first to the death of her husband and then, as a result, of her son.

After this, or at about the same time, 9 people were burned alive in the Q'anjob'al Evangelical church. I presume that they were the 4 men captured the day before, 3 people whom the soldiers had brought with them, and 2 Q'anjob'als unknown to the witness who watched the soldiers start the fire.

The witness was the man carrying three knapsacks who had been captured by the army as it made its way toward Xalbal. He remembers seeing these 9 people when the soldiers put them in the church kitchen and set it afire following the officer's order: "The lieutenant told the soldiers: 'Make them into guacamole!' Then they hit them with their rifle butts and tied two up by their legs in a squatting position. Then the lieutenant said: 'Take them to the church kitchen!' The kitchen was an open shed thatched with palm. They took the others out too and the lieutenant again said: 'Make them all into guacamole and tie a little packet on each of them!' So they put them in the center of the kitchen. There were nine people, all alive. And they set the building and people on fire. But then the helicopter arrived and we had to leave." The witness therefore did not hear the screams of those being burned alive, but some scouts did: "We saw a lot of smoke and heard the screaming as they were burning the people. The people were inside the house and the house was on fire."[8]

Two of the three who had been captured the day before and burned there were Romualdo Mejía (aged thirty-two) and Rufino Pérez (aged eighteen). According to the witness, they were killed because Romualdo had proved to be an inefficient guide in pursuing the local population. The lieutenant called him a "shit" for being useless and deceitful, telling him he was worthless and deserved to die. They told Rufino that he deserved the same, as he was providing no service to the army.

The third person to be captured en route was an old man, Bartolomé Tomás: "He was 102 years old" and had "white hair"—"a little old man," according to the different witnesses. He could not have been a rebel. His crime was to be carrying several green shirts and pants in his bag and to be wearing two hats. This seemed very odd to the lieutenant but "he was going to make a scarecrow in his cornfield."

The remains of the burned corpses were found in the kitchen shed several days later by those who went to have a look: "We saw all the bones and intestines, lots of ashes. They were in the kitchen, which had also been burned. There were bits of clothing that had been slashed by machetes. Tomás Sebastián's mule had been thrown onto the fire with his owner."

The burning of this group of people in the chapel kitchen was part of the soldiers' effort to burn down the town that Thursday morning. "At about 9:00 A.M. they set the town alight. We watched it happen. We saw fire emerging from Xalbal. The entire center around the landing strip was in flames." Another witness recalls: "They burned the cooperative store, houses, buildings, neighbors' stores, and articles of value such as refrigerators. ... Who knows how much merchandise they destroyed. Each market stall was brimming."

As in Cuarto Pueblo, the battalion killed animals to feed 300 soldiers. But they also slaughtered cattle to send provisions to the military base in Playa Grande: "They killed cattle, and a helicopter arrived and they sent the meat to Playa Grande," according to a witness. The scorched-earth offensive was accompanied by plundering (including the taking away of live animals). This kind of plundering increased later with the creation of civil patrols in some of the plots of land near Xalbal.

That Thursday the army also captured a widow, Lucía Antonio, with her three children and killed them that afternoon. An eyewitness recalls seeing her captured. He also heard the soldiers' intentions to make her work for them and then rape her, as they had done to the young women in Cuarto Pueblo. The witness remembers: "We were still outside, in front of the church," before being taken away by helicopter, "when a woman came along with two children and a baby in arms. Each child was carrying a live duck. 'Good morning, where is your husband?' asked the lieutenant. 'Who knows. ...' She didn't speak Spanish. 'Change your clothes,' the lieutenant ordered the soldiers. They changed clothing and ordered the woman to wash their uniforms. 'And then we're going to screw you in that room over there,' they said. I don't know if they killed the woman," the witness adds, as he did not see what happened next. But other witnesses who knew her claim that "she was killed with her three little boys; they stuffed the children down the latrine." Another says: "The enemies raped her and then dumped her in a place they set fire to." The latrine, a "big hole" like a cesspool, appears to have belonged to the same Evangelical church. According to one witness, she was not burned with her children; "they killed them, piled them together, and threw them down the latrine."

Captures and Chain Killings (2 April)

After this tragic day the army abandoned Xalbal by night. As it marched out of Xalbal it searched houses on the plots of land along the way, taking the young Sebastián Tomás as guide. According to most of the informants, the soldiers found more people, whom they either killed or captured to massacre later.

The army's first step was to capture the Charismatic catechist Alfonso Ramírez Gómez (thirty-five years old) and two of his sons. Ramírez was not Chuj, but a Mam Indian from San Idelfonso Ixtahuacán. He and Pascual Paiz were the most important catechists in the Charismatic renewal movement in Xalbal. But in contrast to Pascual, who was soft-spoken and polite, Ramírez "was very fierce when spoken to." When his neighbors tried to convince him to leave, "he was rude to them, saying they were a load of lazy thieves" because going into the jungle implied suspending agricultural activities. When the soldiers passed by, he handed himself in with his ten- and twelve-year-old children, whom he had taught: "If the army comes by, hand yourselves in." The catechist's wife, however, was not captured.[9]

The soldiers' second step was to go to Inocencio's house at midnight to the appointment he had made in the note with the scout Sebastián. The army, accompanied by the scout, took over Inocencio's house, but there was no one there, as he had gone with his family to sleep in the jungle. The soldiers laid ambush, surrounding the house and waiting for Inocencio to return the following morning. But when he did return, the soldiers, hungry and half-asleep, were unprepared, and he found them "having an early breakfast under the coffee shrub" and making noise. He therefore was made aware of their presence in time and escaped, collecting his family and heading toward the river. They did leave tracks, though, which the army followed later.

The man we have called Inocencio was saved but two of Pascual Paiz's sons, Gaspar, twenty-one, and Pascual, thirteen, fell into the ambush when they went to Inocencio's house to visit. They "were going to have a meeting with Inocencio at 7:00 A.M."; it seems they were going to organize a group to seek the whereabouts of Pascual Paiz and the rest of his family. Inocencio knew that they were coming but had no way of warning them of the army ambush. The two sons fell into the trap. Gaspar had been a student at the Santiago Indigenous Institute in Guatemala City and showed the soldiers a certificate as proof, but to no avail. They undoubtedly tortured Gaspar in the house to make him tell them of Inocencio's whereabouts, and they killed him in front of his younger brother, Pascual, and his friend, the scout Sebastián, who had become an army guide. But they did not live to tell their tale.

Still on their way out of Xalbal, the soldiers then traced Inocencio's tracks. They came to the house of another Chuj Indian, called Miguel Carmelo, who was "just starting breakfast," according to a witness from Xalbal. He and his two sons were captured.[10] The only one to escape was a seventeen-year-old son who had tried to convince his father to leave his home: "The youth was trying to make his father leave, but he didn't want to."

Miguel Carmelo's wife had abandoned him. He had then killed the man with whom she had gone off and as a result spent many years in prison in Santa Cruz del Quiché. He had "just returned to his family when he was killed," recalls another witness. His commitment to the Charismatic movement seems to have been related to his family crisis.

The capture of Miguel Carmelo and his children must have taken place very quickly, as the army was in pursuit of Inocencio. The soldiers must have tied Carmelo up and pushed him along with their other bound captives: the catechist Alfonso Ramírez, Pascual Paiz's son, and the scout-guide Sebastián Tomás. They were all killed by the river and their bodies were left as a warning: "They left Miguel Carmelo hanging there." Another witness adds that the soldiers left some grenades under the corpses; that was why they could not bury them: "They covered the dead and placed bombs under some *cortes*. Pascual was taken near the river with Miguel Carmelo and Alfonso Ramírez, who were captured that night. But we didn't go to bury them."[11]

Massacre in Kaibil (2 April)

The army continued to follow Inocencio's tracks. It discovered the spot he had spent the night and pursued him until it reached the river. The soldiers crossed the Xalbal River and again picked up some tracks. But these belonged to Inocencio's father-in-law, who had separated from his son-in-law to put the army off. The father-in-law advanced and managed to warn the first house in Kaibil of the army's proximity, but the inhabitants did not pay heed to him, putting down the army's approach as routine. The army then arrived at the house and massacred almost everyone inside with immense cruelty. Let us listen to a Kaibil witness who saw the victims:

> Crisanto Gómez had a house on the banks of the Xalbal River. He did not want to leave for the jungle—he wanted to stay home. When the soldiers came upon a camp of people in Xalbal, the people fled exactly in the direction of his house. But he did not flee. The soldiers went in pursuit of the people.
>
> Seven people were killed in Kaibil: Crisanto, about thirty years old, his wife, his son Manuel, who was about twenty, Manuel's wife and their baby, and two more of Crisanto's children.
>
> He had a lime oven. They burned two people in it as it blazed; his daughter-in-law had her eight-day-old baby. They placed it on stones where the flames came out of the oven. The baby melted like oil on the stones.

We asked the witness if he had seen this:

> I went the following day. The woman had been burned. Only a bit of her sash was left. The woman and her baby's burned bodies were in the oven.
>
> The rest were killed on the other side of the river where they [the soldiers] had chased the people from Xalbal. They placed the man's son in a kneeling position. They left him there as if praying. The man was hung from a tree, as though crucified, like Jesus Christ, tied with reeds from one tree to another. The woman had been thrown onto the ground. They placed a tape recorder on her and wrapped her in her own *corte.*

As in La Nueva Concepción, a boy was an eyewitness to the massacre. He escaped and watched the army put the woman and her newborn baby in the oven. She had left the house but could not run, having recently given birth. When she saw the soldiers tying up her parents-in-law by the neck she "let out a scream," whereupon a soldier discovered her, tied her up, and dragged her to the oven: "They put her in the fire and threw the little one into the oven," affirms a witness other than the one from Kaibil. He heard the surviving boy's account.

For some surviving Charismatic witnesses who did not trust in the army, the massacre had religious connotations. The army's mockery of the religious made them interpret the massacre as a way of following Christ. Crisanto was "crucified like Jesus Christ." A witness from Xalbal confirms the deed and interpretation, although he says that more people were crucified: "Three people from Kaibil were crucified."[12] So badly has the witness wanted to identify his memory of the Passion of Christ with the passion of Xalbal that he has confused exact dates of the army's arrival: "The army arrived on Good Thursday and on Good Friday threw the people into the fire." Good Friday was a week later, on 9 April.

After finishing the massacre, the army returned on the Xalbal road, reached the transversal highway, and crossed the river over the bridge.

This was to be the end of the army's first scorched-earth offensive in Ixcán Grande. It would not return until May.

Last Event: A Grenade Explodes (5 April)

After the army had left, friends and relatives went to bury the corpses. One of the bodies was that of Gaspar Paiz, the young student. The army had placed a grenade under his body and left him on a table at Inocencio's house. Three peasants entered the house and dug a grave right there, but they were unable to finish the burial because the bomb exploded when they moved the corpse. One of the three, Matías Miguel, was killed. The witness was wounded and the third escaped unscathed. Let us listen to the witness, who was Gaspar's brother-in-law: "We began digging a hole, but we had dug the hole at the head of the corpse. 'Why didn't we dig the hole next to his body so we could just roll him in?' we thought afterward. The stench of his corpse was great, as he had been there three days. We looked for bits of cord to straighten him out. I pulled his head and another pulled his feet. But a bomb had been placed under his T-shirt! God is so bountiful and powerful and helps us a lot. I saw the bomb fall on some wood on the floor. I shouted 'bomb,' and threw myself onto the ground. The bomb didn't explode on us, but nothing remained of the corpse, only bits on the ceiling and wooden column. I was standing, and his other brother was protected by the wooden column. My arm and legs were wounded [he shows me the scars]. The other companion, Miguel Matías, was about three meters farther away; the bomb did kill him. He died at 10:00 that night."[13]

Matías Miguel was very religious, the witness remembers, because when they went to bury Gaspar he had told him: "We know we are believers and our bodies are all going to be buried." But Gaspar was not buried because the grenade "turned him into paste" and his remains "even stuck to the faces" of the friends who had gone to bury him.

Nor were buried the bodies of those left as a warning by the river. The witness was sure that bombs had been placed under them. The bodies of those massacred in the town were not buried either, as all that remained was their charred bones. The many remains were dangerous to get near.

Beginning Collective Agricultural Production

When the army withdrew from the entire area, not only from Xalbal, the inhabitants of Xalbal and other cooperatives had to decide whether to continue or interrupt their agricultural activities. The decision to sow was a sign of resistance, of people opting to bear the difficult conditions in the jungle for a long time and not wanting to return to their birthplaces in the cold highlands or to leave the country: "Everyone asked me whether we should continue sowing or leave the country. And we all agreed, even after Xalbal had been burned down, and we began to sow," recalls a witness who promoted the decision.

Although agricultural activities continued, they were carried out very differently in the jungle from those in normal open conditions. The witness who headed the first attempts at collective production tells of the first changes introduced: "A small group of us decided to sow collectively on the plots of land we had prepared by slashing and burning individually. We began to sow collectively and to keep watch on 20 or 25 May." "How many of you were there in the group?" I asked him. "There were five families. 'If the offensive continues we will have to work collectively and not think only about one's own corn,' we said, 'better to sow quickly.'"

The first steps in the process of collective work had far-reaching consequences because it meant a change in the mode of production.[14] The change did not stem from a desire to increase production or from a conviction of the excellence of working collectively, but from the need for the people to defend themselves from the army. Working together meant that they could take turns keeping watch and sending out the alert if the soldiers arrived.

During the first stages of working together, corn from previous crops was not shared. Each family in the small group had its granary on its plot of land, and as these were near the camp in the jungle, each one could go get its own corn. However, the fields that year were sown on the understanding that the harvest would be shared.

Collective work was carried out with the idea of reciprocity. The group of men started to plant first one plot of land and then another until all the land that had been previously prepared was sown. At this point, the corn in each field was still visualized as belonging to the field's owner, and during this initial stage, property, products, and lands were not yet considered collective. In retrospect, though, the witness sees that the collective work would lead to collectively sharing the harvest and that "each person would no longer think only about his own corn."

The last thing before the massacre that the peasants did individually was to prepare their plots of land for sowing by slashing and burning. New seeds would be sown on these lands by the small group. The radical and transcendental implications of this act contrasts with the small size of the group and area covered. But the idea of mutual collaboration was taken up by other groups: "My group set the example and another group saw how we were working collectively."

List of Those Massacred in Xalbal and Kaibil

Name	*Age*	*Origin*	*Other*
La Chuchilla, Xalbal: 7 March 1982			
1. Petrona Ramírez		Concepción Huista	
Xalbal: 31 March to 2 April (S1)[15]			
2. Bartolomé Tomás	102	Barillas	
3. Rufino Pérez	18	San Miguel Ixtahuacán	
4. Romaldo Mejía	32	San Miguel Ixtahuacán	3's brother-in-law
5. Pascual Paiz	52	San Miguel Ixtahuacán[16]	
6. María Lucas	50	San Miguel Ixtahuacán	5's wife
7. Eulalia Paiz	18	San Miguel Ixtahuacán	5's son
8. Pascual Paiz	13	San Miguel Ixtahuacán	5's son
9. Miguel Paiz	10	San Miguel Ixtahuacán	5's daughter
10. Sebastián Torres	60	San Miguel Ixtahuacán	
11. María Tomás	60	San Miguel Ixtahuacán	10's wife
12. José Torres	20	San Miguel Ixtahuacán	10's son
13. Isabela Pascual	8	San Miguel Ixtahuacán	11's daughter
14. Fabiana Pascual	8	San Miguel Ixtahuacán	11's daughter[17]
15. Tomás Sebastián	40	San Miguel Ixtahuacán	
16. Sebastián Tomás	18	San Miguel Ixtahuacán	15's son
17. Lucía Antonio	45	Barillas	
18. Guillermo Antonio	12	Barillas	17's son[18]
19. Rey Antonio	10	Barillas	17's son
20. Jacobo Antonio		Barillas	17's son
21. Gaspar Paiz	21	San Mateo Ixtatán	5's son
22. Miguel Carmelo	64	San Mateo Ixtatán	
23.		San Mateo Ixtatán	22's child
24. María[19]			22's daughter
25. Alfonso Ramírez Gómez[20]	35	San Ildefonso Ixtahuacán	
26. Victor Ramírez	12	San Ildefonso Ixtahuacán	25's son
27. Alicia Ramírez	10	San Ildefonso Ixtahuacán	25's daughter
Xalbal: 5 April 1982 (S2)			
28. Matías Miguel		San Miguel Acatán[21]	
Kaibil: 2 April 1982 (S3)[22]			
29. Crisanto Gómez	52		
30. Concepción Hernández	50		
31. Santiago Gómez	18		
32. Susana Gómez	10 days		
33. María Ordóñez	55		
34. Santos Gómez	4		

35. Manuel Gómez Sales   30
36. Juana Gómez   24
    Hernández
37. Cristina Gómez   5
    Hernández
38. Pedro Gómez   3
    Hernández

NOTES

1. I do not have the exact figure, but there could not have been very many soldiers, as it took some time for one of the witnesses who arrived in the town to realize that there were soldiers in the church with the people who had been captured. The army apparently did not have enough qualified troops to launch their offensive in two parts of Ixcán Grande on the same day, Cuarto Pueblo in the north and Xalbal in the south.

2. There's a certain likeness to the pacification technique called "village festival" or "district fair" mentioned in Tho (1980, 98), which was "a combination of cordoning off and searching, civic action and information gathering."

3. I have based my account on twenty-six interviews, mostly with people from Xalbal. But the information gathering was "asymptotic." As asymptotes never reach the parabola, the interviews never achieve a perfect exactness. There is always a witness who was closest to particular events who changes the account and draws it nearer to the complete historic truth. I have gone over events in Xalbal with other witnesses, and there was always another aspect to correct. This fact should be taken into consideration by critics who wish to check out this account with other informants. The inexactness of certain details does not invalidate the account as a whole. To do so would demonstrate the critic's ignorance of writing history based on oral accounts.

4. The two families together came to seven people; this is the number estimated by the witness I have quoted. The witnesses are not completely sure that that was where Pascual Paiz's family was burned, though they are sure that Sebastián Torres's family was burned there; they deduce this from the number of remains, the nearness of the houses, and the absence of remains in the homes of Pascual Paiz and Sebastián Torres. As to the form of death, whether they were burned alive or killed and subsequently burned, one witness affirms that they were burned alive, but he probably just presumes this. The other says that there was blood on the *corte*, which would indicate that the woman was first killed and then burned. However, on the following day, as we shall see in a moment, there was a firsthand eyewitness to people being burned alive.

5. These are the accounts of two women who heard the tale of Pascual Paiz's surviving daughter.

6. With this I do not wish to say that all "visions" were false, as some people had clear premonitions of the army's approach and were thus able to save the lives of entire groups. But this time the woman was sadly mistaken. Discernment is needed to distinguish the truth, as are objective facts, as far as these can be gleaned. This pre-

vents relying merely on subjectivity, although subjectivity can contribute to the interpretation of hard facts.

7. Let us not get confused by so many Sebastiáns. One is Sebastián Torres, who was returning from the religious ceremony with his son, the guitar player. Another is Tomás Sebastián, who had gone to get his mule. And the third is this explorer, Sebastián Tomás, son of Tomás Sebastián. It is a Chuj and Q'anjob'al custom to use the father's first name as a surname. In this way, first and last names go back and forth indefinitely. They are not really surnames but names used in memory of their ancestors. That is why the father is called Tomás Sebastián and the son Sebastián Tomás; a grandson would again be called Tomás Sebastián.

8. Note that there is a small discrepancy between the witness who speaks of the kitchen and the previous witness, who had mentioned the chapel latrine as the place where the burning took place.

9. One testimony says that "the woman screamed." Another woman said that they tied her up and left her there.

10. According to three witnesses, two sons were captured. A fourth witness refers to three sons.

11. However, I was unable to establish from any of the witnesses who had personally seen their bodies whether they had been killed there. All the Xalbal witnesses agree that they were killed. But there appears to be a certain overlap of images with the corpses of the Kaibil victims, one hanging and the others strewn on the river bank. See the following section.

12. According to the Kaibil witness, there were 7 dead. Another witness's list gives 10 names. The list seems to have certain errors in the transcription of some of the last names and ages.

13. He did not die that day, but on Wednesday, 7 April. According to a witness, "He died a day and a half later, as some metal fragments had penetrated his stomach."

14. Remember the first Christian communities (Acts 2). The CPR (Communities of Population in Resistance) in Ixcán refers to them in its January 1991 declaration.

15. Nos. 2–4: residents of La Unión center, Xalbal (S1). Nos. 5–16 and 22–28: residents of the Río Cinco center, Xalbal (S1). Nos. 17–20: residents of San Lorenzo center, Xalbal (S4). No. 29: resident of Santa Rosa center (S5).

16. An animator of the faith, according to S2.

17. Nos. 13 and 14 were eight-year-old twins, according to S2.

18. According to S2, no. 17's name was Lucía Ramón and no. 18's was Santana Ramírez.

19. According to S6.

20. An animator of the faith, according to S2.

21. According to S7, he was from San Miguel Acatán.

22. S3, the source for the following list of names, is not the source who was used in the text. For this reason some of the ages are different.

CHAPTER 11

Circular Offensives: Piedras Blancas

[18 to 30 May 1982]

After the army withdrew to Playa Grande there was a month (April) of relative calm. But in May the government armed forces returned with a new kind of offensive. They settled in and formed certain points of control in the area they had abandoned in November 1981, in places where the population supported them or where conditions were favorable for them to stay. These points were at the foot of the Cuchumatanes mountains. The aim of settling was to impede the guerrillas in the jungle from uniting with the guerrillas in the Ixil highlands. Witnesses mention three places: Asunción Copón, next to the Copón River; Santiago Ixcán, between the Tzejá and Xalbal rivers; and San Luis, to the west of Xalbal. The first and third had large landing strips. Tightest control was kept there.

The offensives that began in May started from the two main points at about the same time. A third offensive was also launched from the transversal highway, once again in an attack on Santa María Tzejá. The three offensives formed a kind of fork or plow, two prongs toward the north and the one in the middle toward the south.

The aim was no longer to attack the towns that had already been razed, but to trap and destroy the camps of people forming in the jungle. We saw how before the Xalbal massacre the army pursued the inhabitants of one of these camps near Pueblo Nuevo. But during the March offensive the pursuit was secondary to the razing of the main towns. Now it became the army's main objective.

The new offensives were also aimed at the towns and villages (usually smaller) that were not touched in previous months. The offensives were quicker, with fewer troops, shorter routes, and using civil patrols. I have called them circular offensives because the army would leave the outpost and make a kind of circle and return a week later more or less to the departure point. A week later, it would repeat the same circle or thereabouts, and again the week after that, until it gained control of the area. The army would raze the villages en route or try to win over the local population and then pursue groups of people that had fled to the jungle to kill or capture them.

Large massacres were carried out in the process, although they did not reach the scale of Cuarto Pueblo, as the most important towns with the exception of Mayalán had already been razed. On the eastern side of Ixcán, the largest massacre was in Rosario Canijá (6 July), when 71 people were killed.[1] In the west, 64 people were killed and 15 captured and forced to disappear in Piedras Blancas in May.

At the beginning of May, the army, perhaps an entire battalion,[2] set camp on the San Luis estate.[3] From there the troops went east to destroy villages that were still standing, such as San Juan Ixcán (burned down on 15 May), combed the jungle, and organized civil patrols, as in Santiago Ixcán. At the same time, troops went west to destroy the small villages and hamlets at the foot of the Cuchumatanes. They massacred and pursued the people in the mountains, as in Piedras Blancas and elsewhere, and organized civil patrols, as we will soon see.

Lands and Villages to the South

To the south of the cooperative project started by the Maryknoll fathers is a place called Malacatán, situated in the southern part of the jungle at the foot of the mountains. There were four dispersed communities there, from north to south: Buena Vista, Nueva Esperanza, Santa Agustina, and Piedras Blancas. Piedras Blancas, a spur of the mountain range, was higher up than the others.

Piedras Blancas was divided into four sections that corresponded to different linguistic groups and forms of organization. Two sections (1 and 2) were inhabited by Mam Indians, and Q'anjob'als lived in the other two (3 and 4). Whereas some were organized in a cooperative, others had contact with trade unions in Guatemala City. Some had bought and registered their farms; others had settled on state lands. These differences caused certain tensions but not to such an extent that the army was able to use them to massacre. The four groups were at different levels of the mountain slopes; group 1 was furthest down, and group 4 was highest up.

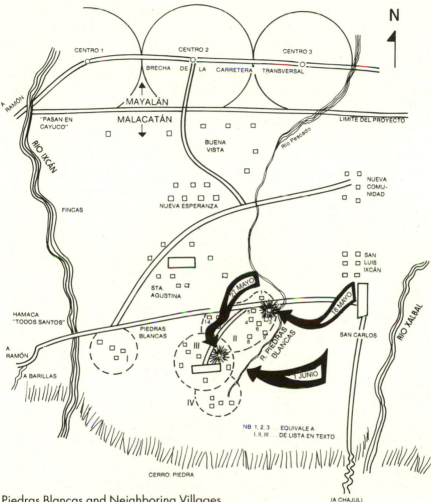

Piedras Blancas and Neighboring Villages

To the east, on the other side of the Piedras Blancas River, which was a tributary of the Ixcán River, were three *ladino* towns bordering on Piedras Blancas and on other communities in Malacatán. From north to south and upward lay La Nueva Comunidad, which was inhabited by 110 families from Chiantla, Huehuetenango. Then there was the San Luis estate, owned by Luis Arenas's heirs. The majority of the people on the estate were Chiantecans and a small number were Q'anjob'als. Then followed San Carlos, also composed of Chiantecans.

The Piedras Blancas River separated the indigenous area in the west from the *ladino* area in the east. The army later took advantage of this division in its scorched-earth policy: Relations between *ladinos* and Indians were already tense because of the guerrillas.[4]

The army set up camp on the San Luis estate at the beginning of May, not apart, as before, but "next to the people from the cooperative" to be shielded by them in case of attack, according to a witness. Many of the inhabitants who had fled in fear of the rebels and had been held by the army in Barillas were now returned to the San Luis estate. The army promised to protect them on the condition that they form civil patrols. "Civil patrol training was very hard. On the first day about thirty or forty men arrived, including old men. ... The army gave the patrol leaders different ranks, posted guards, and everything. The soldiers told them: 'You have to do your duty and patrol with us.'"

Army Summons

According to a Mam witness from Santa Agustina, after setting up camp in San Luis the army sent out word to all the indigenous and *ladino* communities summoning "the representatives from each village" to present themselves. The *ladinos* in La Nueva Comunidad obeyed the army order, saying when they returned that "the army was very kind and friendly." They also sent word to all the communities[5] that the army would wait for fifteen days but that if the representatives had not arrived by then it meant they had done something wrong. The officer had compared the communities that "had done something wrong" to rotten oranges that had to be picked out from the basket so that the others would not rot too. He told this to the members of La Nueva Comunidad, and they told the other communities.

There was a lot of internal discussion in the indigenous communities about whether to present themselves. They also consulted other communities, seeking a general consensus: Either we all go or we all stay. For example, the Mam military commissioner from group 2 in Piedras Blancas consulted with the commissioners in Santa Agustina, who were also Mam. (Group 2 from Piedras Blancas was later the first to be massacred.) In this way the witness learned of the community's reaction to the army summons.

The reason for not going was the same as that of the Cuarto Pueblo commissioners: The army could simply kill them in the military outpost. But San Carlos, like La Nueva Comunidad, obeyed the army call. The *ladino* communities supported the army, whereas the indigenous communities were highly suspicious.

Members of La Nueva Comunidad continued having contact with the army, and they informed other communities that the lieutenant had said that those who had not presented themselves "should be prepared." There was always some indigenous person living among the *ladinos* who acted as a go-between, repeating these statements to the indigenous communities.

The logical alternative to not presenting oneself to the army should have been fleeing to the jungle. But in group 2 in Piedras Blancas, according to the same Mam witness, "most people did not want to leave, as 'we have identity cards, we pay municipal taxes.' Then they said, 'We'll see what the army says.'" That is, they were of two minds, not fully convinced of the need to escape from the army control.

"The time came when the army finished what it had set out to do, but before that it sent a telegram to the commissioner. He told us this personally. The telegram said that the army was going to arrive on Thursday to hold a meeting." The "telegram" was a note taken by hand by anyone who happened to be going that way, as group 2 was on the road from San Luis to the hanging bridge over the Ixcán River. The road was used often, even in such days of danger. Group 2 was only forty-five minutes away from San Luis and was like an entry point to all the indigenous communities.

The twelve families in group 2 again consulted each other and decided to wait for the army on the day it had indicated. The army's arrival was imminent, as the date set was three or four days after the telegram had arrived. The commissioner felt it best not to wait but agreed to the majority decision to do so and informed the neighboring communities. "He told us," the witness from Santa Agustina recalls. "We said to him, 'Do as you please.'" The neighbors tried to dissuade them, but they could not force them to change their minds.

It was corn-sowing time, and because the plots of land were near the houses, the men decided to go out to work, thinking that their families would call them when the soldiers arrived. They also kept watch on the main road to have advance warning of the soldiers' arrival so that "those who want to go into the jungle can do so."

Genocide Massacre (18 May)

The army arrived at noon, not on the day it had announced but on Tuesday, 18 May. It used surprise techniques in changing the date of arrival and also in the way of entering: The soldiers did not take the main road "but entered from a path farther up" so that the person on guard did not see them coming, continues the same Mam witness.

There were about 100 soldiers and no civil patrollers.[6] They came down the hill to the houses, which were close together in a hollow. The women, who were alone because their husbands were still out working, grew frightened when the soldiers suddenly appeared. They "ran into the *chuj* [steam bath]." Having no previous experience of being pursued, they went to hide as though they were in a bombardment instead of fleeing to the jungle. The soldiers searched and took them out of the *chuj*. What the witness calls a *chuj* in this case was a trench, like an underground steam bath, protected on top by beautiful tree trunks that do not rot. The trench was designed for a possible bombardment, like the one in Cuarto Pueblo on 30 April 1981. The witnesses remember that the army knew about the trenches earlier because many strangers passed that way and had seen them. This form of self-defense made the army think that the community was "a rotten orange."[7]

Some children went to call the men planting corn and the one keeping a lookout on the road. The Mam witness remembers that he was cooking brown sugar with his uncle; he observed nothing out of the ordinary in the neighboring community until the workers saw a lot of smoke rising from the group 2 community. He recalls: "We ran to see from the lookout point and thought that they had deserted their houses." They assumed that the soldiers were burning the empty community.

To make sure, a man from the witness's community went to an empty house halfway between the two communities. The empty house had been established as a contact point between the two communities in case of emergencies. But the go-between waited for more than an hour and nobody from group 2 appeared. The people from Santa Agustina were perplexed but still spent the night in their homes. On the following day they again tried to establish contact but were unsuccessful. They came to the conclusion that the people from group 2 "have surely been killed."

Two days later the witness and another man from his community went to the site of the massacre to have a look: "We entered fearfully. From the edge of the village we saw that all the houses had been burned down. I felt terribly sad and I'm sure my companion did too. Very quietly we went to the commissioner's house. We saw a lot of bodies there; they were strewn on the ground. The men were all bound. A rope was tied to a tree near the commissioner's house. All the men were lying outside, close to the house. And the house had been burned."

The soldiers used a single piece of rope to tie up the men with their hands behind their backs. When the rope burned, their bodies keeled over on the ground outside the house.

Inside the house lay the bodies of the women and children. There were three pregnant women. You could just make out the small corpses of the fetuses inside their mothers' wombs. You could see their heads as they hadn't burned well. Their mothers' bodies had been completely burned, but not the babies inside. We saw all of that.

I didn't start counting but my companion did. I was seized by a great fear, a great sadness. My heart ached when I saw all of this. The men lying on the ground had been decapitated with a hachet; the hachet was lying there. That's how we realized their heads had been cut off with a hachet. Only one man had been shot, you could see the bullet wound. He was lying about five or six meters away from the rest. He wasn't armed. So we thought: 'He obviously tried to escape, but they shot him and there he fell.' Only one of the other men lying there had been burned. As the house was nearby, the heat of the fire scorched him, and part of his body had been roasted.

The witness's companion counted 61 corpses. Another Mam witness went to see the dead and counted 65 in all; 13 were men.

A week later more men returned and found 3 children in a small sugar cane plantation: a thirteen-year-old girl, a boy of eight, and a one-year-old who the girl was carrying. They were sucking sugar cane to appease their hunger. These children were the only survivors of the massacre: They had managed to escape from the soldiers, as had the children who survived in Kaibil and La Nueva Concepción. They witnessed what the army did and told me that the women had been burned alive.

The girl recounted how she grabbed her brother's hand when the soldiers locked their mother in the house. "She said that all the women began to scream when they set the house on fire. And how they screamed! They screamed really loud. … She also saw how they hit the men with a hachet one by one. … The children said that the men were killed first, but the women had already been locked into the house. The soldiers tied up the men after locking the women in. The women were screaming as the soldiers killed the men, one by one, one by one. The girl saw how the soldiers set fire to the house with the women inside. She was the person who gave us this information."[8]

Another witness confirms that the women and children had been burned alive: "The children and women were screaming. We were watching from above. The women were alive when they entered the house and then they were burned. The women were crying while they were being burned."

The massacre, an attempt to exterminate the entire village, is a clear example of genocide. The army wanted to exterminate even the seeds still inside the mothers' wombs. The intention of genocide likens this massacre to the one in Cuarto Pueblo but differs in two aspects: First, the aim of genocide was almost completely successful in the group 2 community, with the exception of the three surviving children, as opposed to Cuarto Pueblo, where the population was not wiped out completely. Second, the massacre was on a smaller scale than the one in Cuarto Pueblo, because the village was smaller and had fewer inhabitants and was less central and important than the cooperative. Precisely because the village was small, the aim of genocide was more easily carried out, and the massacre became a clear sign of the army's genocidal intention.[9]

The change of government on 23 March did nothing to protect the sacred right to life, despite the head of state's claim to be a born-again Christian.

The officers' claim in Los Angeles after the coup d'état that the army did not kill proved completely false.

List of Those Massacred

How many died? The witnesses refer to three different figures: (1) the total number of adult men who were killed, (2) the total number of all persons killed, and (3) the number of families affected (in which some or all the members were killed). One witness counted 13 men who were killed. Two of the above-mentioned witnesses refer respectively to altogether 61 and 65 people killed. Twelve families were affected: "the twelve families living in the hollow."

The list was drawn up by a Mam witness from Buena Vista village who saw and counted the dead. He told me the names of the 12 decapitated men from memory. He also looked for people from his village, acquaintances and fellow countrymen of the dead, who together drew up the list of 55 dead, who were grouped together in fourteen families in twelve houses. There are two families whose married children lived with their parents. There were also two families who had recently moved to the village: I refer to them as the "irregulars" (numbers 50 and 55). The couple whose children managed to escape appears on the list (numbers 38 and 39).

Massacre of Group 2, Piedras Blancas (18 May 1982)

Name	Age	Origin	Other
I			
1. Marcos Sales	45	San Ildefonso Ixtahuacán	
2. Francisca Pérez	43	San Ildefonso Ixtahuacán	1's wife
3. Fabiana		San Ildefonso Ixtahuacán	1's daughter
4. Miguel		San Ildefonso Ixtahuacán	1's son
II			
5. Marcos Jacinto	35	San Ildefonso Ixtahuacán	
6. Francisca Ramírez	32	San Ildefonso Ixtahuacán	5's wife
7. Faustino Jacinto		San Ildefonso Ixtahuacán	5's son
8. Juana Jacinto		San Ildefonso Ixtahuacán	5's daughter
III			
9. Sebastián Morales	33	San Ildefonso Ixtahuacán	
10. Juana Gómez		San Ildefonso Ixtahuacán	
11. Marcos Morales G.		San Ildefonso Ixtahuacán	
12. Romelia Morales G.		San Ildefonso Ixtahuacán	
IV			
13. Alonso Morales	38	San Ildefonso Ixtahuacán	
14. María Gómez	36	San Ildefonso Ixtahuacán	
15. María Morales		San Ildefonso Ixtahuacán	

16. Víctor Morales		San Ildefonso Ixtahuacán	
17. Antonio Morales		San Ildefonso Ixtahuacán	
18. Cristina		San Ildefonso Ixtahuacán	
19. Juan		San Ildefonso Ixtahuacán	

V

20. Pascual García	42	Colotenango	
21. Eulalia López	40	Colotenango	
22. Juan García		Colotenango	
23. Marcos García		Colotenango	

VI

24. Bonifacio García	35	Colotenango	
25. María Pérez	32	Colotenango	
26. Víctor García P.		Colotenango	
27. Julia García		Colotenango	
28. Rolando García		Colotenango	

VII

29. Juan Jiménez	31	San Ildefonso Ixtahuacán	
30. Fabiana Ortiz	30	San Ildefonso Ixtahuacán	
31. Luiz [*sic*] Jiménez O.		San Ildefonso Ixtahuacán	
32. María Jiménez Ortiz		San Ildefonso Ixtahuacán	
33. Rafael Jiménez Ortiz		San Ildefonso Ixtahuacán	

VIII

34. Diego Francisco Diego	35	Barillas	Q'anjob'al
35. María Diego	23	Barillas	
36.	7	Barillas	child
37.	$1^1/_2$	Barillas	child

IX

38. Marcos Alonzo Jiménez	30	Colotenango	parents of the sur-viving children
39. Natividad Sales Pérez	30	San Ildefonso Ixtahuacán	

X

40. José Méndez	18	San Ildefonso Ixtahuacán	
41. Fabiana Méndez		San Ildefonso Ixtahuacán	
42. Cruz Méndez M.		San Ildefonso Ixtahuacán	
43. Catarina M.		San Ildefonso Ixtahuacán	
44. José Méndez M.		San Ildefonso Ixtahuacán	

Married Children

XI

45. José García	19	Colotenango	24's son
46. Catarina Sales P.		San Ildefonso Ixtahuacán	1's daughter
47. Rosa García S.			

XII

48. Alejandro Sales	19	San Ildefonso Ixtahuacán	1's son
49. María Méndez	18		

Irregulars

XIII

50. Pascual Morales	San Ildefonso Ixtahuacán(?)	
51. María Velásquez		
52.		child
53.		child
54.		child

XIV

55. Marcos Jiménez	San Ildefonso Ixtahuacán

Pursuit and Massacre (27 May)

On 19 and 20 May, after exterminating the Mam Indians in group 2, the army stayed on, burning down the houses nearby and further up in Piedras Blancas. On 19 May at 2:00 P.M. the soldiers began to burn down the central cooperative in the group 3 community, higher up from group 2. Because it was a clear summer night, the fire could be seen from above.

On 21 May the army descended on Santa Agustina, burning down houses and the Catholic chapel, and on 22 May it returned to San Luis; the excursion lasted about a week. After the massacre of group 2, the soldiers did not kill anyone else, as everyone had escaped into the jungle.[10] The massacre of group 2 drove the entire indigenous population in the area to seek shelter in the jungle.

When the army left the area, a man from group 3 who showed leadership qualities—we will refer to him as Justino (not his real name)—called a meeting to organize a camp around his house. He said that the people should build their huts from bits of burned metal sheeting. The huts could be built under the shade of the cardamom plants surrounding his house. The people would not be protected by the jungle, but being together seemed sufficient to him, as he was (alas mistakenly) certain that the rebels would defend them if the army arrived. They could keep continual watch over the road from San Luis in case the army arrived. Many people were convinced, so they built temporary shelters around his house. There were about fifteen families.

The soldiers arrived on 27 May at about noon, when everyone was busy doing chores.[11] The men were out in the fields, others were having lunch, and some women were bathing in the river or washing clothes. That is how the "thirty soldiers and 'gangs'"[12] (civil patrols) found them.

There was no alert prior to the army's approach because the two young men on guard were eating and joking. When they saw the soldiers approach, dressed in olive green, they mistook them for rebels. Like the owner of the main house, they had the idea that the rebels were near. The witness reconstructs what the soldiers said to them: "'Don't go, you don't need to leave, we're companions.' But when they got close, there were more behind. Then they realized that they were soldiers. But it was too late to leave by then, and they were captured."

While this exchange was taking place at the lookout point, the inhabitants went on in the hollow unalarmed until a teenager at Justino's house, which was also high up, saw the soldiers going up the hill and shot at them with a hunting rifle. The soldiers then opened fire on the people in the hollow, who were occupying an empty house that was being used as a refuge by some of the families. Let us hear the emotional words of the witness:

> There was a house nearby, about four *cuerdas* [100 meters] further down from the lookout point. No one realized when the soldiers arrived. They climbed up the slope and captured the youngsters keeping watch, so they couldn't warn anybody. Then Justino's son saw a lot of people dressed in olive green climbing up the slope. "Who are they? Maybe they're soldiers," he thought. And he went inside the house without saying anything. He found a .22-caliber shotgun and went out to attack. They were soldiers, and he shot once at them.
>
> Then the soldiers opened fire on the people. Who was not going to be frightened? It was terrible. How were the people going to leave the hollow? And those bathing in the stream? The soldiers were nearby now, about 100 meters away. It was so steep, no one could get away.

When the soldiers heard the shot from the opposite slope (see the map), they changed direction: Instead of continuing their climb up to the cooperative, they made a U-turn, going down to capture the people in the hollow and firing a shower of bullets. The stream where the women were washing flowed between the two slopes in the middle of the hollow. The abandoned house was also in the hollow near the stream. The two youths keeping watch were taken there and later were burned. Others were also taken to the abandoned house, where a total of 9 people were massacred. The massacre is described in more detail by the witnesses closest to the event.

Of the 9 people, 4 died outside the house and 5 inside. The first 4 were shot dead while trying to escape. Two surviving girls saw this happen. The little girls' older brother remembers, "My mother was killed by a burst of machine-gun fire." The soldiers hastily buried them where they had been killed. The other 5 died inside the house, which the soldiers had set on fire.

A young man recalls how he and another scout found the two groups of corpses on different visits:

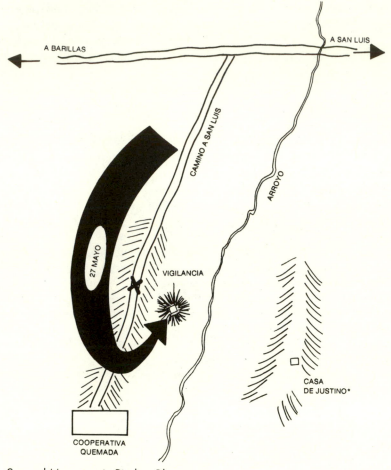

A BARILLAS

A SAN LUIS

CAMINO A SAN LUIS

ARROYO

27 MAYO

VIGILANCIA

CASA
DE JUSTINO*

COOPERATIVA
QUEMADA

Second Massacre in Piedras Blancas

That same day we got near the house and saw that they were still burning it, so we left. At 5:00 P.M. we went to the house again as the soldiers had left by then. We saw that there were people strewn over the floor of the house. The next morning at 7:00 we went to see who had been killed. There were 5 people in the house, including the two young watchmen, lying on the floor. Their faces were unrecognizable, as they had been blown up. It was easier to recognize their pants and belts, but their shirts and hair were burned. We only recognized them by their belts. There were also some women and a girl of ten, but we left quickly because the soldiers were still near the cooperative.

About four or five days later we went again. That was when we discovered the people who had been buried outside the house. There were 4, Eulalia Antonio and her 2 children and someone else. I imagine that those captured alive were taken to the house to be burned, while the people who tried to run away were shot dead about thirty meters away. After setting the house afire, the soldiers buried them on the spot where they had been killed.

On 28 May the soldiers returned to San Luis.

List of Those Massacred

Name	Age	Other
1. Eulalia Antonio	30	
2. Antonio Francisco Regino	8	1's son
3. Regino Francisco Antonio	2	1's son[13]
4. María Caño	15	1's daughter-in-law
5. Pablo	12	4's brother
6. Juan	2	4's brother[14]
7. Angelina Mateo	15	4's cousin
8. Francisco Caño	18	watchman
9. Diego Antonio	18	watchman

Civil Patrol Captures (30 May to 1 June)

After the massacre the army sent civil patrollers to San Luis to make two rounds: the first (30 May) with some soldiers and the second (1 June) alone. The aim was to capture people who had fled to the jungle and to destroy their belongings. Now that the villages had been razed, the army wanted to root out the people from the jungle, and the civil patrols were in a better position to do this because they were familiar with the area.

On the first round, seven people who had camped out on a plot of land were captured. According to a witness who lost his wife, Rosa Bernabé, they were trapped by the soldiers and gangs. When the witness realized that the soldiers were approaching he shouted out: "'They're coming, let's go.' Then my wife started to run, but she didn't manage to get away; the soldiers were shouting, 'Grab those wild boars!' and they began shooting at us." He managed to escape but the three women in his family were trapped by the army. The soldiers also captured another family of four in the same place. They were all taken to the military outpost in San Luis.

On the second round, another eight people were captured; seven belonged to Juan Regino's family, and there was also a young scout. This time the thirty civil patrollers did not come up the road but "arrived out of the blue," taking the hidden group by surprise. Two of Juan Regino's sons who were not with their father at the time recall what happened. They remember that the two of them drew near when they saw smoke from a distant fire: "The patrollers were burning down a small palm-leaf hut and had taken the people with them. They were already walking. There were a lot of people, a lot of civil patrollers, all Chiantecans. There weren't any soldiers. They were armed with machetes, sticks, and rifles. They burned all our clothing and our blankets. They burned our coffee, our cardamom, every-thing, everything we had. They destroyed the corn mill. And they took two harnesses and three mules with them. They also took the radio, tape re-corder, and a .22 shotgun."

Another witness tells how Juan Regino tried to defend himself before be-ing captured, wounding a civil patroller. He was ill and unable to escape, but he decided to hide out behind some rocks. The witness heard the tale from someone who saw it happen as he was searching for his wife, who had got lost in the jungle. "He saw it happen. The Chiantecans came down the hills. Juan Regino climbed up behind some rocks above his family. Per-haps his family was hiding under the rocks [in a cave], as they know the area. … It was a big rock, maybe they were inside. Suddenly the civil pa-trollers arrived and surrounded the rock. 'As I'm going to die anyway I'll try to kill one of them,' he must have thought. Who knows how the man heard them coming. So he climbed on top of the rock above Regino's family. Sud-denly, when they arrived, he started attacking. He got one but only wounded him. Then they began to shoot. As Regino's rifle could only shoot one bullet at a time, when would he be able to reload the gun? They arrived and captured him. They tied a rope around his neck and took him away."

The witnesses do not know whether Regino and his family survived. They were taken away alive but the relatives tell that "some say they were killed and burned on reaching the military outpost because everyone who is taken there is killed. We listened to Radio Maya (from Barillas) that year and there was no letter, no greetings, while we did get a letter from Justino."

On the same day another group of patrollers caught a young man who had climbed a tree. He was trying to observe the army from afar and did not realize that it was behind him. The patrollers did not come along the road but went higher up to surprise the people, who were expecting the soldiers to come from below. The young man, Juan Esteban, was taken to San Luis.

This was the first time that the civil patrollers carried out an operation of this kind in the area under consideration. This operation was carried out by civilians, not soldiers. These civilians, who were of a different ethnic group and from nearby villages, had recently been organized by the army. They used more refined and apt methods to surprise the people hidden in the jungle. The patrollers captured the people but did not kill them there and then, although their whereabouts have never been established. Their aim was to make living in the jungle impossible. They destroyed everything that was not easy to carry and stole their valuable goods and beasts of bur-den. Their tendency to destroy and rob earned the patrollers the name of "gangs," as they acted like highway robbers and thieves.

List of Those Captured[15]

Name	Age	Other
30 May		
1. Rosa Bernabé	25	
2. Eulalia Francisco		1's daughter
3. Ana Sebastián	40	1's mother
4. Pablo Francisco	25	
5. Minga Tomás	18	4's wife
6.	3	child
7.	1	child
1 June		
8. Juan Regino	35	
9. Eulalia Diego	35	8's wife
10. Francisco Regino Diego	14	8 & 9's son
11. Mario Regino Diego	12	8 & 9's son
12. Francisco Regino Diego	8	8 & 9's son
13. Mariquita Regino Diego	5	8 & 9's daughter
14. Micaela Regino Diego	1	8 & 9's daughter
15. Juan Esteban	25	

Death Through Illness

The people's flight from the army and civil patrols caused many children to die, as some of their mothers were lost in the jungle for weeks on end. I interviewed a woman, for example, who had escaped a barrage of bullets with four children; the oldest was seven and the youngest was twenty-three days old. After they had been lost a week the newborn girl died. "I no longer had any milk; I only drank water," the mother remembers. Her hands and feet were swollen, and she was thin and pale—"white as a handkerchief." Five weeks later, the woman was found half crazed: "Mine was a very dark path." She survived, but her remaining three children died in the camp.

Hundreds of children died during the first months in the jungle. A man in charge of one of the camps in Piedras Blancas remembers that 30 children died in his group of 280 people between July and September: "Some days two children would die. If a day passed without one dying, two would die the next. … A day didn't pass without someone dying, and one had to watch over the sick every night. … They started with diarrhea, with dysentery." The children's hands, feet, and faces would swell, and they would grow pale and thinner.

After the children had died, the older women started to die. A witness from the same camp recalls: "Facundo*'s mother's face began to swell. Her feet, her hands were all very swollen. She couldn't go on like that. She was full of water. She looked very white, like paper. It's anemia, I told myself, there was no food. The cold of the jungle gave her anemia. If only there were some medicine. Slowly she began to die. Chepe*'s wife died and was buried. Then Efraín*'s wife began to be poorly, she died and was buried there too. Then Gómez*'s wife suddenly died, and Mundo*'s wife died too. One of Mundo's daughters, who was already grown up, died too. Only adult women died. By then, only another three or four children died as well."

Their deaths were caused by the combination of lack of light and heat in the wet jungle, lack of shelter from the torrential rains, lack of varied food, lack of hygiene with so many people living crowded together, and lack of psychological adjustment to the new seminomadic way of life, which was full of sudden frights because of the army pursuing them. These deaths outnumbered those caused by the army directly, but they, too, are the result of the army repression. I realized too late in preparing this book that I had not gathered information around this central issue; thus I cannot back up what I have affirmed with concrete figures.

A Final Word

Coming to the end of this chapter, the reader may be asking the following question: Why did the people of Piedras Blancas, first the Mam and then the Q'anjob'al Indians, allow themselves to be caught after the experience of Cuarto Pueblo and, nearer still, of Xalbal? I believe there are several reasons:

1. The massacres of Xalbal and Cuarto Pueblo still seemed remote because the people did not experience the direct impact of seeing smoke from houses being burned down and because survivors did not escape along their paths.
2. April, the month prior to the new spate of massacres, had been peaceful, which gave the people a false sense of confidence.
3. When the army arrived on the San Luis estate, it did not massacre the *ladino* villagers nearby. Word spread that although it was forcing people to join the civil patrols, it was not killing anyone.
4. The massacres took place in May, which was planting time. The people were focusing all their attention on production, not on self-defense.
5. Many still believed in the rule of law and in the validity of their papers.

---

*Fictitious names have been used.

6. There was still a great lack of experience in facing situations of this kind.
7. Perhaps most important of all, the people did not have a clear attitude toward the army. They did not consider the soldiers enemies, as they turned out to be.

It is worth noting that none of the witnesses bring in religious factors in either of the Piedras Blancas massacres. The people's motives for staying were not shrouded in Charismatic ideology. This helps us to see that in the other massacres, where the religious factor was important, the Charismatic arguments were merely the expression of something deeper, which also affected the people massacred in Piedras Blancas, Cuarto Pueblo, and Xalbal: an undefined attitude toward the army or even a secret trust. But the army did not understand their lack of definition; it interpreted its manifestations as clear signs of hostility and thus massacred the people. Obviously I do not imply that the army was justified in massacring hostile civilian populations, as it also did but to a lesser extent.

Finally, for the first time we see the army using ethnic differences to divide and control the population and to massacre. Its use of *ladino* communities was facilitated by the treatment they had received from the guerrillas. Later on we shall see how the army began to use religion as a way of dividing communities, not by pitting Charismatic Catholics against traditional Catholics but by pitting Evangelicals against Catholics. The new head of state was a born-again Evangelical.

NOTES

1. I had access to four witnesses to the massacre. There were about 350 Q'echi' Indians in the camp. Fleeing from the army in the jungle for two days, they stopped to eat; when they got up to go they were ambushed by the army. The army started shooting and seven young men tried to resist, defending the population in an uneven match. The young men were killed. The rest were sick and helpless: "It was a large massacre, especially of children, women who were beginning to swell from hunger, and sick people." One blind man miraculously escaped. The massacre took place in July, a different time from when the Piedras Blancas massacre took place (May), as the amnesty period was over.

2. There must have been about 300 soldiers, as from San Luis they carried out offensives toward the east (one witness says 250 were in action in San Juan Ixcán, which is probably an exaggeration) and toward the west (a witness says 50 soldiers moved into Piedras Blancas, which is probably an underestimation). Furthermore, the outpost could not be left unattended. Perhaps the number of soldiers decreased as civil patrols were organized..

3. San Luis, like La Perla, was owned by Luis Arenas, the "tiger of Ixcán." As mentioned in Chapter 1, he was killed in 1975. The estates now belonged to his heirs.

4. Various *ladinos* who were army collaborators were killed by the guerrillas before May.

5. Through this message the witness learned of the army's reaction to La Nueva Comunidad.

6. Another witness says that there were a few patrollers. A witness from group 4 says that there were 50 soldiers, and another from Buena Vista says that there were 300. There could not have been 300 during a week's excursion because the military outpost was only forty-five minutes away. But I think there must have been more than 50—probably 75 or 100.

7. This is the testimony of the witness from Santa Agustina. I have filled in his account with others. No one saw firsthand how the people reacted except the three children who managed to escape; we will come to them presently.

8. As can be seen by the change of style, this witness is not the same as the Mam Indian quoted earlier. This Q'anjob'al witness heard the story from the man who found the girl. Both interviews were taped.

9. Genocide is realized when groups of people are killed "with the intention of destroying totally or partially a national, ethnic, racial or religious group as such" (United Nations 1948, article 2). I do not believe that the army tried to exterminate the entire indigenous population, as some then believed, because it makes up most of the country's agricultural work force. But it did want to exterminate entire groups of both Indians and *ladinos*. It is difficult to prove the genocidal nature of the massacres, as they can also be put down to political motives. However, I feel that the intention of genocide is present when the army kills to exterminate the biological seed of the group. See Falla 1984a, 1984b.

10. The Mam witness from Santa Agustina remembers, however, that his father-in-law's mother, who was 105, died of starvation ("she died more of hunger"). Because of her age she was unable to flee to the jungle, and those who did flee could not feed her well. They could bring her only *totoposte* (toasted and ground corn) but no corn refreshment to drink. She was not shot dead or burned because even the soldiers respected her life and left her two pieces of bread. But she died of hunger as a result of the scorched-earth offensive. Her name was Juana Domingo.

11. I have been unable to establish the precise date of the massacre—only that it was two or three days before 30 May.

12. The Spanish term is *banda*, as in a band of robbers.—TRANS.

13. Two younger sisters (ten and five years old) managed to escape. One of their older brothers was also not killed, because he was not there at the time. He was the person who testified, basing his story on his sisters' account. Their father was not killed, because he was out working.

14. The father of the three was wounded in the buttocks on returning from work. An eight-year-old brother managed to escape.

15. The main sources are, for 30 May, no. 1's husband, and for 1 June, two of no. 8's children.

CHAPTER 12

Place of Torment

(1982)

Torture by Fire

The witness had just been captured in the jungle. He was careless for a moment and they trapped him. After kicking and pushing him, they tied him up and tortured him in an empty house. It was military campaign torture; unsophisticated methods such as firebrands and fire were used while pursuing camps. In previous chapters we have heard of many people being burned alive. Now the witness tells what happened to him.[1]

At about 2:00 P.M. we reached a house and a school. They tied us up inside the house and set it on fire. What huge flames! When the lieutenant saw that the fire was blazing, he said to the soldiers: "Hang this shit up and make him tell us who's a rebel and where the people are." "That's me," I thought. "Where are the people?" he asked. "I don't control the people," I answered, "I don't know." So he told the soldiers: "Hang him up there." They had already tied me up so they hung me from a rafter. There I was, hanging. "Tell us," a soldier ordered me, and they kicked me in the stomach about twenty times. I lost my senses and felt I had died. I did feel the blows, though. Thanks to the grace of God I am deeply convinced that it's better to give up one's life than to squeal on people. "It's better for me to die!" I thought, and I never squealed on anyone.

They stuck my arm in the fire and burned it. I still have the scar! [We look at the scar on his arm.] And they burned the nape of my neck, my fingers, mouth, and the scar on my arm opened up, like a knife wound. But they could get nothing out of me.

Later, from afar. ... A sergeant moved back and said: "Are you a person or an animal?" And he brought out a knife and threw it at me from where he was; it went past my stomach. He threw another at my neck but it didn't hit me. Then he threw another, which stabbed me near my waist.

"May I see the scar?" I asked him. The witness unbuttoned his shirt and showed it to me.

He said to me, "Are you going to tell us who your companions are?" "I know nothing," I replied. Then I felt the scorching heat as he rammed the burning firebrand in as far as the bone. And again. Blood was streaming onto the floor, and my pants were all dirty and torn.

The lieutenant then said to the soldier: "Take him down now, you shit; what the fuck," and they lowered me onto the floor. I was left lying like a poor child by the door of the house. (Source 1)

El Quiché Barracks, a Slaughterhouse

They threw the witness into a helicopter and took him to El Quiché's main town to be interrogated by the officers. He was brought to "the barracks in the center of town, near El Quiché church." Then they shut him into a room that looked like a slaughterhouse. From there he could hear the *Gobernación* clock chime.[2]

A soldier took me to the second floor of the barracks. He shut me in a room. The room was like a slaughterhouse where people were killed, like a butcher's slaughterhouse for animals. The soldier left me there in a room full of blood. It was overflowing in blood and really did give me a fright.

"What do you mean, full of blood?" I asked him.

They'd killed a lot of people. I could tell by all the boots, shoes, sandals, belts, rubber sandals, too. There were a lot—the pile was almost a meter and a half high, and about three or four meters wide at the base. I thought to myself, who knows how many hundreds of people have been killed here. And that's why the room was full of blood; it had thickened. I couldn't really feel the wooden floorboard when I stood on it; it was like a mass of blood. The soldier left me there. "Sit here," he said. "OK." I had to sit in a pool of blood. You couldn't see the wooden floor, only blood.

Then he left me there. He went out and closed the door; I was locked in. I hadn't eaten for two days and was really thirsty from all the burning. I could bear it no longer, so when he came in again a little later and asked how I was, I said: "Forgive me, could I go drink some water?" "Are you thirsty?" he asked. "Yes," I said. "OK," he said, "I'll tell the boss." He came back again a bit later. "OK, go quickly" he told me. But I couldn't walk quickly—I could hardly drag myself to the outside sink. I drank about two gallons of water I think, more or less.

The following day some people came in to ask me: "And what about that place, Dimas [not his real name]?" I didn't say anything. "How are you?" "I'm OK." "You're fine, aren't you? And what did you dream last night?" "I didn't dream anything," I said. "You didn't dream of some dogs or coyotes?" he asked me. "No, I didn't dream of anything," I answered. "You didn't see some buz-

zards coming to peck at you or eat you here?" they asked. "No, I didn't see anything. What I see is the light of the sky," I said. "For crying out loud, I'm not
asking you that," and he left. He didn't like it when I said that. (Source 2)

Playa Grande Crematorium

The witness was taken to the military base in Playa Grande, where he was
to see even more horror: not only clotted blood but the butchers themselves.[3]

Before thirty days were up they took me to the place where heads are cut off.
There are two butchers. They have a star on their foreheads and a cross on
their arms and in the center of the cross a sword. They are never on duty, nor
do they patrol. They are the soldiers who only wait.

Three times they took me to the pit where they burn people. I'll never forget
it! They take the poor people outside and lead them to the pit. Before this they
write down each prisoner's name, where he is from, where he was captured.
The captain says, "Take Víctor out, take out Juan. ... Take them to the
butcher." And they take them out and first ask them if they want to go home,
free. "Don't worry," the captain tells them, "You're going home now, the truck
will take you part of the way." For example, if they were from San Lucas or
Raxujá or Chisec, they told them they would take them part of the way.

The captain brings out a big book, opens it on the table and reads aloud: "On
14 March, so-and-so was brought here at a neighbor's complaint, but now we
have decided he didn't do anything wrong and he will be forgiven. He is asked
not to join the ranks of subversion ... !" But afterward he threatens the prisoner: "Now, if the soldiers find you with the guerrillas, we'll send you to the pit.
There's a big pit just waiting!" They sign and then they put the hood over the
prisoner's head and kick him hard. Then they say: "Get into the truck," but he
falls and they throw him into the truck. That's the way they take down two or
three prisoners' information at a time.

They took me to the pit three times.

"Did they take down your information?"

They didn't take down my information—they only threw me into the truck and
took me to the banks of the Chixoy River, about half a kilometer down the
river. There is a field there and that's where the truck turns back. There is a big
two-by-two-meter pit there.

Other soldiers kick the poor people off the truck. Then who knows how the
butchers do it. They grab them, one by one. They make them kneel and wham,
they stab them. Then they take out the bloody knife and lick it!

The witness imitated the gesture of licking the knife.

"Delicious chicken," the soldiers, killers of people, say. And they grab another,
and another, and another ... and they go on killing them and throwing them
into the pit.

The soldiers grab firewood, because there is chopped firewood right there. They dump the people into the pit, and throw more and more firewood over them. They pour gasoline over the firewood. They drench the firewood with gasoline. Then they stand back and light a match and throw it in. When it reaches the firewood, it explodes like a bomb. Bang, … a huge fire. The whole mouth of the pit is full of flames. It burns for about twenty minutes. The firewood still moves, because the dead are still kicking. Their spirits are alive. When the soldiers see that the fire is dying down, they pour on more gasoline! In half an hour the fire dies. And the corpses have become pure ash. Their hands crumble. What a lot of lard there is on their bodies! The fire sizzles with the lard and soon consumes the poor people.

They took me to see the pit so I would give them information, but, thank God, I didn't change my story. (Source 1)

Underground for Five Months

The witness was held in a small hole dug out of a hillside in Playa Grande. He was kept there incommunicado and imprisoned for five months. They took him out only once every two weeks to dunk him into the river.

I was confined in a hole. Many say it was a cell, but I say it was a hole. I was locked in there for five months.

"Was it a hole going downward?" I asked him.

No, it was like a hole in a wall. There was a hill there and the hole was in the hill, like a cave. It was very dark and closed off by a metal door. There was no light; it was pitch dark. They shut me into that hole. It was very low, about a meter high. I had to kneel, I couldn't stand up.

"How wide was it?" I asked the witness.

I think it wasn't even twelve inches wide, because my shoulders and chest just squeezed in. I couldn't turn around.

"And how deep was it?" I asked him.

It was … well, I could sleep lying down. About a meter high and twelve or thirteen inches wide.

I was like this for five months, almost without food. They gave me half a tortilla for breakfast. Sometimes they'd give me a whole one. The good soldiers would give me a whole one. And when the really mean soldiers were on duty, they'd scarcely give me half a tortilla. Other soldiers took pity on me. What saved my life there was water, and because I had a gallon can, that plastic can helped me out while I was in the hole. I'd ask … I'd knock on the door and say when the soldiers came up: "Excuse me soldier, I'd like some water." "You want some water? Are you thirsty?" "Yes," I answered. "Then drink your urine," he said, "and if you're hungry, eat your shit." I just kept quiet. He didn't give me any water. And sometimes the door would be slightly ajar and I could see a bit of light. I could see a streak of light. I could just make it out—the space was about an inch and a half wide. That crack of light gave me life.

The soldiers went off duty and others arrived. When they arrived I again knocked on the door, asking for water. And the soldiers asked: "Do you have something to put it in?" "Yes, here is my can." "OK," they told me. And they went to bring me water in the can.

I could hardly stand it over five months. But God always brought me light. I would weep from time to time, sometimes every day. I would be sitting in the hole when I would see a light from above, like a light bulb, but it wasn't a light bulb. It was as if the cell suddenly lit up, as if a light went on, and then he would speak to me: "Look Dimas, don't be sad" he would tell me. "What you are going to do is follow this light, this star." And he showed me the morning star. I would look at it for a good while. "Thank you," I'd say to him. But to thank him I wanted to see clearly who was speaking to me. There was nothing, the light would go out again.

So I thought it was God's angel talking to me. I always trusted that God would liberate me from the punishment I was suffering. (Source 2)

The Great Liberation

The army took the witness out of the cell in the hope that he would help them patrol the jungle and turn people in from the camps. On one of the outings he managed to escape, shouting for joy and insulting the soldiers, who fired a shower of bullets and bombs at him to no avail.

At 6:00 A.M. we started marching again. We walked about twenty *cuerdas* [half a kilometer]. There was thick, short undergrowth on both sides of the path. Further on I saw a large hill and thought: "Maybe it's clearer." It was clear and there was a place where one could run.

"From here on let God's will be done," I said to myself and made the sign of the cross on my forehead, as I had decided that I would either get out or be killed there. I said to the civil patroller: "I'm going to have a shit." About fifty soldiers were walking in front, another fifty behind, and about twenty-five soldiers were scattered along the path. "I'm going to have a shit, I can't hold on any longer," I said and put down the pack. "You, Dimas, where are you going?" they asked me. "I'm going to have a shit," I told them. "Quickly, you pig," the soldiers said to me.

The next thing they saw was that I was ten meters away. They said to me: "That's enough. Sit down!" But I didn't stop. Maybe I was twenty meters away when they started firing. "Sit down!" they yelled.

But as I went on, I came to a slope and rolled down. The motherfuckers were behind, following me. When they reached the slope they started shooting. But I went the other way, to the right, and climbed up a hill. I heard them swearing at each other. Who knows what they were saying; they were beside themselves!

I was tired of running, so I had a rest. When I recovered I felt so proud of myself. I was calm. They were still swearing at each other, and I shouted out: "Wow! Motherfuckers, shits, bastards, idiots, bugger off!" And they shouted back: "Dimas, you bastard, you shit, you got away!" They started firing heavily, and then a bomb went off near me. "What the hell," I said, and I got the hell out. (Source 1)

A Religious Experience

Both witnesses (Source 1 and Source 2), intertwined as one, illustrate a kind of religious experience very different from that of the Charismatic Catholics. Two main themes are involved. The first is the link between resistance to torture and imprisonment and God's grace in giving the prisoners strength. The resistance is motivated by the prisoner's love for his people, and he is prepared to sacrifice his own life for them. He interprets his love for his people as a favor and a grace of God. The witness says: "Thanks to the grace of God I am deeply convinced that it's better to give up one's life than to squeal on people."

The second theme is that liberation through death is God's work. The witness's visions, which resemble those of the Charismatic Catholics, promise him liberation from the frightful dungeon, and this promise brings him comfort during such great suffering. When the promise becomes a real possibility, trust in God's liberating force is symbolized by the sign of the cross the witness makes at the decisive moment between life or death, when he will either escape or be killed. The act of escaping is like a prayer, so the witness crosses himself before venturing forth.

The testimonies express the religious experience of two prisoners who escaped from the army. They are personal testimonies and each one has its own seal: one is sober (S1) whereas the other is very imaginative (S2). However, both reflect the people's belief that the force of God has freed them from death. If the Charismatic Catholics' reflection was that one had to submit oneself passively to the will of God, the prisoners' reflection was that God's protecting force was realized through their resistance and actions, not by waiting passively.

Whether the reader is a religious believer or not, the testimonies are an annunciation of life before the darkness of death. They proclaim that the power of death (the crematorium, the bloody slaughterhouse, torture by fire, the underground dungeons) can and is overcome by the power of life.

NOTES

1. In this chapter I have intertwined parts of two valuable testimonies (Sources 1 and 2) as though they were the same witness. The differences in narrative style make it clear that there are two persons, particularly because one testimony was taped and

the other was not. But the content of the accounts makes us forget these differences. The moment comes when one does not know which voice is speaking. I have not been specific about dates and places of capture to protect their identities.

2. Guatemala has twenty-two departments. The highest civilian authority in each department is the governor (*gobernador*).

3. Some of this testimony is given in the Introduction.

CHAPTER 13

Paths Toward Dawn: Population in Resistance and Refugees

(June to October 1982)

Under the shadow's heavy mantle
There also hides
The sure path towards dawn.

—Alaíde Foppa,
"Aunque es de noche"
("Even If It Is Night")

It would seem that all was lost for the civilian population during 1982: The "shadow's mantle" had been heavy indeed. But through the darkness, as we have shown, is found "the sure path towards dawn."

Four factors contributed to making the shadow's mantle heavier for the people of Ixcán Grande: (1) The most important cooperative, Mayalán, was burned down on 7 and 8 June; (2) a military outpost was established on 13 July in the far northwestern corner of the area, in Ixtahuacán Chiquito; (3) there was intense and cruel army patrolling from the new military outpost as well as from San Luis, in the southeast of Ixcán Grande; and (4) the creation took place of the first successful strategic hamlet in the Evangelical village, Samaritano, at the end of October, from which extensive and intensive patrols would be carried out to capture or massacre groups hidden in the jungle.

The army action in the area was supported by the consolidation of the coup d'état of Ríos Montt, who on 9 June put an end to the ruling military junta and became head of state. On 1 July he declared a state of siege after a month-long amnesty. The state of siege and the new scorched-earth policy in the neighboring department, Huehuetenango, also meant greater persecution of the civilian population in Ixcán.

As we shall see, the increase of army control had the effect of strengthening the population's determination and conviction to resist. It also gave rise to an avalanche of people fleeing from Guatemala and seeking refuge in Mexico at the end of October. Both of these factors contributed to the creation of a new society.

The Burning of Mayalán (7 and 8 June)

The army took over Mayalán in a new kind of operation that combined various patrols. A single battalion had been used in Cuarto Pueblo and Xalbal; in Piedras Blancas and its environs, only a military company had been used. In contrast, three patrols descended on Mayalán.[1] One patrol, made up of about sixty men, was taken by helicopter to a center called Altamira, to the east of Mayalán. Another arrived from a farm estate to the west of the Ixcán River. And the third approached from Cuarto Pueblo and Los Angeles in the north.[2] Meanwhile, another patrol was making its way from San Luis, burning houses and pursuing people in the centers to the south of Mayalán, which gave rise to a mass exodus of more than a thousand people, who headed north.

The army entered Mayalán but was unable to massacre anyone because the town was empty. It razed the town to the ground, burning everything it could. The following witness recounts the buildings that were burned down, remembering with pride the progress the Mayalán cooperative had made:

> On 8 June the Mayalán cooperative was burned down. The cooperative store was very big—it had three rooms. The convent was next door, and next to it the cooperative's offices and the office that had been rented from INACOP.[3] Inside the store there were two refrigerators and a large amount of materials that David, the engineer used. All of these were burned.
>
> The priest had a lot of furniture in the convent. We were hardly able to take anything out. The cooperative office near the store was made of cement blocks and had a metal roof. They burned it down. We had a typewriter, tables, and files; they were all taken away, it seems. Some people took their land titles and buried them.
>
> The safe, weighing more than 100 pounds, and documents were burned. The largest warehouse, which all the cooperatives had built together, was burned down. All the wood stored there for another building was burned. Two

buildings, the parish kitchen and teachers' dormitory, were also burned down. The largest church, which was a big building, was burned down, and the small house next to it, where children studying at the parish school slept. They burned down the health center, a wooden building with a corrugated asbestos roof built by the army. The roof cracked when the building was burned down. The six-classroom state school, built entirely by the local inhabitants, was completely burned down. In front of the school was the parish clinic, a pretty wooden house with a corrugated metal roof and a cement floor; this too was burned down. Next to the clinic was the two-room court, this was burned down completely.[4]

Mayalán was burned down, but no one was killed. The factors that contributed to the population's successful self-defense included the following:

1. The people saw or heard various signs of the army's approach, such as the Piedras Blancas massacre and the burning down of Santa Agustina and other Mayalán centers (center 4).
2. The operation did not have a surprise element—the people saw and heard helicopters bringing in the troops.
3. The people were more organized before leaving for the jungle.
4. The dreadful conditions of the mass exodus of people from the south had a great emotional impact on the inhabitants of Mayalán. A man from Mayalán who saw them go by recalls, "I saw them from the side of the path. They were crying. My heart went out to them, and I wept for these people; so many children crying!"

New Military Outpost: Ixtahuacán Chiquito
(13 July)

A month after destroying Mayalán, a patrol of about 150 men left San Luis to Mayalán and followed the Ixcán River to the Mexican border. Ixtahuacán Chiquito, on the border, lies on the corner of the river and the border. The people living on the plots of land were all originally from San Ildefonso Ixtahuacán. The army had not patrolled the area since 1981. Now it would station itself there, ending the scorched-earth offensive it had started in March. The army set up an outpost and tried to form a strategic hamlet;[5] the attempt failed because the population fled.

The patrol failed in its attempt to surround the people still in their houses, as those civilians keeping watch realized from the cattle's movements that soldiers were in a nearby pasture. They warned the people, who promptly escaped to the jungle. Some also crossed the border that same day.

Once the soldiers took over the town, they began sweep operations in the jungle. During the following fortnight, six people died in the sweeps.

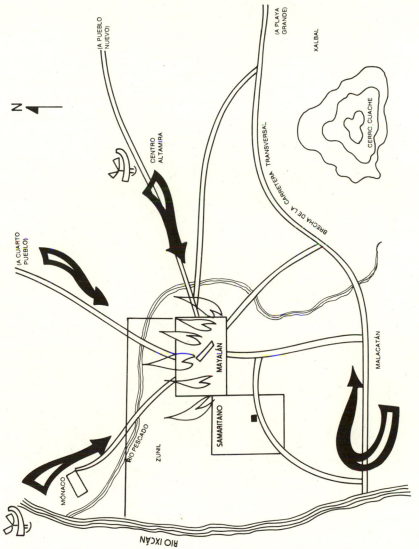

(A PUEBLO NUEVO)

CENTRO ALTAMIRA

N

(A CUARTO PUEBLO)

(A PLAYA GRANDE)

XALBAL

CERRO CUACHE

BRECHA DE LA CARRETERA TRANSVERSAL

MÓNACO

RIO PESCADO

ZUNIL

MAYALÁN

SAMARITANO

MALACATÁN

RIO IXCÁN

Mayalán

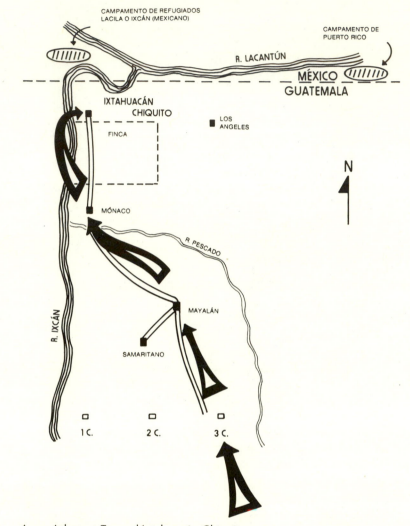

Army Advance Toward Ixtahuacán Chiquito

First, a woman and her son were captured when the army took a small camp of fifteen people by surprise. The woman and her son were unable to escape because she was "washing clothes in a small stream." Second, three men fell to the army in the same camp. Not realizing the soldiers were there, they entered the camp on hearing the crying of the boy who had been captured the day before. A fourth who was with them survived, though he was wounded by a bullet. Traveling from another camp, the four arrived at the small camp in search of food on 24 July. Third, a man was ambushed in a house where he was to make contact with someone bringing provisions. The army shot him dead, put him in a rice granary, and set the building afire on 26 July. Of the six victims, his was the only body to be found by the witnesses. (Their names appear later in the chapter.)[6]

The army burned Ixtahuacán Chiquito on 26 July. It burned down houses, the school, the only church (the Catholic church), the meeting room, and other buildings. Because it completely lacked popular support, it left nothing standing that could be used for a strategic village. The metal sheeting from the burnt buildings was used to set up their outpost.

The blow dealt to the victims and the burning down of the town gave rise to a wave of refugees from Ixtahuacán Chiquito to the CILA[7] camp in Mexico next to the Ixcán River. Almost a hundred families, including those who had crossed the border when the army occupied the town, sought refuge in Mexico.

When the army realized that there was no one around, it began to patrol further afield in an attempt to control two neighboring towns, Mónaco in the south and Los Angeles in the east. Ixtahuacán Chiquito became a center for patrolling platoons coming from different directions. An informant from Mayalán remembers that the movements in August and September included "a patrol that came from the bridge [over the Xalbal River] to Cuarto Pueblo; another from the bridge to Pueblo Nuevo and Los Angeles; a third from San Luis to Mayalán and Mónaco; and a fourth from San Luis to the first center and across the river banks to Mónaco. They all gathered in Ixtahuacán."

The soldiers divided the area into squares, apparently to take possession of Ixcán symbolically. They divided not only the razed villages but also the jungle and the farm plots, where thousands of people were hiding. The army, which at first did not go into the jungle but only patrolled on the roads and paths, now began to act more like the guerrillas, venturing into the undergrowth with the aid of only a compass.

The result was not massive massacres, or even selective killings, but the death of those who occasionally came upon the army. Following is an incomplete list of victims who died as the army combed the jungle.

List of Victims from Army Patrollings (July to October 1982)

Name	Age	Place	Date
Patrolling from Ixtahuacán Chiquito			
1. Marta Jacinta		Ixtahuacán Chiquito	23 July
2. Juan Pedro Esteban	8	Ixtahuacán Chiquito	23 July
3. Alonso Jacinto	30	Ixtahuacán Chiquito	24 July
4. Juan Domingo	25	Ixtahuacán Chiquito	24 July
5. Emilio Hernández	20	Ixtahuacán Chiquito	24 July
6. Juan Ordóñez	20	Ixtahuacán Chiquito	26 July

Other Patrols

7. A man	60	center 1	about 20 Sept.
8. An old man		center 1	about 20 Sept.
9. A woman	21	center 1	about 20 Sept.
10. A woman		La Diez	about 20 Sept.
11. A man		center 1	about 20 Sept.
12. Nicolás Mendoza		Mayalán	21 Sept.
13. Francisca Mendoza	15	Mayalán	21 Sept.
14. Francisca Morales		Nueva Esperanza	6 Oct.
15. Rosa López	12	Nueva Esperanza	6 Oct.
16. Amparo López	6	Nueva Esperanza	6 Oct.
17. Alejandro López	4	Nueva Esperanza	6 Oct.
18. José Ordóñez	45	Buena Vista	13 Oct.
19. Clemente Matías		Samaritano	20 Oct.

On Their Way to Mexico

20. Modesta Aquilón	32	Río Pescado	25 Oct.
21.	1	Río Pescado	25 Oct.
22. Alfonso López		Pueblo Nuevo	23 Oct.
23. Pedro Domingo Pérez		Pueblo Nuevo	26 Oct.
24. José López		Pueblo Nuevo	26 Oct.

Notes: This list is not exhaustive.

Numbers 12 and 13: According to another source, the date was 21 August. If the latter were correct, numbers 7–11 would also correspond to August.

Number 22: According to another source, he was killed on "Friday, 23 October," but Friday was 22 October.

To simplify the lists, I have included the names of 5 people (numbers 20–24) who were killed on the way to Mexico.

For those from Ixtahuacán (numbers 1–6), the source is a man from there.

For the other victims there are different sources, usually from the places where the victims were killed.

The death of these victims frightened and disheartened much of the surviving population, though others were outraged. After the loss of loved ones and also crops (both in the fields and already harvested, such as that in the rice granary), it is hardly surprising that groups abandoned the jungle and sought refuge in Mexico: "We decided to go to Mexico. We didn't return home, or even go to have a look. We made our way to Mexico, as we could no longer live there," a witness from Buena Vista says.

Samaritano, a Strategic Hamlet (end of October)

Remember that the army tried unsuccessfully to form a strategic hamlet in Los Angeles in March and in Ixtahuacán Chiquito in July with indigenous people from Ixcán Grande. It was successful only in San Luis and in two other *ladino* communities. It had played on ethnic differences in San Luis; now it would resort to religious divisions at a national level to form a strategic hamlet.

Samaritano, made up of a group of farm lots, was a project started by the Evangelical church. The army sought church support by inviting, through Radio Maya, the Evangelical radio station in Barillas, the village's former inhabitants to a meeting. But most of its former inhabitants were in the jungle, and only eight families (10 percent of the village inhabitants) had returned to the highlands. According to an Evangelical witness from Samaritano, those hiding in the jungle did not respond: "None of us answered the army's call." Only some of the families who had fled to the highlands returned on the army's request.

Before the army entered Samaritano, it came upon two camps and on 20 October killed a man, Clemente Matías from Todos Santos, who was wearing the red pants typically worn by men of Todos Santos. For many, his death was a clear example of how the army was lying when it said it was not going to kill the civilian population. Army persecution around Samaritano made many flee to Mexico at the end of October so as not to form part of the strategic hamlet.

So the hamlet was formed with people from other places. In October 1983, United Nations special rapporteur Lord Colville visited Samaritano. According to Lord Colville, there were 160 inhabitants, about a third of the village's former population of close to 500 (Colville of Culross 1984).

The following can be seen on the map, drawn by a witness: the barbed wire surrounding the village; two watchtowers, one looking out toward the hill and the other toward the river; the outpost, made up of three houses bordering the landing strip; the soccer field, used by helicopters for landing; one of the Evangelical churches, on the corner of the soccer field; and the houses, all built in rows. The witness has drawn the cattle and banana trees inside the enclosed village.

The Experience of the Communities of Population in Resistance

Many people fled to refuge in October, but others stayed in resistance, creating a new kind of society. The most novel change was probably their means of production. The leap forward, in response to the army persecution, would transform the entire life of the community, which was made up of a network of camps in the jungle. Many factors were involved in this transformation; I will mention a few.

First, the destination of their product changed. As the months went by, the corn stored from the previous harvest came to an end. A witness recalls, "The harvest that everyone had stored away came to an end and then

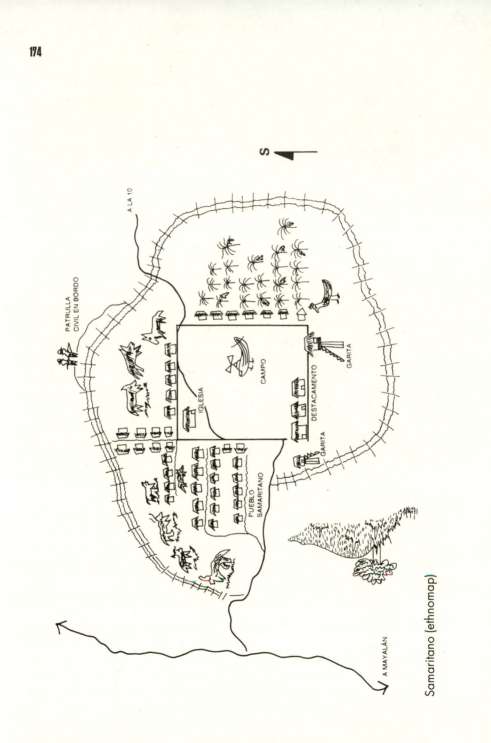

Samaritano (ethnomap)

we began to speak of a true collective." Remember that in the months immediately following the massacres, the corn stored away was still considered family property and the sowing in May, though carried out collectively (people took turns working on each person's field), was still intended for each family's private consumption, not for the group as a whole. However, when the corn from the previous harvest came to an end, the groups decided to store the new harvest collectively, rather than in family granaries, for the consumption of the entire camp. The change was also brought about by the exodus of the refugees, which forced many to leave their fields unharvested. The harvest went to the group that stayed. The group was thus strengthened and collective work became more consolidated.

Second was the proliferation of wild animals. For security reasons, the camps decided to stop hunting, as shooting could attract the army's attention to the camp. Once the hunting stopped, the number of wild animals grew, which was a problem because *cochemontes* (a kind of wild boar) and *tepescuintles* (a small, furry animal) finished the corn in the fields. With the increase in wild animals, the system of taking turns cultivating each person's plot of land became unfeasible because individual attention to fields dispersed the people and put them in danger. It also meant that the group had to work more. So it was safer and more economical to look after a single large field than lots of small ones. Because of the wild animals, the groups decided to plant larger areas, thus abandoning the previous method. By doing this, the restriction of reciprocity, that is, doing the same amount of work on each person's field, was lifted, and the group grew.

Third was the mobility of the camps. Given the army persecution, the camps had to move around, sometimes for months on end, and the people had to cultivate lands that were not their own or the group's. And as a result of the repression many camps divided, and the size of the groups diminished when some of their members sought refuge in Mexico. Some camps joined together and formed new groups. Thus, although the core assemblage of people might have remained in its center, other people who did not belong to the center joined it. The result of the internal migration (of camps or families) meant that the sense of ownership of plots or communal land was increasingly lost. Instead, a wider relationship was established whereby the displaced groups would claim the right over lands whenever these were needed.

The fourth factor contributing to the transformation of the community was the solidarity in difficult circumstances. Solidarity extended from one camp to another because some camps, instead of moving elsewhere once their crops had been destroyed by the army, requested that other groups give them corn. When help was given, the camp in need would send men to harvest corn sown by the others as if it were their own.

Fifth was the distribution of the product. Shortages and the division of labor made the just distribution of the product important. This, among other reasons, made it necessary for one person to be in charge of distribution. This person had to calculate how much each family would receive, depending on the number and age of their members. People involved in nonproductive tasks, such as scouts, messengers, teachers, health promoters, and camp leaders, also received rations. A man responsible for a camp recalls, "If periods went by when there was no corn, we rationed bananas and limes. You couldn't just put the fruit out for people to take, as some would take more than others. Everything was fairly divided." Widows and orphans, like those involved in nonproductive tasks, were also supported by the collective.

Sixth was the flexibility of the collective. The collective was not rigidly imposed: The camp members decided at their meetings that collective work should constitute an improvement, not a burden. Examples of the flexibility included, most important, the designation of one day a week (Saturday) to be free for individual or family chores, such as growing beans for family consumption or cleaning one's own coffee shrubs. The tastes and customs of different indigenous groups from the highlands were respected (for instance, some liked green beans whereas others liked them dried). These differences explain in part why cooking was carried out in families, not collectively. It was understood that if someone harvested a bit of coffee and sold it in Mexico, as the *parcelistas* on the border had always done, the money from its sale would belong to that person, even though coffee beans were also sold collectively to the Mexican buyer by the group's representative in charge of sales.

Life accompanying the collective mode of production would be a book in itself. The army massacred, but from death something new emerged. A witness says, speaking of the destruction of crops and people: "One dies, but more are already on their way. ... The army cut the banana trees to the ground, but new shoots sprang up. It also cut down the cassava that had just been planted, but it also started sprouting again. The same happened to the sugar cane: The soldiers cut it to bits, but it began to grow again. More appear. That's what happens to us—one dies, but more are on their way."

The Experience of the Refugees

The experience of the refugees also gave root to a new society. We have seen how they were forced to leave. They grouped together in three main areas and formed large camps: Chajul, Puerto Rico, and CILA, next to the Xalbal, Lacantún, and Ixcán rivers respectively. The three were very near the border, but in 1984 the refugees were forcibly relocated to Campeche and Quintana Roo. The crisis made many decide to return to Guatemala to join the communities in resistance.

What seeds for a new society can be found in the experience of the refugees? There are four main aspects: community life, political struggle, the strengthening of a national consciousness, and the assimilation of the suffering caused by repression. First, community life is based on collective work, not so much in production but in building infrastructure in the camps. It is also based on the distribution of rations from UNHCR (United Nations High Commissioner for Refugees [Alto Comisionado de las Naciones Unidas para Refugiados, ACNUR]) through the Mexican organization COMAR (Mexican Commission of Aid to Refugees [Comisión Mexicana al Ayuda a Refugiados]). Weekly rations to groups and families have refined the feeling of distributive justice and have long been the force that has best structured the camps.

Finally, community life is based on the need to maintain the group's cohesion to ensure that its demands at different levels of community integration are respected by the host country. The first level of integration is that of the different linguistic and ethnic groups; the second level is the community of camps in each Mexican state; and the third is the community of all the refugees in Mexico. The demand that their rights be respected has brought the refugee community together most. Although the refugees had experienced community life before leaving for Mexico, both as indigenous communities in the Guatemalan highlands and as cooperatives in the jungle, in exile this experience has become more vast and deep rooted.

Second, the experience of acting politically has been enriching, combining a mixture of diplomacy, direct action, and peaceful resistance. The refugees have learned to use the scarce power they have. They have done so in the following ways, among others: negotiating with the authorities, seeking delay mechanisms, showing willingness to compromise, resorting to alternative national and international forces, denouncing injustice, resisting forced relocation, and moving to places nearby without permission. Their struggle has been intelligent and versatile, particularly in their relations with the Mexican government. Their negotiations with the Guatemalan government have centered primarily on the issue of return; they have developed political discernment so as not to be deceived. And the refugees have affirmed their autonomy as far as possible in Guatemala's internal conflict, despite the army calling them subversives. They have suffered internal divisions intended to weaken their cohesion and resistance; this has made the identification with the refugee community a freer and more conscious choice. This likens the refugee community to a popular organization with democratically chosen representatives. In contrast, the freedom to choose one's membership does not occur in communities where one is born, as it is understood that one belongs and will always belong there.[8]

Third, the strengthening of a national consciousness is another important experience. When persecuted peasants cross the border, they are immediately given a new label, unknown to them before, and a new identity: that of refugee. Recalls a refugee, "We were told: 'You are refugees.' We didn't know that there was a name for being in another country." This new identity has contributed greatly to their identification as Guatemalans. And it will remain important in the future, as it has meant that to achieve a wider sense of identification one must identify not only almost exclusively with the community where one was born, with one's ethnic group, and with the area from which one was forced to emigrate but also with the nation. Guatemala, far from being a consolidated nation, is fragmented by people who refer to their municipality as the center of the universe. It is an important leap forward when these identities are no longer barriers but form part of and contribute to a national consciousness. This national consciousness has been strengthened by the refugees' political struggle, both in distinguishing themselves as Guatemalans in Mexico and in negotiating with and confronting the Guatemalan government. Pressure is put on the refugees by the Mexican government and by the circumstance of living peacefully in Mexico to erode such consciousness so that they will stop being refugees and integrate into their host country as Mexicans. The dilemma of the refugees is therefore whether they should be recognized as Guatemalans. Such a critical situation makes nationality an existential question to be answered by the people themselves.

Fourth, being in refuge has allowed these individuals to assimilate the experience of repression recounted by the witnesses in this book. Their situation has given them a relative respite that has allowed them to think about, comment on, and record the terrible things they suffered. Once assimilated, the experience of repression exerts a considerable influence on the future. It is not merely a question of remembering things that have happened but of creating a project for the future. That is when the time of refuge comes to an end and the temptation to change one's nationality can be overcome only by the will to return. But the refugees feel that if they return they would not be betraying those ideals that have cost so much bloodshed.

There is much common ground shared by the refugees and the communities in resistance, as both suffered the massacres described in this book.

NOTES

1. There were two for sure. Only one witness refers to the patrol that was on its way from Cuarto Pueblo.

2. No information is available as to the number of men in the second and third patrols; there were probably about sixty, as in the first.

3. INACOP: The National Institute of Cooperatives (Instituto Nacional de Cooperativas).

4. During July and August the army also burned down Samaritano, near Mayalán (10 and 11 July), Ixtahuacán Chiquito (13 July), Mónaco (at the end of July), and Los Angeles (August). All these villages were in the west, near the Ixcán River. Finally, according to some witnesses, Pueblo Nuevo was burned down in August, since it had not been razed in March.

5. I know of the army's intentions because, before arriving, the soldiers found some peasants near Mónaco and told them to go to Ixtahuacán Chiquito the following day to be organized by the military.

6. The international media reported the six victims (*New York Times*, 9 October 1982). Alan Riding interviewed the refugees from Ixtahuacán Chiquito in the CILA camp in Mexico (see note 7).

7. CILA: Comisión Internacional de Límites y Aguas. A station where the river's water level is gauged.

8. But there are certain parameters of flexibility in the community where one is born: One can choose to leave or to remain. Think of those who emigrate, those who leave to marry, and others.

Conclusions

The Victims

I have documented the cases of 773 civilian victims of Guatemalan counter-insurgency in Ixcán between 1975 and 1982. Although my study is not exhaustive, particularly for the eastern part of Ixcán, I estimate the total number of victims to be between 1,000 and 1,200. That is, between 2 percent and 2.7 percent of the total population.[1]

The victimization occurred in two stages: selective repression (1975–1981) and the scorched-earth offensive (1982). The zones can be broken down between east and west of the Xalbal River. The categories of repression include killings and forced disappearance. The following table synthesizes the information presented in this book.

	Date	Western Ixcán		Eastern Ixcán	
		Killed	*Disappeared*	*Killed*	*Disappeared*
First Stage (1975–1981)					
Xalbal	1975		15		1
Church	1976	7^2			
Captures	1979–1981	5	17		
San José	1980			17	
La 20					
Cuarto Pueblo	1981	10	9		
Subtotals					
Victims		22	41	17	1
Per zone			63		18
First stage				81	
Second Stage (1982)					
East	13–28 Feb.			117	

	Date	Western Ixcán		Eastern Ixcán	
		Killed	*Disappeared*	*Killed*	*Disappeared*
Nueva Concepción	14 Mar.	35	3		
Cuarto Pueblo	14–17 Mar.	324			
Pueblo Nuevo	29 Mar.	1			
Xalbal	31 Mar.	28		10	
Piedras Blancas	18 May	55			
Piedras Blancas	27 May	9			
Piedras Blancas	30 May	15			
Canijá	6 July			71	
Patrolling	July–Oct.	24			
Subtotals					
Victims		476	18	198	0
Per zone			494		198
Second stage				692	
Total				773	

Counterinsurgency policies continued over the following years, and numerous and indiscriminate massacres were carried out, no longer in towns and villages but in the camps hidden in the jungle.[3] Many families were captured and killed; the army bombed the camps or fired machine guns from the air, threw mortars at them, and destroyed their crops with machetes. Conditions brought illnesses and hunger, and many people died, particularly between 1983 and 1985. But this study reaches as far as only 1982.

To estimate the number of victims in the country as a whole, I concluded that the proportion of victims in relation to the area's total population is greater in zones where people could not seek refuge across the border than in Ixcán (for example, in Rabinal, San Martín Jilotepeque, and the Ixil Triangle).

The Stages of Counterinsurgency

I have referred to two stages of counterinsurgency: selective repression, 1975–1981, and scorched earth, 1982.

The first stage contains different phases that help us chart the increase in repression. The first, in 1975, was the attempt to violently eradicate the guerrilla forces. The first abductions were carried out in Xalbal at this time in an attempt to kill off the burgeoning insurgency by severing it at its roots. The death of Father Woods and the people accompanying him, which was widely believed not to have been an accident, belongs to this period, although it took place in 1976.

The second phase, 1976–1981, is characterized by civic action. The army increased its presence in the cooperatives, made landing strips, set up outposts, and tried to appear benevolent by helping to market the local population's agricultural products through the use of planes. This phase begins to break down during 1979, with an increasing number of abductions. The impact of the Sandinista revolution in Nicaragua contributes to the collapse of this phase.

The third phase comprises preparations for the army's scorched-earth offensive. This began in Ixcán with the combat on 30 April 1981 in Cuarto Pueblo. The rebel action made the military abandon their civic action, although several weeks later the army inaugurated the health center in Pueblo Nuevo. Yet it blew up the center a few weeks after that, blaming the action on the guerrillas. The differences between the army officers advocating civic action and those in favor of military action became apparent: The colonel in charge of civic action in Ixcán was labeled a Communist and a guerrilla by officers and troops alike.

The third phase in turn divides into two parts: During the first part, the army abandoned civic action but remained in the area to punish the population with escalating repression. During the second part the army was absent from the area and concentrated in Guatemala's central highlands to start its scorched-earth offensive. The date that divides the two parts is 17 November 1981, when the army left Ixcán. During the months that the army was absent there was a kind of popular insurrection in the area: Empty army outposts were burned down and landing strips were sabotaged. For the army these actions confirmed the need for scorched earth and the massive and indiscriminate extermination of entire villages and towns.

The first stage comes to an end at this point, giving way to the second stage, the scorched-earth offensive. The army returned to the area at the beginning of February 1982 and began its systematic offensive from east to west, in an operation to "sweep" the rebels and their sympathizers among the civilian population toward the Mexican border. (Sweep operations are a standard technique in counterinsurgency manuals.)

In the period examined in this book, the second stage consisted of two phases. The first was scorched-earth or sweep operations that did not try to control the population, and the second phase was sweep operations that did. The first phase, February and March, included the army's trek through the eastern part of Ixcán during February and through the west (the area examined here) in March. During March there was a hiatus of a few days in the army's bloody fervor: It distinguishes the period previous to the coup d'état of 23 March from the period following the coup.

The second phase began in May, as the army was absent during April. One can speculate that the army used this absence to prepare a more elaborate counterinsurgency campaign as part of the National Security and Development Plan drawn up by the new ruling military junta. A characteristic of the plan was the army's attempt to control the population by forming strategic hamlets and civil patrols, an attempt that did not succeed in most cases. When the local people fled or did not heed the army's call, the army retaliated by razing the empty villages or, when the villages were not deserted, massacring their inhabitants with the aim of genocide, as in the terrible case of the Mam indians in Piedras Blancas. During this stage, sometimes with the aid of the *ladino* inhabitants from some of the communities, the army searched out hidden camps, combed the jungle, and generally killed anyone it came across. This time was a watershed for the local population: Some stayed in resistance, defending their lives and lands, and some sought refuge in Mexico, defending only their lives. This is as far as we come in this book.

Increasing Violence

Counterinsurgency violence escalated in geometric proportions. It began with abductions that were either secret or open (in full view at the marketplace) and progressed to sporadic spates of abductions (with many in the same month) or abductions carried out on groups of victims, as in the case of the cooperative members in Cuarto Pueblo. Then there were hidden individual killings and only occasional open killings, when a civilian victim was passed off as a guerrilla. The escalation of repression gave way to selective massacres, that is, the killing of a group of selected people according to certain criteria. A growing degree of violence was used in the abductions, killings, and selective massacres: Disfigured corpses were dumped and bodies were hung from trees in an attempt to instill terror. The warning to the local population was no longer conveyed by forced disappearance but by the mutilated bodies of the victims. Although the army took pains not to kill in front of anyone, the population knew who the executioners were and the army assumed that they knew but preferred not to leave proof. Repression reached its peak when the massacres were no longer selective but indiscriminate, as in La Nueva Concepción, Cuarto Pueblo, Xalbal, and Piedras Blancas. In these attacks, no distinction was made between civilians and combatants or between collaborators, sympathizers, and people indifferent or opposed to the insurgency. Distinctions were not made between men and women (in the previous stages of repression, the victims were always men). Unlike with the interrogations, in the massacres there was no differentiation between young and old, between children and adults. The entire population was seen as "a rotten orange," in the words of the San Luis officer, and everyone, absolutely everyone, should be thrown onto the demolishing fire. The army regarded the local population as an infected whole, and the possibility of there being any healthy cells was discarded; thus the massacres were genocidal.

Systematic torture was integral to every level of repression. Sometimes obtaining information from the victim was emphasized and sometimes the torture was aimed at terrorizing others. Terror may have two objectives: to inhibit all activity against the army and to force people to provide information. I have found evidence of individual torture, by well-known methods (burning with firebrands, submerging in water, asphyxiating), and also of collective torture. I believe that burning people alive, a practice documented so often in this book, can be considered collective torture. Collective torture was used to glean information from or instill terror in others, be they in captivity or nearby. The depths of savagery are symbolized by the places of torture and death: pits in the military outposts, tunnels where prisoners are held, the room in the military barracks in Santa Cruz del Quiché that was thickly coated in clotted blood, and the crematorium of freshly butchered bodies in Playa Grande. These places were all carefully hidden by the army. When they came to light they become symbols, like the Nazi gas chambers.

In this way the chronological sequence of events reflects an abstract, ascending scale of violence. It bears out the idea that an intrinsic element in the dynamics of counterinsurgency is the violation of the most sacred of all rights, the right to life. Counterinsurgency tries to restrain the will of the people. The more clearly articulated and the more urgent the will of the people, the bloodier the restraints.

Racism

The massacres should also be interpreted as a new expression of the existing conflict between the corporate indigenous community and the *ladino* state.[4] The racist and discriminatory nature of *ladino* society is embodied in the state and army, making counterinsurgency particularly cruel.

In this case, the corporate indigenous community was not a monolingual society made up of individuals who had settled in the municipality in which they were born and who had ancestral ties to the land but was rather a new, multilingual, and even multiethnic settlement, as *ladinos* were not excluded, of people who had emigrated from different indigenous municipalities. The settlement was corporately organized in a cooperative with collective land tenure. It was subdivided into local cooperatives that operated with community leadership, with meetings and decisionmaking at the grass-roots level. As a social class, the peasant population was uniform, though they had come from two very different ecological areas and backgrounds before migrating: the experience of semiproletarian, intense labor on the large estates on the southern coast and the experience of opening up new agricultural horizons in the northern jungles. The previous experiences also seem to have given rise to different religious expressions, the more traditional Catholics in the former and the Charismatic Catholics in the latter. These differences threatened to fragment the community's unity. But unity was preserved in the shared experience, like a rite of passage, of migrating in search of new land as well as in the threat of losing the land to the state and the large estate owners. Possessing the fertile lands of Ixcán was too beautiful a dream to be true.

Because of the rebel presence in the area, the state or army tried to interfere with the community by reducing its autonomy. To this end, it denied the Church a role in the tasks of legalizing land tenure and marketing the local population's agricultural products, as these did not fit in with the Church's traditional role of legitimizing the *ladino* state. The army also interfered with the appointment of cooperative leaders, the decisionmaking, and the meetings themselves. It tried to win recognition by carrying out cultural activities, such as indigenous beauty contests, and gave out benefits with strings attached. The army later used brute force against the cooperative members to put an end to the community's form of cooperative organization.

In the process of interfering with and trying to control the indigenous community, the *ladino* state, represented by its *ladino* army, came across an increasingly impenetrable information barrier. The more it tried to break down the barrier, the more united became the community, as one can see at an individual level with persons refusing to talk under torture and at a community level at the meetings when the officer slammed his gun on the table in frustration at not obtaining information on the rebels, whether the local population knew about their activities or not.

In the interviews I did not hear about the officers attributing the lack of information to ethnic differences. But the National Security and Development Plan refers to the ethnic groups' lack of integration as a problem related to subversion, thus making the *ladino*'s stereotype of the Indian perfectly congruent with events. I believe that the army in the field and in Guatemala City was influenced by this stereotype to massacre the indigenous communities.[5] The stereotype contains three salient aspects: (1) that the Indian is a vile and despicable being, whose life is worth less than a normal person's and whom one can therefore exterminate without scruples to save the country from a great evil such as communism; (2) that Indians lie and are by nature treacherous, so that even if an Indian is not lying the *ladino* suspects that he is deceiving him and thinks he does not need to prove it, even if the Indian's life is in the balance; and (3) that Indians are like children—easy prey to the deceit of others.[6]

The decision to massacre lays bare the *ladino*'s uncertainty of his own identity, a hidden insecurity. The decision deceptively overcomes this sense of insecurity. Take, for example, the officer in the cooperative who asked about the rebels: He was met with laughter and evasion until he lost control, picked up his gun, and aimed it at them, telling them their uncooperative attitude would be punished. The officer was hurt and humiliated by the whole community; he felt impotent, unable to fathom or control their world. Matters were made worse by the stereotype he had of Indians as being easy to deceive. Why then could he not control them? How could a child or a vile and despicable being trick him? His hurt pride and frustration gave way to great anger, which motivated him to exterminate not just one person but the whole community. I can't control you? Well, you'll see; I'll wipe you off the face of the earth. These reactions must have taken place not only in the low-ranking officers but also all the way up the military hierarchy. The officers in charge of counterinsurgency were probably influenced by the psychological and social need to overcome their sense of humiliation.

But why did the army also kill *ladinos* in these communities? One reason could be that many of the *ladinos* had the physical appearance of the indigenous people. But this explanation does not seem sufficient, as the army also massacred "old *ladinos*" of white descent. The most plausible reason is that the army identified the indigenous community as a whole and could not conceive of it having a "healthy part," as the indigenous majority had infected the *ladino* minority with its way of being, of deciding for and defending itself.

One can also ask why the army did not try to wipe out all indigenous communities. The answer is that the army would never want to exterminate the entire indigenous population, despite what the persecuted Indians themselves might have felt, for two reasons. First, the indigenous population is the backbone of the country's work force, and second, not all indigenous areas of the country had insurgency groups. Racism is a specific trait of counterinsurgency in Guatemala, but it is not the main motivation for it.

Nor did the army decide to massacre an entire organized indigenous community—a municipality or all of Ixcán, for example—instead it selected small communities, villages, or towns, which could be the targets of "control-and-search" operations because it was impossible to control and search an entire municipality in one operation. The massacre plan must have taken into consideration many of the communities' characteristics, such as geographic location, to provoke foreseen population displacements. I believe that the plan was not to carry out a systematic racial or ethnic extermination but to apply conventional counterinsurgency theory. However, counterinsurgency was altered or given specific characteristics by the racial and ethnic conflict between the *ladino* army and the indigenous communities. The alteration lay in applying the stereotype of the despicable, lying, and gullible Indian to the smaller indigenous communities through coercive indiscriminate massacres. Thus a "control-and-search" operation became a "control-and-massacre" operation, as what was understood in the manuals as a sign of submission was interpreted in Guatemala as a sign of deceit. The army took for granted that everyone was infected and that everyone was a liar.

Only in this light can one understand how the army promised to protect Pascual Paiz's life in Xalbal in return for his gathering the people and staying in town but then subsequently exterminated him. The army's previous warning not to flee was a deceitful warning that corresponded to the stereotype, since it was the same as saying: "Because they are trying to deceive us, we will deceive them first." In turn, the indigenous communities' stereotype of the army is that it is destructive and always fabricates lies. The cleaning up of the army implies not only removing its repressive elements but also changing its image.

As a result of the scorched-earth offensives, other corporately organized indigenous communities have been formed, the Communities of Population in Resistance (CPR) and the refugees. These communities have continued to resist and distrust the army and Guatemalan state. But their vision has widened as a result of the level of confrontation and the mixture of tongues and ethnic groups and contact with different government and nongovernmental forces. Their situation has transcended the interests of the community and has a national relevance beyond that of the local indigenous community in conflict with the state. As indigenous communities these people have been able to take their place alongside other groups, such as the internally displaced, women affected by the repression, and peasants, although these groups are only popular organizations and not communities.

Religious Persecution

Army repression, during the periods of both selective repression and indiscriminate violence and destruction, involved persecution of the Catholic and Evangelical churches alike.[7] The persecution demonstrated the army's deep mistrust of the Church, which was no longer playing the traditional role of legitimizing the *ladino* state.[8] The offending image of the Church was that of an institution that, out of faith, promoted the liberation of the poor ("incited them to subversion," the army would say). Mistrust was an attitude, like racism and discrimination, that caused the army to misinterpret the behavior of those with the Church and gave another slant to Guatemalan counterinsurgency. The army marginalized, deported, and killed priests like Woods, Stetter, and Gran, perceiving them as promoters of the liberation of the poor and as actual or potential supporters of the guerrillas.

The army restricted and infiltrated the religious ceremonies, deceived the leaders of the Church, and threatened the members. It killed catechists[9] and massacred religious groups, surrounding them during church services and burning them in their temples, particularly in Evangelical chapels. The army considered the religious activities deceitful, not so much a front for nonbelievers as an authentically religious screen that fomented subversion while attempting to project the false image of innocuous prayers and singing. The army used religious symbols to punish the population, hanging or crucifying people and leaving corpses in kneeling positions. It destroyed churches and religious symbols, including those of saints, to make people's lives difficult. Only later, after the Ríos Montt coup d'état, did the army make a distinction between the churches in an attempt to manipulate them, using religion to curtail the force of liberating faith. Pitting one religious group against another had been tried out locally before the indiscriminate massacres during the army's civic action phase within the Catholic Church itself but had been written off as unviable and unproductive by the time of the scorched-earth offensive.

The persecution of the Church, that is, of all believers, created a faith among the believers that had the following characteristics, among others:

1. The experience of a God who is on the side of the just and persecuted and saves them from death at each step, and, to a lesser degree, the experience of being like Jesus, who was persecuted from childhood (as a refugee) and later massacred.

2. The experience of a saving, tangible, and practical faith—a faith that does not undervalue the importance of security precautions, of human intervention, and of the people's struggle.

3. The experience of solidarity, which is so much stronger and more indispensable in times of great repression.

4. The experience of a grass-roots ecumenism that is not promoted from outside and an absence of or reduction in the sectarian divisions that so plague Guatemala.

5. Faith in the institutional Church, albeit with certain reserves, symbolized in the martyrdom of priests like William Woods.

Faith was purified by persecution, like embers that the wind brings to a blaze, but the Church fell apart and religion was greatly weakened. The Church has been reconstructed both in the communities in resistance and in the refugee camps. The embers, which could have gone out as a result of the dispersal, have come together again and been rekindled. Most important, however, is not that there be religious expression but that the Church be nurtured by that experience of faith in times of persecution.[10]

Hope for the Future

Seeds of new life have emerged from the massacres, which are not only a wretched end to life but are also, paradoxically, like fertilizer that makes the earth fruitful, blossoming with something new. Out of the Ixcán experience, the communities in resistance and the refugees blossom.

In resistance, from the moment the people escape from the army, life begins to vanquish death. For some of the fugitives who almost fell, their escape was through the grace of God. After this liberation, the concern of those who sought out the refugees or the love for one's relatives and neighbors are like sparks of life that bring together the lost and the dispersed, starting the first small camps in the jungle. The new form of organization is accompanied by weeping, as is natural in the psychology of disaster victims. But weeping is also life, as it brings solace and, like a threshold, leads to a new way of life. Weeping is accompanied by another sign of life: the feeling of brotherhood, which overrides family, language, and ethnic and religious barriers—their shared bond as people who have lost everything. Their houses have been burned down, their belongings stolen or destroyed, their animals eaten by the soldiers, their cornfields demolished by machetes, their churches wiped off the map, their tranquility snatched away. A new family is born, in which orphans are the new sons and daughters. A new community is born, whose members are brothers and companions. A new church is born, in which Charismatic and traditional Catholics and Evangelicals come together. The walls of the houses and temples have fallen down. All this is life. Life is the deep structure that gives the experience substance, so that it does not fade with the passing of the emergency. By deep structure, I refer to the form of collective production adopted for self-defense against the soldiers and wild animals that devour corn. But it is a human and flexible collective that does not intrude on the sense of home (meals are cooked in the family, not collectively). Nor does it discard personal and cultural likes and necessities (family plots of land are maintained) or destroy ethnic identities or the sense of people's places of origin. The collective merely makes them relative, including them in the community, where each person is assigned tasks in production or other activities during group meetings. The witnesses highlight more or less explicitly the arrival of a new dawn following death and massacre. That is why this book brings good news.

Life also blossoms anew among the refugees. The solidarity among refugees and the Mexican peasants' solidarity with the refugees are sparks of life, motivating the refugees to form camps based on the work of all and to appoint their representatives on leaving Guatemala to justly distribute the international aid that has begun to flow. The consciousness of their nationality as Guatemalans, from the perspective of their new identity as refugees, is also a manifestation of life. Indigenous localism is lost, as the refugees realize that it is more important to be from Guatemala than from a certain village. But the links between people with the same background are not broken, nor is the ethnic identity of the different indigenous groups lost in the camps that bring together so many languages and regional clothings, which heighten the consciousness of the refugees' nationality. Their national identity is also deepened as the result of political negotiations with the Mexican and Guatemalan governments, when the refugees fight for their right to a dignified life and to return to Guatemala in safe conditions. The blood shed by the refugees' families, neighbors, and communities cannot be forgotten. (See Manz 1988a, 145–166.)

In this book I have wanted to share the good news of the witnesses who survived the repression in Ixcán. But the acceptance of good news requires faith, like the faith of the witnesses who believed in self-defense mechanisms to save their lives. Thanks to this faith that I have witnessed and shared with the reader, I see spilling "heavy wines"—wines of hope—and "ruby splendor" in the torrents of blood shed in the massacres.

NOTES

1. I estimate the population of Ixcán to have been between 45,000 and 50,000 in 1982; no census was carried out at that time and previous counts do not break down figures for the municipality of Ixcán.

2. I have included Father José María Gran and his sexton although they were not actually killed in Ixcán; their deaths were related to their work in the area.

3. On 4 January 1983, for example, the army killed 17 people, including children, in a camp of civilians in the Betel center in Xalbal.

4. See Smith 1990, particularly her enlightening chapter "Social Relations in Guatemala over Time and Space," pp. 1–30.

5. Once inside information is available from the army as to how the decisions were made, I will be able to test this hypothesis.

6. See Adams 1990.

7. In Ixcán there were no groups of *costumbristas*, believers of the traditional Mayan religion.

8. See Smith 1990 to understand the legitimizing role of the Church during the colonial period.

9. Catechists were killed, for example, in Cuarto Pueblo in 1981 even though the army's practice was to kill leaders in general, not just religious leaders.

10. It is always possible, of course, that the religious flowering in times of peace eats away at the experience of faith during persecution.

EPILOGUE

Exodus, Resistance, and Readjustments in the Aftermath of Massacres

BEATRIZ MANZ

The relationship between the Indian majority and the state in Guatemala has been characterized historically by conflict and the subordination of the Indians. In the 1970s vibrant new Indian organizations in local and regional coalitions began to challenge these traditional social arrangements. To preserve the subordination of the Indians, the state intensified the conflict, escalating the repression and violence to heretofore unimaginable levels. The onslaught had two major components: first, the widespread murder of individuals and destruction of communities in the most heinous of ways, which led to the second, the sowing of terror and paralysis among the survivors. The state was to penetrate every aspect of Indian community life, leaving no sanctuaries.

State terror is not unique to the Central American republics but has torn the social fabric of many South American countries as well (Corradi, Weiss Fagen, and Garretón 1992). The consequence, as one scholar notes, is that

Beatriz Manz is director, Center for Latin American Studies, and associate professor of geography and ethnic studies, University of California at Berkeley.

fear creates "a sense of defeat, a perception of the overwhelming power of the enemy, a feeling of failure or weakness that cannot be blamed on others, and sense of having lost the opportunity for personal or collective realization" (Garretón 1992:14). That collective fear was certainly pervasive in the years immediately following the terror in Guatemala. Despite the highly visible nature of the crimes, none of the perpetrators were brought to trial nor did the military even hint at excess let alone apologize, reasoning that the Indians deserved what they got for having allowed themselves to be manipulated by "subversive" elements. Although the scars from the experience of mass terror will not fade from the collective memory soon, Indian communities displayed a remarkable resilience, finding ways not only to survive but to actively resist, escape, and readjust. The military remains dominant, operating with impunity; the Indians remain vulnerable, living in fear, but the survival and internal strength of Indian communities itself represents a triumph.

The struggle of people confronted by military repression has been studied by Central American social scientists, who are often the victims of terror themselves. These social scientists have provided important insights into the dynamic relationship between hegemonic states and citizens—the objects of the repression (Martín-Baró 1989, Aguilera Peralta and Romero Imery 1981, Aguilera Peralta 1980, Pacheco and Jiménez 1990, Torres Rivas 1989). A recognition of the debilitating effects of state-sponsored violence is balanced against an awareness that individuals are more than passive victims—they are also psychologically resourceful agents. As Ignacio Martín-Baró states, the evidence shows "the essentially active role groups and individuals play as subjects no matter how alienated they may be" (Martín-Baró 1989:15). The horror may bend or even break its victims physically, but it does not necessarily dominate their spirits.

Nowhere has the repression been more overwhelming than in Guatemala. The best documentation of this shocking violence, unprecedented even measured against the devastating standards of Guatemala, has been produced by anthropologist and Jesuit Ricardo Falla. In *Massacres in the Jungle*, Falla documents with painstaking detail and extraordinary humanity horrific human rights abuses and assassinations of peasant jungle colonizers in the Ixcán region of Guatemala. Falla insists on detailing numbers, locations, and events in a way that does not allow the enormity of the crimes to slip into an anonymous historical night. But Falla is not satisfied merely to provide the outline of events and general facts: He recalls the names, ages, and kinship relations of the victims, honoring them by sliding back a veil of anonymity that would make these tragedies easier to accept. We no longer confront faceless and unfathomable numbers—1,000 or 10,000 dead—but rather poignant portraits of Isabela Francisco, age seventeen, daughter of Nicolas Francisco, age fifty-one, and María Marcos, age forty-nine, originally from Santa Eulalia, married to Andrés de Juan, age twenty, originally from San Juan Ixcoy. All of these individuals and Isabela's brothers and sisters were murdered in the massacre of Cuarto Pueblo on March 14–17, 1982. A total of 324 human beings were killed in this one community. No anthropologist, no Guatemalan, has so concretely shifted the horror from the private to the public domain.

This powerful book guides us through one of the darkest periods in Guatemala's history: 1975–1982. Its very effectiveness, however, raises some important questions: How have individuals and communities coped with the aftermath of the terror that Falla has documented, and what has happened since? The shape of Guatemala's nightmare has shifted, but the country has not been freed of its long night of terror. In the Ixcán three broad alternatives presented themselves for many of those who survived the violence: (1) fleeing to Mexico as refugees, (2) living under army domination, or (3) forming communities of displaced peoples in resistance to army domination, the Comunidades de Población en Resistencia, CPRs (Communities of Population in Resistance).[1] I would like to briefly examine each of these experiences in the years since 1982.[2]

Few outsiders have journeyed to the Ixcán and fewer have spent significant time there. I took my first trip to the Ixcán in 1973, where I visited the cooperatives in Ixcán Grande and stayed in the village of Santa María Tzejá in the Zona Reyna (Manz 1988a, 1988b).[3] The Ixcán offered a glimmer of hope to many who had experienced degradation and deprivation. It was not easy. Courageous highland people struggled against all the uncertainties and problems of establishing a settlement in a tropical rain forest with few tools and minimal resources. Under the most arduous of circumstances they carved out a life over which they would have some control. Aided by two Catholic dioceses, they obtained land and thus severed their links to the dreaded, enslaving migrant plantation work. Incredibly, these Indian colonizers not only survived, they prospered. They provided food for themselves and cash crops for the market. Moreover, they developed highly successful cooperatives to purchase their goods and sell their products.

I was very moved by the early experience of these rain forest colonizers. Not only was their courage and resourcefulness impressive, but their optimism was infectious. They had few illusions about conditions becoming easier, but they had enormous pride in what they had accomplished and this pride generated confidence and hope for the future.

In 1981 and 1982 terrifying reports of vicious military repression and widespread destruction began filtering out of this region. What had taken years of the most painstaking dedication to build was wiped out in an afternoon in village after village. In the wake of these calamities, tens of thousands of people fled. I went to the Lacandón Forest in Mexico to hear firsthand what was happening in what had appeared to be a promised land only a decade earlier (Manz 1981, 1983, 1984, 1988c).

The Refugee Experience

Whether an individual or family fled to Mexico, remained in army territory, or became part of the CPRs was often as much a product of circumstance as conscious choice. Some who may have preferred to become part of the CPRs were forced to cross the border to survive, and others remained in army territory because they could not make it to the border. The mass exodus to Mexico was perhaps the most visible response to the calamities that were unfolding. These refugees, predominantly Indians, came from the Ixcán region of El Quiché as well as from municipalities in other departments along the border such as El Petén, Huehuetenango, Quetzaltenango, and San Marcos.

From the Ixcán some fled for safety to Mexico in February 1982 within days of the army's scorched-earth policies, the ashes of their burnt homes still warm. Others waited within the Ixcán for a year before moving on to Mexico, hoping that they had seen the last of the destruction but ended up seeing more. At this point provisional camps were set up in Mexico along the border. Few went north of the Mexican state of Chiapas because they hoped their stay might be short and they wanted to be as near as possible to their land for the return.

Reality set in for those still holding out in the jungle by the end of 1982: The army was staying and had definite plans for the future of the Ixcán and the resources and will to carry them out. Within a year or so the only place one could hide was in the northwestern part of the Ixcán, a geographically more difficult place for the army to penetrate. The bulk of the villagers from what was to become CPR territory were either refugees in Mexico or had returned to their original villages in the highlands. It was more difficult for the army to make incursions into this area because of the guerrilla presence. The Guerrilla Army of the Poor (EGP) had retreated to this northwest corner and dug in. The army was able to maneuver but not to reclaim this territory, thus with few exceptions—and these along the periphery—it was not able to repopulate the entire area under its control. But people who fled the overwhelming force of the army were able to establish their own communities, in defiance of the military and with the tacit assent of the guerrillas. These displaced people found a certain sanctuary in this predominantly EGP territory.

The early days in exile in Mexico were extremely difficult, especially as the number of people burgeoned. Months of hiding in the forest took a harsh toll: People became ill, malnourished, and psychologically worn. They arrived in Mexico exhausted, frightened, devastated. Some fled with only what they had on, some without shoes. Many had survived on roots and cold tortillas for months, cooking only at night, if at all, so as not to reveal their presence. Whereas those who came earlier might have been able to attain assistance or work from a border Mexican *ejido* (federal system of communal land tenure), those who came later became immediately dependent on institutional aid.

At this point the Mexican government created a special agency for refugee assistance, the Comisión Mexicana de Ayuda a Refugiados (COMAR). This new agency and the United Nations High Commissioner for Refugees (UNHCR) responded to the emergency. These groups were important, but the mobilization of the San Cristóbal Diocese, local solidarity organizations, and nongovernmental organizations proved pivotal. At the beginning the refugees lived under nylon tarps in the rainy and muddy Lacandón jungle. In late 1982 when I visited the Puerto Rico camp near the Guatemalan border, many refugees still had nothing more than nylon to cover themselves from the torrential rains. One day about 800 people arrived from Guatemala after having wandered and hid for nearly ten months in the rain forest. As they slowly straggled into camp, the burden of their long journey was visible on their drawn faces and in the slowness of their gait. Among them were the very old and sick, orphans, and women carrying babies born in the jungle. Two completely naked orphans found in the jungle—so dazed and frightened they could hardly respond to anything—came in with the group.

The refugee camps began to stabilize by 1983. The largest and least accessible were those in the Lacandón forest along the Lacantún and Usumacinta rivers. These remote camps, which included Puerto Rico, La Cila, and Chajul, had landing strips, food distribution, and medical care and were effectively organized and democratically run (Manz 1983).

A year later, in 1984, the Mexican government decided to move all the Guatemalan refugees from Chiapas—in camps near the Guatemalan border—to the more distant states of Campeche and Quintana Roo. The ostensible reason for the relocation was the refugees' own security. A more likely rationale, however, was the Mexican government's desire to stop the Guatemalan army's persistent incursions into Mexican territory in pursuit of elusive guerrilla units. Thus, the relocation of the camps away from the border was a concession made by Mexico to the Guatemalan military. The Guatemalan high command wanted the refugees either in Guatemala under its control or, failing that, as far away from the border as possible, thereby depriving the guerrilla units of a potential rest and support base. The Mexican military made the decision known with particular assertiveness in the more isolated camps. In Puerto Rico the Mexicans forcefully relocated some refugees, and to make the point especially clear to those who were refusing to leave, they burnt the camp to the ground, destroying some 1,000 homes in the process. Despite this destruction, about 3,500 of the 5,080 refugees in the camp signaled their resistance to being moved further away from their land and relatives in the Ixcán by hiding in the Mexican jungle. Ultimately, the camps along the rivers were closed. Of the 46,000 official Guatemalan refugees in Mexico, a total of about 20,000 ended up in the designated camps in Campeche and, later, Quintana Roo. The majority successfully fought relocation and remained in camps in the southwestern part of Chiapas, some returned to Guatemala to join the Communities of Population in Resistance, and others moved to the United States or elsewhere in Mexico (Manz 1984:51–52).

The makeup of the refugee population is heterogeneous not just in ethnicity, language, and religion but also in political views. What the refugees do have in common is that they are peasants and share an unspeakable experience—they have fled the army's violence. Moreover, the military uniformly dismissed them as subversives and the Guatemalan government therefore wrote them off. On the surface the attitude toward the refugees changed with the new Christian Democratic government of Vinicio Cerezo in 1986. In an attempt to create a better international image and thereby obtain needed European and U.S. aid, his government expressed interest in the refugees' repatriation. Consequently, Cerezo formed the Special Commission to Aid Refugees, CEAR (in 1988 renamed CEARD to include the internally displaced). Despite solicitous public pronouncements and visits by government officials, few refugees returned, in large part, because the repatriation procedure was heavily dominated by the feared and hated armed forces. The army had little inclination to negotiate with the refugees whom it still viewed as subversives but was anxious to exert its control over this population. The military offered amnesty, as though the refugees and not the generals had committed a crime.

The Catholic Church of Guatemala took a strong position on behalf of the refugees and their right to return. Even though human rights violations continued, especially in Huehuetenango, this diocese, unlike El Quiché's in 1980, did not close down but persisted in its mission. Guatemalan bishops visited the refugees to learn of their plight and to compare it to living under military occupation.

One significant issue in the camps concerned the situation of young people. Thousands had been born in Mexico and many others had grown up in the camps, knowing Guatemala only through hearing the recollections of adults. Although many social activities and development projects took place in the camps, the young were not working in the fields of the Ixcán forest, a place where they would acquire the skills they needed to become successful agricultural producers and learn to survive. Many found employment in the city of Campeche, in Chetumal, Villa Hermosa, and, most incongruously, in the deluxe international tourist hotels of Cancún. In these resorts, young refugee women would shed their *huipil* (traditional blouses) and *corte* (skirts) for tank tops and shorts. Bicycles, unfathomable in the muddy, roadless villages of the Ixcán, became a common site in the camps.

The economic situation in the camps was quite varied by the 1990s. Camps such as Kesté, in the state of Campeche, contained solid, large, and spread-out houses with cement foundations and walls, potable water, and land parcels.[4] In contrast, the Chiapas camps (numbering about forty) had more difficult conditions, a reflection of the land pressures in the state. What the Chiapas camps lacked materially they made up for in organization, solidarity, and support from the Church in Chiapas, especially through the efforts of the popular bishop of San Cristóbal de las Casas, Don Samuel Ruiz. In contrast, the dioceses of Campeche and Quintana Roo had little interest or understanding of the refugees.

The refugee saga took its first formal turn toward resolution with the formation in 1987 of the Permanent Commissions, which represented refugees before governmental and international bodies, and the United Nations resolution in December 1988 to form the Conferencia Internacional sobre los Refugiados Centroamericanos (CIREFCA). The refugees' efforts culminated with the successful negotiated return on January 20, 1993. In Guatemala, the returnees have shown impressive levels of organization. At the returnees' site of Polígano 14, also known as Victoria 20 de Enero, numerous organizations exist to address issues of women, health, education, security, land, and public relations, among others. A common sight are men and women carrying notebooks and pens, sitting down over tree trunks or whatever else they can find to write things down so that they can more effectively report to their respective organizations. Meetings are held early in the morning or late into the night. All of the people I spoke with expressed great optimism and confidence about the future. Although conditions may not yet warrant this optimism, the refugees' enthusiasm mirrors their own achievements.[5]

Militarized Villages

Another alternative followed or forced upon villagers was to subject themselves to military dictates.[6] For villagers who remained in the army-controlled sector of the Ixcán, the military's presence in the first year was onerous and extensive. Some villages in the northeastern section of the Ixcán were abandoned for just a few weeks. This area was the least conflictive and therefore there was an early, though slow and cautious, return to these communities. People in the rest of the Ixcán who hid from a month to six months were taken to the military zone 22 of Playa Grande. If cleared following an intelligence check, they were set up in temporary settlements near the military base. Among this population were those who voluntarily came out of hiding when they heard of General Efraín Ríos Montt's[7] amnesty over the radio and others who were caught. Those who were caught and identified by informers as guerrillas or guerrilla sympathizers were separated, tortured, killed, or "disappeared." Women were raped and practically all men were pressed into involuntary labor. Ironically, this labor was used to protect the military itself by constructing the massive concrete wall around the base as well as building and repairing roads and airfields. In exchange for work, villagers were given food. The army sought credit for this largess, even though the international community had provided the food to the military government for distribution and had not intended it to be used in support of involuntary servitude (Garst and Barry 1990). The army also successfully pressed the population into military service, forming columns of villagers and soldiers to identify cornfields, corn storage *trojes* (granaries) and places where fellow villagers were hiding, a task far more difficult for the military to carry out on its own. The army took people into helicopters to identify areas and speak into loudspeakers to their fellow villagers. In interviewing survivors—either among refugees in Mexico or those living in militarized villages in Ixcán—it is clear that a combination of three devastating events broke their resistance: the total eradication of food supplies, their fellow villagers' involvement in that destruction, and the lack of accurate or sensible analysis presented by the insurgent forces.

People who remained hiding in the dense rain forest near their villages in the Ixcán the longest, at times up to a year, seemed to have done so based on the flawed information that the army's occupation was temporary. The guerrillas actively encouraged people in this incorrect assessment. It was only when extreme hunger, fatigue, disillusionment, and lack of organization combined with the recognition that the army was firmly in control that people decided to leave their areas and head toward the border. At this point, weakened, doubtful, and demoralized, they limped and staggered as much as walked. They express the devastation and demoralization experienced at seeing their own fellow villagers—relatives and former neighbors acting as willing or reluctant army collaborators—destroying the crops that were to provide food for those in hiding for the months ahead.

A year later the army allowed villagers to resettle their destroyed villages as long as new inhabitants replaced those that fled or had been killed. Radio announcements in key areas of the country blared the availability of land in the Ixcán. The ones most likely to take up the offer and least fearful of military persecution were Evangelicals, perhaps because a fellow Evangelical, General Efraín Ríos Montt, was the self-appointed president of the country—the first Evangelical to hold that position. Moreover, Evangelicals dominated many of the rural army/government counterinsurgency projects as well as Non-Governmental Organizations (NGOs), especially in the hard-hit areas of conflict. In part this Evangelical presence resulted from the fact that the crucial diocese of El Quiché had closed down and did not have a bishop until 1987.[8] In particular, the NGOs linked to Evangelical fundamentalist churches in the United States had a monopoly for several years in many of the most conflictive rural regions. Catholic villagers also trekked back to their original highland communities to recruit desperate landless peasants for the Ixcán.

The new settlers came from varied backgrounds. Often an Evangelical pastor would go to the Ixcán with several members of his church. Other would-be colonizers were former soldiers who, having participated in the destruction of villages and massacres, would know of the availability of land and would present themselves at the military base with several relatives, *compadres*, or friends. People heard about land in the Ixcán in the predominantly *ladino* Oriente, the South Coast, and also land-starved departments such as Alta and Baja Verapaz, Huehuetenango, and so on. The new arrivals would show their safe conduct passes to demonstrate that they were in good standing and would then be sent either at random or certainly without regard to linguistic and cultural affinities to any one of a hundred villages.[9] Some would argue that the culturally mixed repopulation was a conscious policy to foment disharmony and prevent the strong unified communities that existed prior to 1982.

Daily life quickly took new forms that necessitated severe adjustments. The military's needs predominated. The villagers first had to prove they had sufficient numbers to staff an effective paramilitary structure that could cover a twenty-four hour period seven days a week. Once this was done, the army accompanied them back, set up garrisons, and forced everyone to take part in a wide range of activities. These activities included general discipline, reeducation based on nationalistic ideology, paramilitary training in weapons, and week-long jungle sweeps to provide intelligence to the military base. All of this was new to the villagers (except those that had been in the military), and the consequences of failing to comply were unambiguous. The army left such a searing impression on these villagers that ten years later few if any are willing to openly declare noncompliance.

The vigilante role of the paramilitary Civil Defense Patrols (PACs) has fomented the most disruptive changes in the communities. Typically, a PAC chief—often a military collaborator rather than a respected elder—threatens a villager by accusing him of subversive activity. This situation can lead to the accused fleeing or winding up dead.[10]

The counterinsurgency campaigns are fueled by nationalism and anti-communism. The subversives—in the military's mind not simply armed combatants but anyone who opposes the status quo—were portrayed as servants of a "foreign ideology" capable of destroying the nation itself. Those who organized cooperatives ceased to be loyal patriotic Guatemalans and became linked to "international communism." Few countries saw the cold-war rationale inflated to such excess. To avoid accusations of being connected with "international communism," villagers dutifully, though perfunctorily, learned to raise the Guatemalan flag at dawn and bring it down at sunset even in the most remote villages.

If this were not a sufficient adjustment for the stunned original villagers, the army ordered them not to occupy their former house lots, which were set back from the village center and connected by jungle paths. Instead, the villagers had to live concentrated in the village center, one house next to the other. They were told that this new arrangement was for their protection, but quite clearly it was for better control of the population. This layout bred personal problems and tensions. As villagers slowly began to accumulate chickens or pigs, these animals constantly invaded other people's houses. In a tense and untrusting situation these small incidents could easily explode. Villagers allied with the military could use these incidents to bully their neighbors, knowing that those who were under suspicion would not dare raise their voices. The victims would not think of bringing these complaints into the open at a village meeting or quietly gather allies among one's relatives to talk to the accuser, even ten years later. The mistrust feeds on itself. People to this day, especially new residents, will often accuse a fellow villager of "suspicious" activity to gain advantage, be it land, claim to a mahogany tree, or sexual favors. The situation created by the military is geared to bring out the worst in those subjected to it. This lack of trust is especially detrimental in an isolated peasant community where cooperation is essential to survive.

In 1985, on my first trip to the Ixcán after the traumas of 1982, I noticed immediately a dramatic contrast. The remaining original settlers were stunned, their fear palpable, and their guilt and sadness conspicuous. All were troubled by the horror that had taken place, and many had a relative or neighbor who was either a refugee in Mexico, disappeared, or dead. Most had lost everything. After surviving the nightmare of the terror and the fear and exhaustion of hiding, they still were uncertain about what could or could not be done and this uncertainty was scaring them in their daily lives. As my visits to the Ixcán continued through the years, I have observed the villagers' extraordinary patience and ability to focus on the daily routine, taking one day at a time. Deep down they seem to hope that eventually things will turn out alright. Ultimately, just to have survived when so many perished is a consolation. Deeply religious to begin with, they look for religious explanations to make sense of what happened, why they are alive, and what the future holds.

Although the civilian patrols are still dutifully, though lackadaisically, performed in the Ixcán in 1993, few take the task seriously. The attitudes toward the PACs fall into two extreme positions: either villagers are wholeheartedly for them or they reluctantly comply with the requirements. Among the first group are those that feel indebted to the military. Some were given land, and others benefited from the terror by seizing property such as cattle from those who were killed or fled. Some villagers informed on the insurgents, often for personal gain, and now fear reprisals; others have abused their position in the past and want to maintain their privilege through the power of a paramilitary organization. Among those who barely go along with the PACs are villagers who have suffered at the hands of the military or at the hands of the first group; they hate the army and see the unpaid shifts as a net loss—a deep burden that tears them away from securing a livelihood for their families.

When villagers in the Ixcán are asked why they perform patrol service, the overwhelming majority respond that they had no choice. When asked if they want to do it, their answer is no: They are afraid to refuse, although many are undertaking the obligation as sporadically as possible. They resist in their own way by missing a turn here and there, by showing up late, by sleeping through the shift, going on errands or social visits for part of it, and so on. None of this halfheartedness would have been imaginable in the first years of the patrols. At this point the only thing the PACs prove is the army's ability to force people into complying to its whims on the most general of levels. There is no open rebellion, but at best a pro forma compliance. Villagers cannot be accused of not doing their duty, but it is clear that the system is not working. The returning refugees have taken noncompliance a major step forward: They quite openly demanded the right *not* to be forced into patrol service. Proudly they succeeded. The second point of the negotiated agreement states the "recognition of the right to free association and organization by the returnees," specifically that "the Government of Guatemala guarantees that the returnees just as all Guatemalans are not obligated to associate with nor form part of self-defense groups or association."[11]

Today significant freedom of movement exists compared to the past. Most villagers reside back in their lots with the army's approval, abandoning the earlier military-imposed concentration in the village center. Moreover, organizational initiatives such as the Médicos del Mundo health promoters' network now exist as well as project-specific organizations such as a cardamom-dryer cooperative, a network of catechists, and others. Rather than reflecting a more tolerant military, this opening indicates that the tight control of earlier years simply was not sustainable. The tight regulations required more resources to enforce than they were worth.

The military repression has left deep scars in the Ixcán, scars that will take time and a significant demonstration of redress to heal. This redress will have to ensure improvement in the paramount areas of personal safety and a fundamental respect for human rights. In addition, the most important military-created problem in the villagers' daily life that needs correction concerns land and the civil patrol obligation. On one level is the resolution of land occupancy issues, and on another level are a range of interconnected ecological issues concerning the fragility of the soil, detrimental ecological practices, extraction of precious lumber, and, in general, serious deforestation. Dissolving the PACs is needed to move in the direction of village harmony. Demilitarization and a functioning system of legal justice need to be instituted.

Although bombings and the military presence have continued into 1993, the arrival of nongovernmental organizations and the international staff associated with the refugee return have created a somewhat more relaxed climate. The army is no longer the sole institutional presence in the Ixcán. Offices housing such nongovernmental institutions as the UNHCR, the United Nations Development Program (UNDP) coordination of refugee assistance (PRODERE), Medicos del Mundo, Veterinarios sin Frontera (the French "Doctors Without Borders" and "Veterinarians Without Borders"), with a visible foreign staff, and dozens of volunteers such as Witness for Peace and other organizations from around the world, have made a substantial difference in the Ixcán. In addition, the Guatemalan human rights ombudsman opened an office. A member of the local human rights committee predicted, "When the office is completed there will be such long lines of people presenting complaints, they will stretch for miles."[12]

The Communities of Population in Resistance (CPRs)

The most conscious and toughest alternative or option was to refuse to come out of hiding and also to refuse to leave the Ixcán for Mexico.[13] Those who followed this path of defiance argued that they had struggled too hard to obtain land to leave, often recalling the pain and hardship of opening up the jungle. They tell an outsider with passion that abandoning their land is abandoning all their hard work and the possibilities for sustenance as well as allowing the military to triumph. As they simply put it: "The land feeds us" (IGE 1989:125). The terrain—thick tropical rain forest—conceals them and protects them "as a mother would do."[14]

These families who refused to leave came together in an organized way, calling themselves Comunidades de Población de Resistencia, or Communities of Population in Resistance (CPRs) in 1983. The name was provocative, lending itself to easy characterization as being part of the guerrillas—but as whole families. The term *comunidad* emphasizes the importance of community in their lives; *población* refers to people; *resistencia* underscores their refusal to accept military domination, although they are not in armed opposition. When aggressively pursued, these villagers found ways to successfully elude the army. By remaining in the Ixcán, they have established a degree of independent control over their lives as well as have aided in preserving the area. Often they describe their actions in religious, almost mystical, terms. As an indigenous catechist put it, "God gave us this land so that we could work it and we could nourish ourselves, so we continue struggling, we must continue forward ... there is no other way" (Communities of Population in Resistance 1992: 5).

The skilled and ruthless Guatemalan army has employed various tactics in this contested terrain—bombings, sweeps, artillery, psychological persuasion—but has seldom succeeded in finding this population, let alone routing the guerrillas. The casualties among the CPRs have been relatively low considering the firepower and repeated army incursions inflicted on the area. Nonetheless, troops have occasionally been able to locate and destroy communities and agricultural production, leaving terror in the wake of its raids. These sweeps produce hardships and alarm during the period of emergency evacuation and considerable work in starting from scratch again and again. Although successfully disrupting the CPRs, the army has been eluded in its main goal of engaging and defeating the guerrillas entrenched in that area. This victory would allow the army to repopulate this area of the Ixcán and maintain it under the military's permanent control.

At first the population remained in hiding in small, mobile groups, but small bands proved ineffective. Agricultural production required not simply work in the fields but an effective security system: protection for those planting as well as for the center of the community, where the women's work largely took place. Consequently, this phase was followed by a further concentration of population into larger communities to facilitate production and security.

The 1984 relocation of the refugees away from Chiapas increased the population of the CPRs. Rather than be relocated to distant Campeche and Quintana Roo, refugees streamed back to Guatemala, some joining the CPRs to avoid the army. The communities were able to accommodate the additional people—though it was often a considerable burden—and adjust to the ill-timed loss of a friendly backdoor ally for trading, rest, and other services. Initially the increase in numbers created food shortage (the food production in 1984 did not have large surpluses), but eventually the influx strengthened the CPRs. Luckily the naturally plentiful fauna and flora relieved the problem. Juxte-tree nuts could be ground and used for tortillas, palms consumed as vegetable, green bananas mixed with maize could stretch the dough for tortillas, and ripe bananas and other tropical fruits (planted in the 1960s by *parcelistas* in their house lots) could be harvested.

By 1986 the CPRs had developed stability in production, appropriate health care, dedicated educational instruction, and an elaborate security system, a remarkable achievement under the circumstances. Because small lapses could have devastating consequences, no detail was too small

to preserve security: Members of the CPRs devised ways to prevent roost-
ers and turkeys from revealing their presence, and children quickly learned
the necessity for complete silence during periods of emergency. All cooking had to be done (and is still done) while dark so as to not reveal their location through the smoke. Within minutes an entire encampment can evac-
uate, and the people, including children, hide in predesignated areas of the
rain forest or huddle in crude bomb shelters to wait out an attack. This un-
breakable discipline has allowed them to survive.

The population expanded considerably because of an increase in births
and the addition of returning refugees. Communities grew to 300 or 400
people each. The coordination of activities needed for survival including
food production and trade, security, or other occupations including health
promotion, catechists, or teachers required significant collective activity
and coordination. Once the coordination of various activities and surplus
was achieved, each family could also dedicate time to individual production.

The bulk of the men engaged in collective agricultural tasks from 7:00
A.M. to 3:00 P.M. Monday through Saturday. From 3:00 P.M. onward they
can join the women engaging in individual cultivation or personal interests.
Along with planting corn, beans, and rice, the CPRs introduced nutritional
new crops such as soya. A conscious effort also exists to preserve the forest. The CPRs proudly point out that their area is the only one that retains
the mahogany and other precious trees, and they point to the ecological
devastation of the rest of the Ixcán over the past ten years.

The communal activities are coordinated by the locally elected Comité
de Ixcán, which also coordinates through general assemblies the needs of
all the CPRs. A high degree of consensus is always sought. For example,
Evangelicals contribute to the sustenance of Catholic catechists (a distinct
difference from the rest of the Ixcán). Two priests joined the CPRs. Father
Julio arrived in November 1986 and began a creative and ambitious pastoral plan and Ricardo Falla (Father Marcos) joined the CPRs in July 1987.

The year 1986 proved to be stable and fruitful, but also the calm before
the storm. An army offensive against the CPRs began in 1987, bringing new
disruption and suffering in its wake. The high command was increasingly
frustrated and embarrassed at not being able to finish off the guerrillas and
exercise some real control over what amounted to a small corner of territory. Worse yet, from the military's viewpoint, the guerrillas were becoming
stronger and more aggressive. Prior to the offensive, the army placed some
600 refugees who had returned to the Ixcán in what was to be a temporary
settlement at Centro Veracruz. The objective of the army and the Cerezo
administration was for these repatriates to settle in the CPR area, pushing
the CPRs out. These unsuccessful efforts combined with the realization that the guerrillas had strengthened prompted the army to announce

their "Fin del Año" offensive. This operation, involving some 2,000 soldiers, was to finish the guerrillas and provoke a definitive displacement of all the CPRs once and for all. The offensive forced one community with Father Julio to escape to Mexico, but it did not accomplish a permanent displacement. Despite the havoc these raids caused, the CPRs were able to persevere as functioning communities. The offensive lasted almost six months and resulted in heavy losses for the army.[15]

Surviving the bitter 1987 offensive gave the communities confidence and new hope. In the aftermath of constant disruption, a return to normalcy was aided by the active presence of a priest, whose role was important to the members of the community not only in religious terms but also because he provided a familiar dimension to daily life. The priest organized activities that relieved the strain of day-to-day survival. The activities might take the form of slide shows (operated with solar energy); showing photos from *National Geographic* (which everybody likes!); doing drawings; visiting the sick, the elders, and newborns; producing the newsletter (in 1989)— the *Correo de la Selva*, printed in stencil—exchanging information; and analyzing the national and international news. Although isolated, these communities are nonetheless surprisingly informed about national and international news. The "media committee" listens to the news and reports to the community. News events pertaining directly to the CPRs are discussed, as are more general themes such as the collapse of the Soviet Union.

A new religious organization, Acción Cristiana Guatemalteca (ACG), was formed in 1989.[16] The ACG, named Christian rather than Catholic to highlight its ecumenical mission, grew out of three experiences: the refugee camps, the CPRs, and the displaced population in Guatemala. At the heart of the ACG are the "groups of reflection." The discussions revolve around linking relevant contemporary issues and examples from the Bible. Each person is encouraged to strive to be both a creative thinker and an actor. Falla explains the dynamics: "A question that could be raised is, What will it mean when the refugees return? What will happen to the land parcels? What will happen to the CPRs? The idea is to discourage the 'well, let's wait and see what will happen.'" Individuals are encouraged to develop their own analyses and not wait to hear what others have to say. As Falla would say, "You, what do *you* say? Where is your voice, where are your thoughts, what are your opinions?"[17]

The two priests in the Ixcán CPR made a concerted effort to organize a solid and creative pastoral structure. The aim, as Ricardo Falla explains, was to be new, fresh, and above all participatory (to avoid falling into a so-called verticalist trap—an undemocratic, centralized way of operating). Religious language, like political rhetoric, inherently has the danger of becoming stale. Asked why it should be so important to be informed and to participate, Falla responds that otherwise the CPRs would "lose perspective. Otherwise they become an island: There is no sense of the world, there is no sense of Guatemala."[18] If that were the case, they would lose sense of what they are doing and why.

Falla organized impressive religious retreats, emphasizing a spiritual and personal dimension. He is exuberant when recalling these experiences. "The retreats left me marveled. I thought it was impossible, to take eight young campesinos up to a mountain to meditate! We would separate ourselves from the community. I thought they would get bored, that it wouldn't work. It was a challenge. They prayed five hours a day. Personal prayers. No talking among themselves. Each person would reflect about their own life, with emotion, with tears, with internal struggle, that is, stirring up their own interior being." The retreat was the place for coming together, and to hear the priest explain passages from the Bible as well as personal questions for reflection. Examples? "Why are you in the resistance? Find out why you are here. What keeps you here?" Questions like that are "fundamental," Falla affirms.[19]

In the CPRs people needed to understand and give meaning to their situation, to interpret what happened to them and their current position as a population in hiding. A meaningful interpretation for them was both political and religious. As one scholar puts it, religion must be conceived "as a process of change; a process of production/reproduction of values, ideas and practices, a process in which the religious actors reproduce or transform their social and natural context. Likewise, reproduce or transform themselves" (Siebers 1992, 11).

Progressives in the Catholic Church metaphorically gave birth to the Ixcán in the 1960s and 1970s, helplessly saw its death in the 1980s, and now are witnessing its resurrection. The Episcopal Conference has come out strongly in support of the CPRs and Ricardo Falla's right to conduct pastoral work among them. As El Quiché's Bishop Julio Cabrera stated, the CPRs have a right to ask for the Church's presence. Of all the parishes, that of Ixcán is one of the "hardest and most difficult" in his diocese (Cabrera 1993:15–16). In a homily to the returnees, Bishop Julio Cabrera stated bluntly and unequivocally his "repugnancy" at the inhumane army actions. He told the returnees that their coming home was a "triumphal" one: "You have come to unite, not to separate" (Cabrera 1993:12–13). In the eyes of the Catholic Church, the refugees and internally displaced peoples have developed a special set of religious values. The returnees, according to Bishop Cabrera, displayed "human, moral and spiritual reserves" (Cabrera 1993:13). He promised that the Church would not abandon them, ending his homily with "Brothers don't be afraid, Jesus is with you and will not leave you" (Cabrera 1993:13).

When interviewed, people from the CPRs reveal an extraordinary confidence and inspire respect. Although they appreciate national and international solidarity, they don't seek sympathy. Except for the violence—army incursions and bombings—and having to live "under the jungle trees" (*bajo la montaña*), they emphasize the positive aspects of their experience. Despite the hardships, community members point out, they avoided the debilitating experience in refugee camps as well as life under military domination.[20] The CPRs experienced territorial isolation from the rest of the Ixcán for eleven years, but not the individual isolation experienced in so many divided and antagonistic villages with few beliefs, visions, or purposes in common. Paradoxically, it also appears that there are more festivities, sports activities, musical bands, cultural events, and political meetings in the CPRs than elsewhere in the Ixcán. Although the CPRs must live with fear, it tends to be collective rather than individual and therefore more tolerable. Risks are assumed as a community instead of being borne by individuals. Feelings of loneliness, abandonment, and lack of trust are more likely to be experienced among the militarized villages in the Ixcán.

Like members of any community, however, individuals in the CPRs embody different views and commitments, which can affect cooperation and can result in conflicts. Their experience mandates a high degree of harmony and consensus, but some individuals are more committed to collective production than others, some are very religious, others would rather rest or play soccer than attend mass, some are more spiritual, and others more political. What is most unusual is their conception that the fate of the individual is tied to the fate of the whole and a passionate belief in a right to remain and produce in that land. Their situation demands an active engagement, organization, consensus, and reaching out to establish solidarity links essential for their survival.

All in all, the CPRs are resourceful and proud of their accomplishments. Since organizing an association—the formidable Comité de Parcelarios del Ixcán—on December 11, 1983, they have learned much from experience. A high degree of communal spirit exists. The political savvy of the refugees' Comisiones Permanentes and the CPRs' Comité de Ixcán are unmatched. Given their activities and their determined resistance, the temptation is to simplistically identify the CPRs politically with the URNG, as the army has done. In talking to community members or Ricardo Falla, however, what one hears challenges easy ideological categorizations.

In the Ixcán the guerrillas have demonstrated that they can survive as armed units but not that they can control territory. The army has demonstrated that it can penetrate guerrilla-dominated territory but not hold it or permanently rout the guerrillas. Thus a military stalemate exists, but a stalemate is not sufficient for a population that would like guarantees for their safety and the right to be normal functioning social communities and agricultural producers.

The CPRs of the Ixcán have, since their public declaration in 1991, captured the fascination and admiration of the country and the international community. Who could have imagined after the terrifying massacres, documented so eloquently by Falla, the emergence of highly resourceful and socially cohesive and economically productive communities? They defended their lives, their rights, and their land and blossomed under the most difficult of circumstances. One cannot help but be impressed by their tenacity, survival skills, and formidable organization. An expression of this confidence and sophistication was the refugees' and the CPRs' persistence in certain broad demands. The refugees demanded voluntary and organized return, and the CPRs demanded the right to be recognized as civilian population and live in the open.

In contrast, the people in Ixcán Development Pole seem overtly more passive. Whatever their resistance, it is more likely to be silent and individual. From the start of the militarization, they have been told what to do. Most of the creativity had to be directed at outsmarting the army by appearing to be complying yet doing what was necessary to ease their condition. This creativity, though pivotal for survival, is more reactive. The Ixcán villages were not born out of resistance but out of surface acceptance and compliance.

The Ixcán villages will recover step by step and with goodwill solve, along with the CPRs and the returnees, the problems that lie ahead—mainly land disputes and human rights violations, so that soon this lowland rain forest municipality will again become a peaceful, thriving region.

NOTES

1. In this epilogue, when I refer to the first group—those that fled the country and are living in United Nations High Commissioner for Refugee (UNHCR) camps in Mexico—I will call these individuals refugees. The second group, who become part of their own or new communities with army approval and supervision, I will simply refer to as the people of the Ixcán, although the Ixcán rain forest municipality is also home to the CPRs. The third group—the CPRs—live in the northwest quarter of the Ixcán, in the territory more or less under military control of one of the insurgent organizations, the Ejército Guerrillero de los Pobres (EGP). It is here that some 5,000 to 6,000 civilian people live in hiding in resistance to the military. Other paths taken included joining the guerrillas, moving to the United States as undocumented migrants, relocating to Mexico as "unofficial" refugees (this population alone numbered some 200,000), returning to their highland villages or resettling in the South Coast, Guatemala City, or elsewhere in the country.

2. For a comprehensive analysis of the disruption emanating from the Guatemalan population displacement, see two illuminating studies done by the Association for the Advancement of Social Sciences in Guatemala (AVANCSO 1990, 1992).

3. Coincidentally, this was one of the first villages visited by a new guerrilla organization—the Ejército Guerrillero de los Pobres (EGP) (Guerrilla Army of the Poor)—even before they made themselves publicly known in 1975 (Payeras 1983).

4. Interviews in Keste, Maya-Tecun, Quetzal-Edzna, and Los Laureles in the state of Campeche and in the Quintana Roo camps of Maya-Balám, Los Lirios, Cuchumatán, and La Laguna, July 1990.

5. Interviews in Polígono 14, also known as Victoria 20 de Enero, March 1993.

6. Although those who came out of hiding after an amnesty was publicized by radio are generally classified as those that turned themselves in to the army (*se entregaron al ejército*), that is too broad a generalization. Some were caught and suffered severely or were even killed. Those who came out voluntarily were those that felt the safest and that suffering in the jungle wasn't worth it. They hoped to be treated relatively well and hoped that once the army investigated their past activities and political sympathies they would pass the test. Often it was from among this population that the army obtained information regarding the past activities of those who were caught. Therefore feelings of guilt, denial, and resentment are not unusual in these once-solid communities. This group recognizes the terrifying actions of the army but are also likely to place blame on the irresponsibility of guerrilla actions and their wishful triumph-around-the-corner perspective. Some view the guerrillas as manipulative, lazy, and irresponsible for putting the defenseless population in vulnerable situations and then fleeing. This assessment could have been arrived at independently or it could be part of the army's reeducation campaign. In 1984 the EGP suffered a serious split, losing significant intellectual leaders and capable cadres. Most of them were in Mexico, where debates and reassessments over previous tactics and future strategies took place.

7. In March 1982, General Efraín Ríos Montt staged a coup and declared himself president. He was overthrown in August 1983.

8. The army accused the Catholic Church—their new theology of liberation—of undermining the traditional subservience of the Indians. The Church had played a significant role in the settlement of the Ixcán, providing peasants with an independence that met the army's definition of subversion.

9. Often the villages in the Ixcán became repopulated with people from five different cultures, who spoke five different languages, belonged to several competing religions, and had experienced different forms of terror. In villages such as Santa María Tzejá, one can find living side by side one person whom the army tortured severely (and still cries when recalling that experience) and another person living right next to him, a new settler, who brags about his tour of duty in the army—the killing, rapes, destruction of homes and crops, and torture that were committed. This ex-soldier displays his army boots and other mementos of his days in the army. The result has been socially, economically, and politically devastating for these villages. In ten years they have not begun to recuperate to the point where they were at the time of the violence.

10. In the municipality of Santa Cruz del Quiché, a rural teacher, Amilcar Méndez, formed a human rights organization aimed particularly at making the PACs live up to their stated name, that is, voluntary. The organization, called the Council of Ethnic Communities "All Are Equal" (CERJ), has been in constant confrontation with the military and their surrogates, the PAC chiefs. No international pressure, not even receiving the Robert F. Kennedy Memorial Center Human Rights Award, has guaranteed the safety of their members. Amilcar Méndez lives in the San Francisco Bay Area.

11. Accord of the Permanent Commissions of the Guatemalan Refugees in Mexico and the Government of the Republic of Guatemala, Guatemala, 8 October 1992.

12. One would have expected this thirty-year-old villager, given his past, to have been low key about a topic this sensitive. His family fled the village prior to its destruction in 1982 and have not yet been able to recover their land parcel, which was taken by a new settler. Just recently he and other villagers were told at 1:00 A.M. to appear at the military base to answer questions concerning subversive activity. Fully confident there was no basis for the accusation and that it was just a result of the normal tensions between original and new settlers, he decided not even to appear. The others went accompanied by the local priest, Tiziano Sofía, who, according to the villagers, told the officers off in so many words, telling them to do something productive, to stop bothering hardworking campesinos, and, if they had a war going, to go fight their real enemy in the jungle and not take cheap shots at the local inhabitants. It should be noted that Father Tiziano, a native of Italy, made so many enemies and became so controversial that the Church transferred him out of the Ixcán and Guatemala. Whether his replacement, a Guatemalan priest, will have the courage to stand up to the military in defense of the local inhabitants remains to be seen. Interview in Cantabál, Ixcán, March 1993.

13. Most of the information in this section was obtained from conversations and correspondence over the past decade with CPR members as well as a recent series of interviews in Guatemala in March 1993. Ricardo Falla provided rich details about the daily life of these people.

14. Interview with CPR members, Guatemala, March 1993.

15. See details of the 1987 offensive in IGE 1989. In 1987 guerrilla units were conducting village takeovers close to the massive military base of Playa Grande. While I was staying in one village of the Zona Reyna, the guerrillas appeared at dawn on 20 and 22 April, in the villages of El Milagro and San Isidro. They congregated people in the village center to listen to a political talk. Before leaving they bought provision from the village store.

16. The ACG with its dedicated pastoral team, Equipo de Trabajo Pastoral (ETP), represents one of the most significant movements of the 1990s.

17. Interview with Ricardo Falla, Santa Tecla, El Salvador, March 1993.

18. Interview with Ricardo Falla, Berkeley, California, March 1993.

19. Interview with Ricardo Falla, Santa Tecla, El Salvador, March 1993.

20. Interview with CPR members, Guatemala City, March 1993.

REFERENCES

Aguilera Peralta, Gabriel. 1980. "Terror and Violence as Weapons of Counter-Insurgency in Guatemala," *Latin American Perspectives*, Vol. 7, Numbers 2–3, Spring/Summer.

Aguilera Peralta, Gabriel, and Jorge Romero Imery. 1981. *Dialéctica del terror en Guatemala*. San José, Costa Rica: Editorial Universitaria Centroamericana.

AVANCSO (Asociación para el Avance de las Ciencias Sociales en Guatemala). 1990. *Assistance and Control: Policies Toward Internally Displaced Populations in Guatemala*. Washington, D.C.: Hemispheric Migration Project/Center for Immigration Policy and Refugee Assistance, Georgetown University.

———. 1992. *¿Dónde está el futuro? Procesos de reintegración en comunidades de retornados.* Guatemala City: AVANCSO, Cuadernos de Investigación, no. 8, julio.

Cabrera, Julio. 1993. "Ustedes no están solos." In *Carta a las Iglesias.* San Salvador, El Salvador: Universidad Centroamericana, 1–16 de febrero.

Communities of Population in Resistance. 1992. *Communities of Population in Resistance.* Washington, D.C.: Guatemala Health Rights Support Project.

Corradi, Juan E., Patricia Weiss Fagen, and Manuel Antonio Garretón. 1992. *Fear at the Edge: State Terror and Resistance in Latin America.* Berkeley: University of California Press.

Garretón, Manuel Antonio. 1992. "Fear in Military Regimes: An Overview." In *Fear at the Edge: State Terror and Resistance in Latin America*, edited by Juan E. Corradi, Patricia Weiss Fagen, and Manuel Antonio Garretón. Berkeley, University of California Press.

Garst, Rachel, and Tom Barry. 1990. *Feeding the Crisis: U.S. Food Aid and Farm Policy in Central America.* Lincoln: University of Nebraska Press.

IGE (Guatemalan Church in Exile). 1989. *Guatemala: Security, Development, and Democracy.* Guatemalan Church in Exile (IGE), April.

Manz, Beatriz. 1981. "Refugees—Guatemalan Troops Clear Peten for Oil Explorations." *Cultural Survival Quarterly* 5:3.

———. 1983. "Guatemalan Refugees: Violence, Displacement and Survival." *Cultural Survival Quarterly* 7:1.

———. 1984. "The Forest Camps in Eastern Chiapas, Mexico." *Cultural Survival Quarterly* 8:3, Fall.

———. 1988a. *Refugees of a Hidden War: The Aftermath of Counterinsurgency in Guatemala.* Albany: State University of New York Press.

———. 1988b. "The Transformation of La Esperanza, in Ixcán Village," In *Harvest of Violence: The Maya Indians and the Guatemalan Crisis*, edited by Robert M. Carmack. Norman: University of Oklahoma Press.

———. 1988c. *Repatriation and Reintegration: An Arduous Process in Guatemala.* Washington, D.C.: Hemispheric Migration Project/Center for Immigration Policy and Refugee Assistance, Georgetown University.

Martín-Baró, Ignacio. 1989. "Political Violence and War as Causes of Psychosocial Trauma in El Salvador." *International Journal of Mental Health* 18 (1):3–20.

Pacheco, Gerardo, and Bernardo Jiménez, compilers. 1990. *Ignacio Martín-Baró (1942–1989): psicología de la liberación para América Latina.* Guadalajara: Instituto Tecnológico y de Estudios Superiores de Occidente, Departmento de Extensión Universitaria, Universidad de Guadalajara.

Payeras, Mario. 1983. *Days of the Jungle: The Testimony of a Guatemalan Guerrillero, 1972–1976.* New York: Monthly Review Press.

Siebers, Hans. 1992. "Religión y sociedad en Guatemala: Un marco interpretativo." In *Voces del tiempo.* Guatemala: Sociedad para el Estudio de la Religión en Guatemala, 4.

Torres Rivas, Edelberto. 1989. *Repression and Resistance.* Boulder, Colo.: Westview Press.

Bibliography

Adams, Richard N. 1990. "Ethnic Images and Strategies in 1944." In *Guatemalan Indians and the State, 1540 to 1988*, edited by Carol A. Smith, pp. 141–162. Austin: University of Texas Press.

Aguilera, Gabriel. 1986. "La guerra oculta: La campaña contrainsurgente en Guatemala." Paper presented at conference, "The United States and Central America: A Five-Year Assessment, 1980–1985," Los Angeles, 20–22 February 1986. San José, Costa Rica: Instituto Centroamericano de Documentación e Investigación Social.

Amnesty International. 1976. *Guatemala*. Briefing Paper No. 8. London: Amnesty International Publications.

AVANCSO (Asociación para el Avance de las Ciencias Sociales en Guatemala). 1992. "¿Dónde está el futuro? Proceso de reintegración en comunidades de retornados." Cuadernos de Investigación No. 8. Guatemala City.

Barton, Allen H. 1969. *Communities in Disaster: A Sociological Analysis of Collective Stress Situations*. Garden City, N.Y.: Doubleday.

Bravo, Carlos. 1986. *Jesús hombre en conflicto*. México: Centro de Reflexión Teológica.

Brett, Donna Whitson, and Edward T. Brett. 1988. *Murdered in Central America: The Stories of Eleven U.S. Missionaries*. New York: Orbis Books.

Carmack, Robert, ed. 1988. *Harvest of Violence: The Mayan Indians and the Guatemalan Crisis*. Norman and London: University of Oklahoma Press.

Colville of Culross, Viscount. 1984. *Report on the Situation of Human Rights in Guatemala*. E/CN.4/1984/30. United Nations Economic and Social Council. Commission on Human Rights, 8 February.

Comité Pro Justicia y Paz de Guatemala. 1982. *Situación de los derechos humanos en Guatemala*. Informe publicado con la colaboración del Consejo Mundial de Iglesias. Guatemala, December.

CPR (Communities of Population in Resistance) in Ixcán. 1991. *Declaración*. Guatemala, January.

Dennis, Philip A., Gary S. Elbow, and Peter L. Heller. 1984. *Final Report: Playa Grande Land Colonization Project, Guatemala*. Lubbock: Texas Tech University.

Falla, Ricardo. 1984a. "Genocidio en Guatemala." In *Tribunal Permanente de los Pueblos. Sesión Guatemala, Madrid, 27–31 enero 1983*, pp. 177–237. Madrid: IEPALA.

———. 1984b. "We Charge Genocide." In *Guatemala, Tyranny on Trial: Testimony of the Permanent People's Tribunal*, pp. 112–119. San Francisco: Synthesis Publications.

214 *Bibliography*

————. 1983. *Masacre de la finca San Francisco, Huehuetenango.* Copenhagen: IWGIA. Also published in *ECA* (Estudios Centro-americanos), July–August 1983: 641–662. San Salvador. Published as "Voices of the Survivors: The Massacre at Finca San Francisco," Cultural Survival, Inc., and Anthropology Resource Center, Boston, 1983.

————. 1979. *Quiché Rebelde.* Guatemala City: Editorial Universitaria.

Foppa, Alaíde. 1982. *Poesía.* Guatemala City: Serviprensa Centroamericana.

Frank, Luisa, and Philip Wheaton. 1984. *Indian Guatemala: Path to Liberation.* Washington, D.C.: Epica Task Force.

Inforpress Centroamericana. Guatemala City.

Kreps, G. A. 1984. "Sociological Inquiry and Disaster Research." *Annual Review of Sociology* 10 (1984): 309–330.

Krueger, Chris, and Kjell Enge. 1985. *Security and Development Conditions in the Guatemalan Highlands.* Washington, D.C.: Washington Office on Latin America.

Manz, Beatriz. 1988a. *Refugees of a Hidden War: The Aftermath of Counterinsurgency in Guatemala.* Albany: State University of New York Press.

————. 1988b. "La Transformación de 'La Esperanza,' una aldea del Ixcán." In *Harvest of Violence: The Mayan Indians and the Guatemalan Crisis,* edited by Robert Carmack, pp. 121–154. Norman and London: University of Oklahoma Press.

McClintock, Michael. 1985. *The American Connection. Volume 2: State Terror and Popular Resistance in Guatemala.* London: Zed Books.

Menéndez Rodríguez, Mario. 1981. *Por Esto,* nos. 1–7 (2 July to 13 August) (México).

Noticias de Guatemala. San José, Costa Rica.

Payeras, Mario. 1983. "Guatemala: Del valle al altiplano." Entrevista por Marta Harnecker. In *Punto Final,* suplemento del no. 205 (January–February).

————. 1982. *Los días de la selva. Relato sobre la implantación de las guerrillas populares en el norte del Quiché, 1972–76.* México City: Nuestro Tiempo.

Plan Nacional de Seguridad y Desarrollo. 1982. Guatemala City.

Sack, John. 1971. *Lieutenant Calley: His Own Story.* New York: Viking Press.

Schell, Jonathan. 1967. *Village of Ben Suc.* New York: Alfred A. Knopf.

Smith, Carol A., ed. 1990. *Guatemalan Indians and the State, 1540 to 1988.* Austin: University of Texas Press.

Tho, Brigadier General Tran Dinh. 1980. *Pacification.* Washington, D.C.: U.S. Army Center of Military History.

Thompson, Robert. 1974. *Defeating Communist Insurgency: Experiences from Malaya and Vietnam.* London: Chatto and Windus.

United Nations. 9 December 1948. Convention on the Punishment of the Crime of Genocide. Geneva.

Wipfler, Rev. William. 1976. *Testimony to Subcommittee on International Organizations of the Committee on International Relations of the House of Representatives.* New York: National Council of Churches of Christ in USA, 9 June.

About the Book and Author

"Falla has produced the first detailed regional history of the Guatemalan holocaust of the 1970s and 1980s. This study of the Selva Ixcán shows the same careful recording and comparing of eyewitness testimonies that characterized his earlier studies—such as that of the San Francisco massacre. It is, however, vastly more important. It shows how the Guatemalan military, from 1975 to 1982, evolved strategies to punish the *campesino* population for the presence of *guerrilleros* in their area. It shows how the victims and their communities were interrelated both in their destruction and survival, how human courage survived the worst the military could invent, and how peoples of all faiths and political preferences were equally victims. It provides the first detailed count of assassinations and disappearances that gives us an actual sample of the human cost of Guatemala's policies.

"Falla is one of the courageous Guatemalan scholars who, in order to seek the truth, have been forced by their own governments to choose between exile or death. It confirms his position as one of Central America's major living social scientists and adds further luster to the work of those Catholic priests who are dedicating their lives to bettering the lives of Central American peoples."

—Richard N. Adams
Professor Emeritus
University of Texas at Austin

Ricardo Falla is an anthropologist and Jesuit priest. He is the author of *Esa muerte que nos hace vivir* and *Quiché Rebelde*.